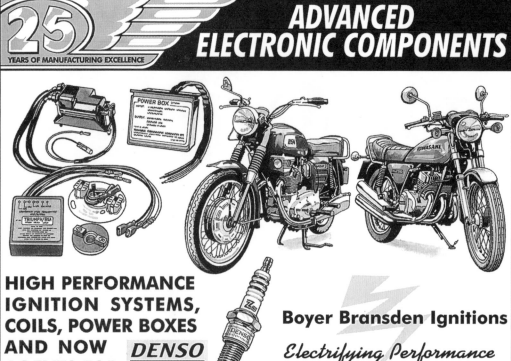

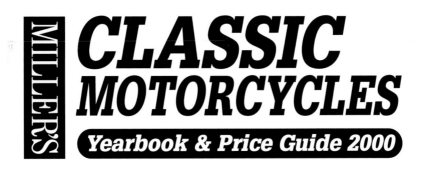

MILLER'S

CLASSIC MOTORCYCLES

Yearbook & Price Guide 2000

MILLER'S CLASSIC MOTORCYCLES YEARBOOK AND PRICE GUIDE 2000

Created and designed by
Miller's Publications
The Cellars, High Street
Tenterden, Kent TN30 6BN
Telephone: 01580 766411
Fax: 01580 766100

General Editor: Mick Walker
Editorial and Production Co-ordinator: Ian Penberthy
Editorial Assistants: Carol Gillings, Jo Wood
Designers: Kari Reeves, Shirley Reeves, Alex Warder
Advertisement Designer: Simon Cook
Advertising Executives: Jill Jackson, Melinda Williams
Production Assistants: Gillian Charles, Léonie Sidgwick
Additional Photography: Ian Booth, David Hawtin,
David Merewether, Robin Saker
Indexer: Hilary Bird

First published in Great Britain in 1999
by Miller's, a division of Mitchell Beazley,
imprints of Octopus Publishing Group Ltd,
2–4 Heron Quays, London E14 4JP

© 1999 Octopus Publishing Group Ltd

A CIP catalogue record for this book is
available from the British Library

ISBN 1 84000 175 5

Colour and black and white Illustrations and film output by CK Litho, Whitstable, Kent
Printed and bound by Toppan Printing Co, (HK) Ltd, China

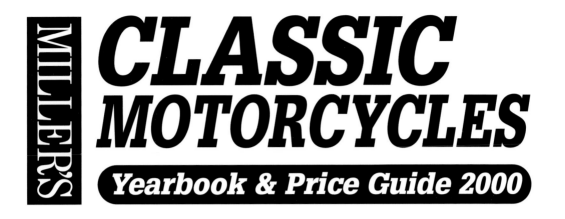

MILLER'S

CLASSIC MOTORCYCLES

Yearbook & Price Guide 2000

General Editor
Mick Walker

Foreword by
Sammy Miller

Don't Throw Away A Fortune!
Invest In
Miller's Price Guides

Please send me the following editions

Contents

Acknowledgements 6
Tuning Four-Stroke Motorcycles 7
How to use this book 8
Foreword 9
The Motorcycle Market 10

Aermacchi 11
AJS 12
Alcyon 15
Ardie 16
Ariel 16
Baker 19
Benelli 19
Bianchi 20
BMW 20
Bradbury 22
Bridgestone 22
Brough-Superior 23
BSA 25
Calthorpe 36
Clement 36
Clyno 36
Coventry Eagle 37
Dayton 38
Diamond 38
DKW 39
DMW 39
Dot 39
Douglas 40
Ducati 42
Excelsior 47
Francis-Barnett 47
Garelli 47
Gilera 48
Gitan 48
Greeves 48
Colour Review *49–56*
Harley-Davidson 57
Henderson 58
Hesketh 59
Hewetson 60
Honda 60
Indian 62
Itom 63
James 63
JAP 64
Kawasaki 64
Kerry 66
Laverda 66
Levis 67
Lube 67
Matchless 68
Minerva 70
Monotrace 70
Motobi 71

Moto Guzzi 71
Moto Morini 74
Motosacoche 78
MV Agusta 78
Neracar 80
New Imperial 80
Norman 80
Norton 81
NSU 85
OEC 85
Ossa 85
Panther 86
Praga 86
Quadrant 87
Raleigh 87
René-Gillet 87
Royal Enfield 88
Royal Ruby 90
Rudge 90
Rumi 90
Scott 91
Singer 92
Sparkbrook 92
Standard 92
Sunbeam 93
Suzuki 96
Terrot 98
Triumph 98
Ultima 106
Velocette 107
Victoria 111
Vincent-HRD 111
Yale 113
Yamaha 113
Dirt Bikes 114
Colour Review *121–128*
Military Motorcycles 129
Monkey Bikes 132
Mopeds 134
Police Bikes 136
Racing Bikes 138
Scooters 149
Sidecars 155
Specials 159
Speedway Bikes 160
Memorabilia 163

Key to Illustrations 167
Glossary 169
Index to Advertisers 170
Bibliography 170
Directory of Museums 171
Directory of Motorcycle Clubs 172
Index 174

Acknowledgements

The publishers would like to acknowledge the great assistance given by our consultants:

Malcolm Barber — 81 Westside, London SW4 9AY Tel: 0171 228 8000

Amedeo Castellani — Raceco UK, Unit 4, St John, Saxmundham, Suffolk IP17 1BE

David Hawkins — 81 Westside, London SW4 9AY Tel: 0171 228 8000

Michael Jackson — Sotheby's, 34–35 New Bond Street, London SW1A 2AA Tel: 0171 493 8080

Ian Kerr — 2 Barley Close, Hazlemere, Bucks HP15 7TU Tel: 01494 817360

Sammy Miller — Sammy Miller Museum, Bashley Manor, New Milton, Hampshire BH25 6TF Tel: 01425 620777

Mike Smith's Motoring Past — Chiltern House, Ashendon, Aylesbury, Bucks HP18 0HB Tel: 01296 651283

Brian Verrall — Caffyns Row, High Street, Handcross, Nr Haywards Heath, West Sussex RH17 6BJ Tel: 01444 400678

We would like to extend our thanks to all auction houses, their press offices, and dealers who have assisted us in the production of this book, along with the organisers and press offices of the following events:

The International Classic Bike Show

Louis Vuitton Classic

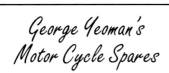

Tuning Four-Stroke Motorcycles

Since its invention, enthusiasts have been obsessed with obtaining more power from the four-stroke, internal-combustion engine. All the principles of producing power were well understood by the turn of the century, but as with any innovative product, engines had to go through an evolutionary process. In the last two decades, the rate of change has been phenomenal. Today, production motorcycles with 200bhp per litre are fast becoming the norm. Even so, there are still individuals out there trying to squeeze even more horsepower from these already mega-fast machines.

The advent of affordable electronic equipment means that the top-flight racing teams have data-logging and computer equipment that is capable of recording every engine parameter. This enables them to fine-tune their engines to a degree of accuracy that was not possible when I first became involved in motorcycle racing. To have witnessed the changes has been truly rewarding. I am sure that over the next decade, even more innovations will astonish us.

At present, motorcycling is going through a boom period in the UK. Publications are full of adverts for tuning companies, and the dynamometer has become a common workshop tool. The problem that the keen motorcycle enthusiast faces is deciding on where to take a machine to obtain more power.

Bearing in mind that the cheapest is not necessarily the best, it is advisable to look for people who are involved with, and have achieved results in, competition, and who have been around for a while. If your type of machine was never used in competition, word of mouth is probably the next best thing, or check out the club magazines. If you are not a member of a club that caters for your marque, it is a very good idea to join one. This will give you instant access to a wealth of information. Speak to friends and acquaintances who have already had work done to see if they are satisfied, especially after the bike has covered some mileage. There is no point in obtaining a large increase in power for the engine to last only 500 miles.

Because of their popularity, the top tuners will usually have a long backlog of work, so speak to them well in advance. Make an appointment, discuss your requirements, and get a written estimate (this may only be possible once the engine has been stripped and checked) and a delivery date.

It is very easy to spend a small fortune on tuning your bike without adding to its value, so look upon it simply as an aspect of your hobby and do it for the satisfaction it will give. In some cases, a premium price may be obtained at the time of resale if the modifications have been sensibly done, especially if they are universally recognised as a real improvement or the solution to a problem inherent in the design of your bike's engine. Some modifications neither add to, nor detract from the value, for example the fitting of electronic ignition, especially if it is possible to revert to the original system. Others that change the machine irreversibly may scare off some potential buyers, so consider your plan carefully before parting with your cash.

Components that are commonly replaced include pistons, camshafts, cylinder heads, carburettors and con-rods. Pistons can be of the same bore in a stronger material with higher compression, or a larger diameter for increased capacity. The latter is one of the easiest ways of obtaining more power, with the benefit of also gaining more torque. To put it simply, torque gives you acceleration, and horsepower gives you top speed. However, they are inter-related, as you cannot have one without the other.

Changing a camshaft can affect the relationship between horsepower and torque. A cam with too much duration will increase horsepower, sometimes at the expense of torque. There is no point in fitting a camshaft that is suitable for racing flat out at Daytona if you also intend riding to the shops.

Cylinder head work is probably the most difficult thing to get right. Professional tuners make extensive use of the flowbench to assess and improve heads, and as long as the results are interpreted correctly, this is definitely the way to go. All the power the engine will ever make is linked directly to the cylinder head, so choose your supplier very carefully.

Larger carburettors may give you more top end to the detriment of bottom-end tractability. However, since some bikes began life under-carbed, this can be an area for improvement. Connecting rods may be lightened, polished and peened for extra strength or, better still, replaced with Carrillo items. The list could go on.

Mixing and matching components can give different results. My tuning business caters predominantly for the Moto Guzzi market, and over the last 20 years, we have built virtually every configuration of engine, so we can predict quite accurately an engine's characteristics. Some customers will want to use a bike every day for riding to work and touring, possibly in Europe. The last thing we want is a telephone call from a customer stuck half-way up a mountain in Portugal with a broken machine. So reliability is a big issue. Others will want to trailer a machine to the race-track for a good thrash. These two diametrically opposed uses illustrate why tuning is such a fascinating subject.

The ability to mix and match components to serve a particular purpose can keep the customer and tuner awake at night considering all the possibilities. When the finished engine performs as it should, it is a source of great satisfaction to both. Some tuners have the same affection for their engines as they do their offspring; nobody wants to be told that their kid is ugly or stupid.

In parting, remember that the main reason for tuning an engine is to put a big grin on your face. Choose your tuner carefully; get it right, and get it right first time. Anyone can do this with a bit of research and forward thinking.

Amedeo Castellani

How to use this book

I t is our aim to make this Guide easy to use. Motorcycle marques are listed alphabetically and then chronologically. Dirt Bikes, Military Motorcycles, Monkey Bikes, Mopeds, Racing Bikes, Scooters, Sidecars and Specials are located after the marques, towards the end of the book. In the Memorabilia section objects are grouped by type. If you cannot find what you are looking for, please consult the index which starts on page 174.

Marque Introduction
provides an overview of the marque including factory changes and in some instances the history of a particular model. Introductions change from year to year and not every section will begin with an introduction.

Sunbeam (British 1912–57)

Sunbeam was at the forefront of bicycle manufacture during the late Victorian/early Edwardian period, offering machines of outstanding quality with advanced features such as 'the little oil bath' chaincase, which improved the life of the drive chain considerably. Therefore, it came as no surprise that when the company began building motorcycles, its products were finished to the same exceptional standard. Introduced in 1911, the first machine broke with convention by adopting a two-speed gearbox and chain final drive, at a time when single-speed, direct belt drives were very much the norm. The benefits of the chain final drive were further enhanced by the adoption of the oil-bath chaincase for motorcycle use. Suddenly, riders were presented with a drive system that was clean and virtually maintenance free.

1923 Sunbeam, 491cc, side-valve single.
£4,800–5,200 VER

1926 Sunbeam Model 1, 346cc, side-valve single.
£2,750–3,050 BKS

Caption
provides a brief description of the motorcycle or item, and could include comments on its history, mileage, any restoration work carried out and current condition.

Vincent-HRD (British 1928–56)

1955 Vincent-HRD Series D 'Open' Black Shadow, 998cc V-twin, rare, but incomplete and in need of restoration.
£10,800–12,800 BKS

The Series D Black Shadow was the last machine produced by the Stevenage factory. While the massive unit-construction V-twin engine and girdraulic forks of previous models were retained, the suspension was altered, with a single shock absorber beneath the saddle. The upper frame oil tank was also modified, and a lifting lever was incorporated to raise the machine on to its centre stand.

Price Guide
these are worked out by a team of trade and auction house experts, and are based on actual prices realised. Remember that Miller's is a PRICE GUIDE not a PRICE LIST and prices are affected by many variables such as location, condition, desirability and so on. Don't forget that if you are selling it is quite likely you will be offered less than the price range. Price ranges for items sold at auction include the buyer's premium.

 Miller's Motorcycle Milestones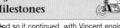

Egli Vincent 1332cc (Swiss/British 1971)
Price range: £10,000–17,000
Although production of the British Vincent-HRD 998cc, overhead-valve V-twin ceased during 1955, the engine didn't disappear. Both before and after the company's demise, Vincent engines were used to power a number of record-breaking speed machines. In America, both Rollie Free and Marty Dickinson used the V-twin to set new world and AMA (American Motorcycle Association) records on Bonneville Salt Flats in Utah. In Britain, George Brown (a Vincent dealer and former racer) created first Nero, and then Super Nero to take on and beat the world of drag racing for over two decades.

And so it continued, with Vincent engines finding their way into other peoples' frames, notably the Norton Featherbed to make the Norvin. Finally, the talented Swiss engineer Fritz Egli (with assistance from Englishman Terry Price) employed the Vincent V-twin during the late 1960s and early 1970s as the motivation for a series of street bikes and racers with considerable success.

With his friend and racer Fritz Peier, Egli used Vincent machines to win the Swiss national hillclimb championships on more than one occasion. At first, Egli retained the standard 998cc (84x90mm) Vincent engine displacement, but tuned the V-twin to increase maximum power from 55 to 70bhp.

SUNBEAM • VINCENT-HRD 28

Source Code
refers to the 'Key to Illustrations' on page 167 which lists the details of where the item was photographed, and whether it is from a dealer, club or auction house. Advertisers are also indicated on this page.

Bold Footnote
covers relevant additional information about a motorcycle's restoration and/or racing history, designer, riders and special events in which it may have participated.

Miller's Motorcycle Milestones
highlights important historic motorcycle events and the effect they have had on the motorcycle industry.

8

Foreword

Miller – same name, but different aspects of our great classic movement. *Miller's Classic Motorcycles Yearbook and Price Guide* is a wonderful reference for new and existing classic enthusiasts, allowing them to check out prices and specifications. Most of the overseas visitors to my museum refer to it, and in Japan it is the classic 'bible'.

I remember happy childhood days when I cycled to watch all the classic Irish races, then later competing in classic road races myself, such as the North West 200, Ulster Grand Prix, Temple 100 and Mid Antrim 150. Bangor and Lugan Park were great Irish road races, led by the likes of Artie Bell, Ernie Lyons and Stanley Woods, where I gained my knowledge of all the different makes and machines. I am also privileged to have worked at the Ariel, BSA, Bultaco and Honda factories, which I found to be a great experience.

I am lucky to have ridden and raced motorcycles for over 50 years. My first win was at the Temple Grass Track 200cc Scratch Race in 1951, and my latest was on 8 July 1999 at the Ringwood Pre-65 Trial. I have competed in road races and trials throughout the world during my career. Now I can marvel at the rare and exotic machines of the past by preserving them for the future in my Sammy Miller Museum, which is a heritage trust, ensuring that the bikes will never be sold.

Here's hoping that through *Miller's Classic Motorcycles Yearbook and Price Guide* you will be able to marvel at similar wonderful machines, and continue to gain valuable information from it for many years to come.

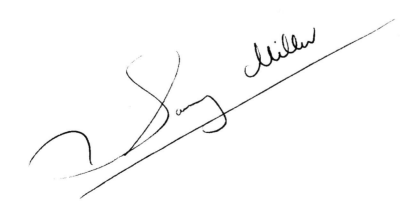

The Motorcycle Market

The 'recession', with which we were all threatened, now appears to have been something of a damp squib, recent UK auction sales of motorcycles indicating a buoyant market. Interest rates have tumbled since last year, which has encouraged a home market and eased exchange rates for overseas buyers, even though sterling remains strong. Brooks, Palmer Snell and Sotheby's remain the main contenders in the motorcycle market, but H&H in Buxton has indicated an intention to begin motorcycle sales in September 1999.

Traditionally, the barometer of the market is the April Stafford sale, but Brooks' October sale at Stafford has also grown in popularity, so much so that in 1998 it siphoned off many bikes that might have been entered for the December sale at Olympia. Sotheby's continued to include motorcycles in the car sales at the RAF Museum, Hendon, and in June 1998 sold three Hesketh prototypes. Not unnaturally, they attracted a good deal of interest, making £12,075, £10,350 and £11,500.

WWII military machines are popular, although those of the Axis forces make better money than those of the Allies. This was epitomised by the 1942 BMW R-75 found in a French château during the war by a British officer, presented in military livery, and sold by Sotheby's for £4,830. The wartime story helped the sale, too. Originality also continues to score over condition. The totally original, unrestored 1921 BSA Model E combination sold by Sotheby's in July 1998 for £3,795, and the £7,000 paid at Brooks in April 1999 for an 1899 Marot Gardon tricycle, are typical of the excitement that genuine 'barn discoveries' generate.

Sporting machines – particularly well-known makes or models – continue to do well. The 1928 AJS K7 and 1929 M7 sold by Brooks in April for £6,600 and £6,000 underline this, as do the 1935 Norton International and 1931 Brough-Superior 680 sold by Sotheby's last December for £5,800 and £7,400 respectively.

American machines have a cult following, and Harley-Davidson, Indian and Henderson are the most popular. All are renowned for their multi-cylinder models, which generally make the best prices. Brooks sold several in April 1999, including a 1918 Harley-Davidson Model 18F combination (£6,900), a 1920 Model J combination (£7,000), a 1968 FLH Electra Glide (£5,405), a 1922 Henderson 1340cc De Luxe (£11,000) and a 1950 Indian Scout (£8,500).

Pioneer machines – those eligible for the Sunbeam Motor Cycle Club's annual Pioneer Run from Epsom to Brighton – have a ready market, although solo machines have not increased in price in recent years. The 1906 3½hp Quadrant sold by Sotheby's for £5,400 last December is typical, but multi-cylinder veterans, like the 1914 Yale 7/8hp model fielded by Brooks last October and sold for £11,500, are far rarer and sought after.

Single-owner collections invariably command a premium over multi-consignment sales, and the more discriminating the collector whose machines are on offer, the more discriminating will be the buyers and the higher the prices. This was apparent in Brooks' sale of the Autokraft Collection in March 1999. With 100 lots, it totalled £568,991, three Vincents – a 1949 Black Lightning, a 1950 Grey Flash and a 1950 Grey Flash Racer – each realising more than £20,000.

Many machines had racing provenance, including a 1928 Works Sunbeam Model 80TT, which doubled its estimate to make £17,250, while other racers that did well included a 1959 Matchless G50 (£14,375) and a rare 1914 Royal Enfield 350cc (£18,400). More modern Japanese racing machines have been conspicuous by their absence from salerooms in the past year, and have proved difficult to sell in the past.

'Bread and butter' machines make up the bulk of most sales, however, and unless their condition is very good (very original or restored to a high standard), they remain cheap. The cost of professional restoration has something to do with this – usually a full restoration will cost more than the value of a finished machine – but more often, it is a case of supply and demand. While there are good supplies of machines in average-to-good condition, buyers will avoid 'basket cases' at anything other than rock-bottom prices. This does not apply to rare or sought-after models, however.

Foreign buyers have continued to present a high profile at British sales, and despite the economic conditions in the Far East, Japanese buyers have been quite active. America's economy is good, however, and interest in bikes at home and abroad has been strong. While American buyers are rarely seen in person, their agents have been strong bidders, and there were few unsold lots at the auction held during the 1999 Daytona Beach Bike Week. European and British bikes were well-represented in the results, but the highest prices (like the $26,500 paid for a 1942 Indian Four) appear to be reserved for indigenous popular makes.

Brooks held a new sale in June 1998 at Beaulieu, achieving many good prices. These included £5,175 for a 1903 Minerva, £12,650 for the former Don Grant 1959 Norton 500cc Manx, and £10,925 for a 1929 Sunbeam Model 80 taken by the factory to the Island for the 1929 Junior TT. Unrestored, but complete and original, its all-important history was unbroken.

When a 1936 Brough-Superior SS100 sold at auction for £31,625 in October 1998, it was clear that the *crème de la crème* will still command prices approaching those of the heady days of the late 1980s. However, that figure was exceeded at Stafford in April, when a 1937 example of the same model achieved £39,100, and a 1925 SS80 doubled usual SS80 prices to make £13,800. That sale totalled £522,000. Such results speak for themselves, and I am delighted with the state of the market and optimistic about the future.

Malcolm Barber

Aermacchi *(Italian 1950–78)*

1957 Aermacchi Chimera 175, 172cc, overhead-valve, horizontal single.
£3,000+ PC

Launched at the Milan show in 1956, the Chimera (Dream) proved a sales flop, but today, it is highly prized for its rarity value.

1966 Aermacchi Ala Verde, 248cc, overhead-valve, horizontal single, unit construction, 5-speed gearbox, modified with twin-leading-shoe front brake, megaphone silencer, alloy rims and racing seat.
£2,200–2,500 PC

1971 Aermacchi Sprint, 344cc, overhead valves, dual exhaust, 5-speed gearbox with right-hand change, open frame, twin-leading-shoe front brake.
£2,000–2,250 PC

1968 Aermacchi Sprint, 248cc, overhead-valve single, completely restored in 1996, little use since.
£1,850–2,000 BKS

Recognising the need to diversify in the face of competition from Japan, Harley-Davidson purchased a 50 per cent share in the Italian Aermacchi concern during 1959 and began marketing the Italian bikes in the States as Aermacchi Harley-Davidsons. They utilised the racer's horizontal, single-cylinder four-stroke, suspended from a spine frame, and were aided in gaining a market share by success on the track. This machine has fully-enclosed valve gear with the one-piece 'ashtray' rocker cover.

1972 Aermacchi SX350, 344cc, overhead valves, one-piece, 'ashtray' rocker cover, high-level single exhaust, 5-speed gearbox, open frame, braced handlebars.
£1,800–1,900 PC

AJS *(British 1909–66)*

1913 AJS V-twin, 770cc, single carburettor feeding both cylinders, magneto ignition, fully enclosed transmission, footboards, completely restored, rare, excellent original condition.
£7,500–8,500 VER

1912 AJS Single, 349cc, inlet-over-exhaust single, magneto ignition, hand-change gearbox, rear brake only.
£5,250–5,750 VER

1922 AJS B1 Sporting, 349cc, overhead-valve single, magneto ignition, chain final drive, brakes on both wheels, TT-pattern handlebars and footrests, restored to original specification.
£5,250–5,750 BKS

Sporting models were fitted with high-lift camshafts and higher-compression pistons.

1926 AJS Model G8, 498cc, overhead-valve single, magneto ignition, unrestored, excellent original condition.
£4,250–4,750 BKS

After victory in the 1920 Junior TT, and in the Junior and Senior events of the following year, the overhead-valve AJS made its production debut in November 1922. Originally built as a 350 only – subsequently known as the Big Port – it became available as a 500 in 1926. Coded G8 ('G' is the AJS letter code for 1926), the new 4½hp model followed the general lines of its successful smaller sibling. The engine combined the latter's 90mm stroke with an 84mm bore. The bike distinguished itself in the 1926 Isle of Man Senior TT, when works rider Jimmy Simpson became the first man to lap at over 70mph. Progressively updated, the Model 8 remained in production until the Matchless take-over in 1931.

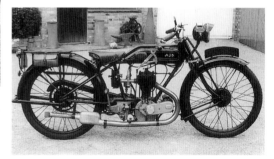

1926 AJS Sporting Model 5, 349cc, side-valve, 4-stroke single, original lighting equipment, restored, good condition.
£4,000–£4,250 VER

Restored Values

The cost of a professional restoration will have an influence on, but no direct relation to, a motorcycle's market value. A restored motorcycle can have a market value lower than the cost of its restoration.

◄ **1927 AJS Big Port,** 498cc, inlet-over-exhaust, single-cylinder engine, 3-speed gearbox with hand-change, pillion pad, complete and original, unrestored, good condition.
£4,500–5,000 PM

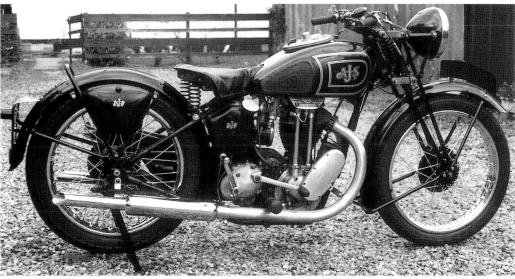

1938 AJS Twin Port, 348cc, overhead-valve single, twin-port head, foot-change gearbox.
£2,400–2,750 CStC

1952 AJS Model 20, 498cc, overhead-valve twin, 66x72.8mm bore and stroke, 4-speed foot-change gearbox, teledraulic forks, 'jam pot' rear suspension units, single-sided brakes front and rear, original specification.
£2,250–2,500 PS

▶ **1952 AJS Model 16MC,** 348cc, overhead-valve single, 69x93mm bore and stroke.
£3,000–£3,200 BLM

The 16MC was designed for trials use, but several have been converted for road use, such as this example. The model was built between 1951 and 1958.

1953 AJS Model 16MS, 348cc, overhead-valve single, forward-mounted magneto, Burman gearbox, full-width front brake hub, 'jam pot' rear suspension units, unrestored.
£1,850–£1,950 CotC

1955 AJS Model 20, 498cc, full-width alloy brake hubs front and rear, 'jam pot' rear suspension units, twin pilot lights, restored.
£3,500–£3,900 BLM

1954 AJS Model 20, 498cc, overhead-valve, twin-cylinder engine, 66x72.8mm bore and stroke, 29bhp at 6,800 rpm, 'jam pot' rear suspension units, very original, restored, good condition.
£2,200–2,400 CStC

The 1954 Model 20 was the first of that model to receive a full-width, light-alloy front hub with straight spokes.

1957 AJS Model 18, 497cc, overhead-valve single, front-mounted magneto, full-width hubs, 'jam pot' rear suspension units, finished in black and gold.
£2,000–2,250 PM

1958 AJS Model 16MS, 348cc, overhead-valve single, restored, good condition.
£1,800–£2,200 BLM

Revised for 1958, the 14MS lost its twin pilot lights and gained an alloy chaincase, modified rear shocks to give a lower ride height, AC electrics, a rectifier under the seat, an ignition coil under the tank, and a small timing cover with points.

◄ **1959 AJS Model 18S,** 497cc, overhead-valve single, 4-speed foot-change gearbox.
£2,000–£2,600 BLM

Equipped with an alternator, the 1959 Model 18S had a much improved alloy primary chaincase and an AMC gearbox.

1961 AJS Model 16MS, 348cc, overhead-valve single, improved primary chaincase, AMC gearbox, Girling rear suspension units, full-width hubs, original specification. **£2,000–2,200 CotC**

1960 AJS Model 8, 348cc, overhead-valve single, 72x85.5 mm bore and stroke, unit construction, composite frame of steel stampings and tubes, in need of restoration. **£700–£800 AT**

> Miller's is a price GUIDE not a price LIST

► **1960 AJS 31 De Luxe,** 646cc, overhead-valve twin, twin carburettors, restored. **£2,000–£2,500 PM**

◄ **1961 AJS Model 8,** 350cc, overhead-valve single, restored, good condition. **£800–1,100 BLM**

Derived from the 250cc Model 14 (also built as a Matchless), the Model 8 was introduced in 1960 and offered as a substitute for the heavyweight Model 16. Production came to an end in 1962.

Alcyon *(French 1902–65)*

1914 Alcyon Single, 250cc, 4-stroke, single-cylinder engine, belt drive, restored, good condition. **£3,750–4,150 YEST**

Very few of these machines survive today.

Ardie *(German 1919–58)*

Founded in Nürnburg during 1919, by Arno Dietrich (the former chief designer of rivals Premier), Ardie's first efforts were 305 and 348cc two-stroke singles with deflector-type pistons. However, after Dietrich was killed in a racing accident in 1922, the firm passed into the hands of Bendit and, from 1925, used British JAP engines. These ranged from 246 to 996cc, but the best-selling models had the 490cc, overhead-valve engine. These very refined machines featured duralumin frames and many top-quality fittings. In the mid 1930s, JAP engines were supplemented by those from Bark, Küchen, Sachs and Sturmey-Archer, and the firm reverted to tubular-steel frames, presumably to cut costs. In 1938, Richard Küchen designed an innovative 348cc machine

with a transverse, overhead-valve V-twin engine, but this never entered production.

Following WWII, the company was acquired by the Bartel-controlled Dürkopp concern of Biefeld, but remained under independent management. Unlike most companies at the time, Ardie built its own power units, its engineering director, Dipl. Ing. Noack, having created a series of crossflow, two-stroke engines, from a 122cc single to a 344cc twin. These were used to power a range consisting, in the main, of modest, but well engineered, commuter-type motorcycles. From 1953, Ardie also produced mopeds. After record sales in 1955, the company suffered the same drastic decline as many other producers in West Germany. It finally went into liquidation in 1958

◀ **1956 Ardie BD176,** 172cc, twin-port, 2-stroke, single-cylinder engine, fully-enclosed final drive chain, valanced mudguards, dualseat, good condition.
£600–650 HERM

Ariel *(British 1902–70)*

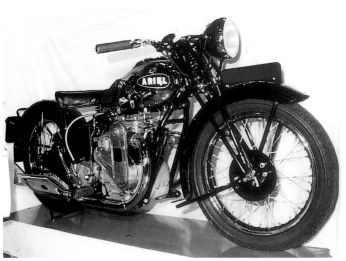 

1932 Ariel 4F/6.32, 601cc, overhead-camshaft square-4, 56x61mm bore and stroke.
£7,000+ AOC/AOM

The Ariel Square Four, a 498cc (51x61mm) model, made its public debut at the London Motorcycle Show in November 1930. Then, at the 1931 show, a 600 version appeared. The Square Four was designed by Edward Turner, later to become chief designer for Triumph. Between 1932 and 1936, some 5,000 examples left the Ariel works.

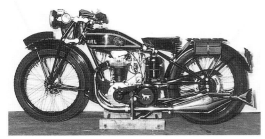

1929 Ariel Colt Model LF, 249cc, overhead-valve single, 65x75mm bore and stroke, twin-port cylinder head, girder forks, rigid frame, restored.
£1,700–1,900 PS

Designed by Val Page, the LF was the main attraction on the Ariel stand at the 1928 Olympia Motorcycle Show.

1949 Ariel 4G Mk 2, 995cc, overhead-valve square-4, 65x75mm bore and stroke, telescopic forks, plunger rear suspension.
£6,000–6,500 BKS

▶ **1953 Ariel 4G Mk 2,** 995cc, overhead-valve square-4, 4-exhaust-pipe model, 4-speed foot-change gearbox, telescopic forks, plunger rear suspension, single-sided brakes, fluted tank, dualseat.
£4000+ BMR

Production of the Mk 2 began in 1953 and continued (albeit with revised specification) until 1959.

1954 Ariel VH Red Hunter, 499cc, overhead-valve single, 81.8x95mm bore and stroke, single-sided brakes, dualseat, restored over 8-year period, excellent condition.
£2,000–2,250 CotC

Nineteen-fifty-four was the first year that a swinging-arm frame was used for this model.

1955 Ariel FH Huntmaster, 647cc, overhead-valve twin, 70x84mm bore and stroke, Burgess silencers, fluted chrome tank, separate headlamp, excellent condition.
£3,000–3,700 BLM

The Huntmaster 650 twin was introduced for 1954 and had a BSA-derived engine fitted in a new Ariel frame.

Ariel Leader 247cc (British 1957)
Price range: £800–1,800

For so many years a separate entity, Ariel finally became a part of the giant BSA Group during the early 1950s. This was a reflection of the fact that, even though it offered the well-known Red Hunter singles and unique Square Four, the company was not strong enough to survive as an independent once the immediate post-war demand for motorcycles had begun to tail off.

At first, BSA introduced Ariel to its influence with models such as the 198cc Colt single (a development of the BSA C-series) and the 646cc Huntmaster twin (based on the BSA A10). However, Ariel's management still had the will to build and design their own hardware. As a result, Ken Whistance and Val Page set to work at Ariel's Selly Oak, Birmingham, headquarters on a programme of research and development that would lead to a new 250cc-class, twin-cylinder, 2-stroke machine.

For a start, Ariel purchased an example of the German Adler MB250 to evaluate. However, Whistance and Page soon discovered that the German bike was so well made, using expensive components, that the British company would have been unable to make full use of the Adler technology and keep the selling price at an acceptable level.

Instead, they concentrated on employing pressings, die-castings and plastics, the use of the latter being truly innovative in the motorcycle industry at the time.

The Leader, as the newcomer was called, was probably the best-kept secret of the British bike industry prior to its launch on 17 July 1958. Its 247cc (54x54mm), piston-port engine offered smooth power and other unique features, making it an outstanding machine.

Subsequently, the Arrow, Golden Arrow and 200 Arrow appeared – all without the rider protection of the Leader. Several of Ariel's two-strokes were raced, notably the Hermann Meier-tuned machine ridden by Michael O'Rourke to seventh place in the 1960 TT.

Sadly, despite such valiant efforts to keep Ariel alive, it ceased to exist at the end of the 1960s.

1957 Ariel NH Red Hunter, 346cc, overhead-valve single, fitted with early-type front mudguard.
£2,000–2,250 CStC

The final version of the Red Hunter was built between 1957 and 1959, having full-width hubs and a cowled headlamp. It was virtually the same machine as the 500 VH, aside from a logo on the timing cover and the different engine displacement.

▶ **1961 Ariel Leader,** 247cc, twin-cylinder 2-stroke, piston-port induction, 54x54mm bore and stroke, fitted with optional indicators and panniers.
£2,950–3,250 AtMC

1958 Ariel FH Huntmaster, 647cc, overhead-valve twin.
£2,000–2,500 BLM

◀ **1961 Ariel Arrow,** 247cc, air-cooled, 2-stroke twin, restored, good condition.
£1,400–1,600 BLM

Ariel undressed the Leader to produce the Arrow. This example is fitted with the optional Avonaire fairing.

Baker *(British 1927–30)*

1925 Baker, 247cc, twin-port, 2-stroke engine, flywheel magneto/generator, automatic lubrication system operated by crankcase depression, 3-speed Albion gearbox.
£400–450 BKS

Founder of the Precision (later Beardmore-Precision) engine manufacturing firm, Frank Baker left the ailing Birmingham-based concern to set up his own marque in the mid-1920s. Introduced in 1927, the Baker line-up consisted of Villiers-engined lightweights ranging from 147 to 247cc. Their major selling point was a robust straight-tube frame that featured only two brazed joints. All Bakers had smart, wedge-shaped tanks finished in yellow and black. Sadly, these promising machines would be short-lived, for Baker sold his company to James in 1930.

Benelli *(Italian 1911–)*

1963 Benelli 125 Sport, 124cc, overhead-valve single, alloy cylinder head, iron barrels, Dell'Orto UFB carburettor, unit construction, 4-speed gearbox, full-width alloy hubs.
£1,400–1,500 RIM

1973 Benelli 250 2C, 231cc, iron-barrelled engine, 32mm Marzocchi front forks, double-sided front brake, stainless steel mudguards.
£600–700 MAY

1981 Benelli 654 Turismo, 603cc, 4 cylinders, chain-driven overhead camshaft, 4-into-2 exhaust, 5-speed gearbox, triple Brembo disc brakes, cast alloy wheels.
£1,500–1,700 IVC

Bianchi *(Italian 1897–1967)*

1957 Bianchi 125 Mendola, 124cc, 2-stroke single, mechanically sound, in need of restoration.
£450–650 MAY

BMW *(German 1923–)*

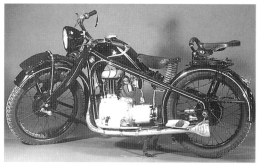

1932 BMW R39, 247cc, overhead-valve, 4-stroke single, 68x68mm bore and stroke.
£1,500–1,650 BERN

The R39 was first shown in December 1924, entering production in 1925. Production ceased in 1939.

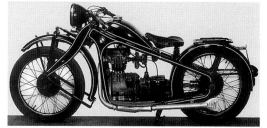

1933 BMW R2, 198cc, overhead-valve, 4-stroke single, 63x64mm bore and stroke.
£1,800–2,000 HERM

In all, 15,207 R2s were built between 1931 and 1936.

> A known continuous history can add value to and enhance the enjoyment of a motorcycle.

 Miller's Motorcycle Milestones

BMW R23 493cc (German 1923)
Price range: £3,000–5,000
At the outset of WWI, BMW's forerunners, Eisenach, Otto and Rapp, were all separate companies, but each would play a vital role in the emergence of BMW. The first step came in March 1916, when the Otto and Rapp aircraft factories merged to form Bayerische Flugzeugwerke AG (BFW), its directors being Karl Rapp and Max Friz. BFW soon gained a reputation as an aero engine builder of the highest order, and in July 1917, it became Bayerische Motoren Werke GmbH (BMW). A year later, the company went public, becoming BMW AG. But just as BMW's rise had been meteoric, so its fall, after Germany's defeat, was equally spectacular. The company was forced to diversify to remain in business. Eventually, in 1920, a completely new avenue opened – motorcycles.

BMW's first attempt was the 148cc, two-stroke Flink, but it was not a success. Then, in 1921, Martin Stolle designed the M2B15, a 493cc, side-valve, flat-twin engine. In the main, this was sold to other manufacturers. Finally, Max Friz designed a masterpiece – the R23.

When the R23 was unveiled at the Paris show in 1923, it created a sensation. Although the engine was still a 493cc flat-twin, it was mounted transversely, in unit with a three-speed gearbox with shaft drive to the rear wheel. The frame was of a full twin-triangle design, the front fork being sprung by a quarter-elliptic leaf spring. It was the beginning of a design concept that was modern enough to last throughout the 20th century.

In all, 3,090 R23s were constructed between 1923 and 1926, and the model's success set BMW on its way in the two-wheel world.

◄ **1952 BMW R67,** 594cc, overhead-valve, horizontally-opposed, twin-cylinder engine, telescopic forks, plunger rear suspension, twin seats, tank-top tool box, virtually original, restored, very good condition.
£5,000+ BMW

1955 BMW R25/3, 247cc, overhead-valve single, telescopic forks, swinging-arm rear suspension.
£1,800–2,000 HERM

In all, 47,700 R25/3s were built between 1953 and 1956.

1960 BMW R60, 594cc twin, Earles forks, separate seats, alternative white finish with black lining, touring trim, original unrestored condition.
£2,500–3,000 BLM

► **1962 BMW R27,** 247cc, overhead-valve single, 68x68mm bore and stroke, shaft final drive, Earles forks, swinging-arm rear suspension.
£2,200–2,400 HERM

In all, 15,364 R27s were built between 1960 and 1966.

1964 BMW R69S, 594cc, overhead-valve, horizontally-opposed, twin-cylinder engine, shaft final drive.
£3,700–4,100 BKS

When BMW introduced the R69S in 1960, it was the most powerful model marketed by the firm up to that point, producing 42bhp at 7,000 rpm, which gave a top speed of 109mph. However, its ability to cruise at high speeds without succumbing to fatigue endeared it to enthusiasts and ensured its reputation as one of the company's classic products. In common with other machines in the range, the R69S featured interchangeable 18in wheels and Earles forks, although optional telescopic forks were offered on US export models from 1967. Between 1960 and 1969, 11,317 R69S models were built.

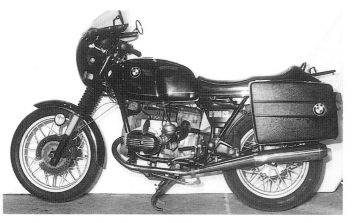

◀ **1982 BMW R100CS,** 980cc, overhead-valve, horizontally-opposed, twin-cylinder engine, 94x70.6mm bore and stroke, 5-speed gearbox, shaft final drive, disc front brake, handlebar fairing, panniers, good condition.
£1,400–1,550 PS

The R100CS was built from 1980 until 1984, but only 6,141 examples left BMW's Spandau, Berlin, production lines, compared to over 33,000 of the R100RS.

Bradbury *(British 1901–25)*

◀ **1912 Bradbury,** 554cc, long-stroke, side-valve, single-cylinder engine, variable gearing, unused since 1959, complete, in need of restoration and recommissioning.
£4,800–5,300 S

Bridgestone *(Japanese 1952–69)*

1966 Bridgestone GTR 350, 344cc, air-cooled, 2-stroke twin, rotary-disc induction.
£3,000+ SWC

No more than 12 of these machines are known to exist in the UK.

Brough-Superior *(British 1919–39)*

The legendary Brough-Superior motorcycles were the work of William Brough and his son, George. In 1919, the latter opened premises in Nottingham and, contrary to his father's favour for flat-twin engines, based the majority of production on the V-twin engine and the use of proprietary parts. In 1920, George announced a new generation of good looking, fast, powerful machines that handled well, becoming the creator of what has been termed 'The Rolls Royce of motorcycles'. By 1924, the pinnacle was reached when the SS100 was introduced.

Each machine was accompanied by a certificate guaranteeing that it had exceeded 100mph on the track. Production continued until 1940, by which time, a total of approximately 3,000 machines of all models had been built.

It is generally acknowledged that the rarer Matchless-engined SS100 is better than the arguably slightly faster, but more common, JAP-powered version. Certainly, it runs smoother, is easier to maintain, has more readily available spares, and is longer lasting. Of the 102 built, it is thought that 81 survive.

◀ **1925 Brough-Superior SS80,** 998cc, JAP side-valve V-twin engine, completely restored to concours condition.
£13,800–15,000 BKS

This machine was fitted with a four-speed Norton gearbox in 1946 to allow its continued use in a variety of sporting events. It was rebuilt during 1990/91, the Norton gearbox being retained and a BSA A7 front brake added.

1931 Brough-Superior 680, 677cc, JAP V-twin engine, 70x88mm bore and stroke, unrestored.
£8,500–9,400 S

This machine was acquired in 1945 by Herbert Guildford, service manager at Alvis Cars. After his death, it lay concealed under a variety of automotive components for many years.

A known continuous history can add value to and enhance the enjoyment of a motorcycle.

1936 Brough-Superior SS100, 982cc, overhead-valve, V-twin engine, 85.5x85.5mm bore and stroke.
£31,500+ BKS

Brough entered the 1930s with an entirely JAP-powered range. Then, after a brief absence, the SS80 reappeared in 1935 as the SS80 Special, this time with an AMC engine. In the following year, the SS100 adopted an overhead-valve version of the AMC power unit, and the two continued to use these engines until production ceased in 1939. This example was supplied new to Richard Laird, who was a famous Brooklands competitor in a supercharged Morgan. He was an entrant in many motorcycle trials of the period and a personal friend of George Brough.

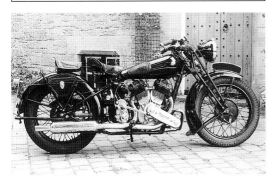

◀ **1936 Brough-Superior SS80,** 998cc, side-valve V-twin, good condition.
£7,000–7,500 BKS

Introduced in 1922, the SS80 (so called because of its guaranteed 80mph top speed in road trim) achieved instant fame when a stripped version, ridden by George Brough, became the first side-valve machine to lap Brooklands at over 100mph. The later AMC-powered machines, such as this example, used an engine that was similar to the Matchless Model X, but incorporated Brough's preferred 'knife-and-fork' big-end bearing arrangement, instead of the side-by-side connecting rods of the Matchless.

1937 Brough-Superior SS100, 998cc, overhead-valve V-twin, matching engine and frame, completely restored, 2,000 miles covered since, excellent condition.
£39,000+ BKS

Most SS100s were fitted with JAP engines, but this particular machine has the rarer Matchless V-twin. It was taken off the road in 1954 and remained unused for 42 years, after which it was completely restored and recommissioned. It was voted the best SS100 at the Brough Rally in August 1997, and also featured in a re-creation of T E Lawrence's famous escapade with a biplane for *Classic Bike* magazine.

1937 Brough-Superior SS80, 982cc, 85.5x85.5mm bore and stroke, in need of restoration.
£6,000–£7,500 YEST

From July 1935, the SS80 was fitted with a Matchless-made side-valve engine. The tappet covers were inscribed 'SS80', while the magneto chain cover carried the Brough-Superior logo.

1939 Brough-Superior 11.50, 1096cc, side-valve V-twin engine, sprung frame, restored, excellent condition.
£10,000–12,000 BLM

This bike was ridden by Chris Packham, director and presenter of BBC2's *Watchout*, during an edition of the programme in August 1998.

BSA *(British 1906–71, late 1970s–)*

1921 BSA E2 DeLuxe, tank-mounted, hand gear-change, calliper brakes, flat tank.
£3,000–4,000 SIP

▶ **1924 BSA Flat Tank,** 349cc, side-valve, caliper brakes, chain final drive.
£2,300–2,350 CotC

c1925 BSA Model B Round Tank, 249cc side-valve engine, good condition.
£3,500–3,800 BKS

A top-selling model for BSA in the 1920s, the versatile Model B – or Round Tank, as it became known – was used for just about every task, especially by tradesmen who needed cheap personal transport. A three-speed version (identifiable by its black tank) was offered in 1926. In the following year, a wedge-shaped tank replaced the much-loved original.

1926 BSA B28, 249cc, side-valve engine, restored, very good condition.
£2,000–2,500 BLM

The B28 model was also known as the Wedge Tank.

1932 BSA Sloper, 493cc, overhead-valve, twin-port single, rear-mounted magneto, hand gear-change, in need of restoration.
£1,850–2,250 AT

The Sloper gained its name from its inclined cylinder; the oil was carried in a sump cast in the crankcase.

1936 BSA G14, 985cc, side-valve, V-twin engine, 80x98mm bore and stroke, good condition.
£4,500–5,000 VMCC

BSA offered a number of V-twins during the 1930s, ranging in capacity from 499 to 985cc.

1933 BSA Blue Star R33, 348cc, overhead-valve, twin-port single, 71x88mm bore and stroke, high-level exhaust, concours condition.
£3,000–3,500 VER

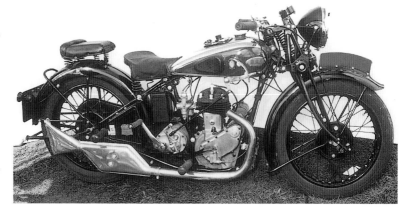

► **1935 BSA W35-6,** 499cc, side-valve single, 85x88mm bore and stroke, front-mounted magneto, Brooklands silencer.
£2,000–2,250 CStC

1936 BSA Y13, 748cc, overhead-valve, V-twin engine, 71x94.5mm bore and stroke, in need of restoration.
£5,500–6,500 AT

The Y13 was built from 1936 until 1938.

1936 BSA 500 Empire Star Q8, 499cc, overhead-valve, twin-port single, 82x94mm bore and stroke, high-level exhaust.
£3,500–3,800 PM

1945 BSA M21, 596cc, side-valve single, good condition. £1,500–1,650 CotC

The M21 was built between 1937 and 1963, making it one of BSA's longest running models.

1939 BSA C10, 249cc, side-valve single, 63x80mm bore and stroke, restored, excellent condition. £600–950 AT

Introduced for the 1938 season, the C10 was also offered post-war, until superseded by the C10L in 1953.

1949 BSA B31, 348cc, overhead-valve single, 71x88mm bore and stroke, good condition. £850–950 BKS

The B31 remained in production from the end of WWII until 1959, offering a good blend of performance and economy. This example has the plunger frame, which was introduced for the 1949 season.

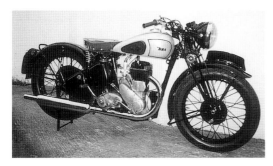

◄ **1946 BSA M20,** 496cc, side-valve single, 82x94mm bore and stroke, girder forks, rigid frame. £2,000–2,150 CotC

BSA Bantam 123–172cc (British 1948)
Price range: £600–1,800
Many would be right to argue that the foundation of a mass-market motorcycle firm lies in the design and production of its bread-and-butter models. As Honda has proved with its multi-million-selling Super Cub step-through, such machines make a vital contribution toward the development of larger, more expensive machines.

The 'Super Cub' of the BSA empire was the Bantam, a model series built in relatively large numbers from the immediate post-war period of the late 1940s until the early 1970s. But surprisingly, what became one of BSA's best-selling machines didn't have its roots in Birmingham. Instead, it came about from the opportunity to make use of German technology; to be precise, the pre-war DKW RT125. This had been designed by Hermann Weber toward the end of the 1930s and entered production on the eve of war in 1939.

The basis of both the DKW design and the Bantam was the engine, a piston-port, single-cylinder two-stroke with bore and stroke dimensions of 52x58mm. This was built in unit with a three-speed, foot-change gearbox.

The new 123cc machine was officially announced in June 1948 as the D1, but it soon became known as the Bantam. At first, it was listed for export only.

The engine was fitted to an all-welded, rigid frame

– at the time, an innovation for BSA – with a single main tube running around the power unit, and rear loops to the wheel. The front forks were simple telescopics with internal springs, but no damping, and the legs slid on grease-lubricated, sintered bronze bushes fitted into the fixed outer tubes.

For 1950, a competition model was added to the Bantam range, and buyers could opt for a plunger chassis rather than a rigid frame. In 1954, a big-fin head and barrel assembly, heavier forks and a flat silencer were introduced for the competition bike, while a larger-engined D3, with a capacity of 148cc, was introduced to complement the D1.

At the end of 1957, the D3 was discontinued, and for 1958, the 172cc D5 made its appearance. However, this lasted only for 12 months before the improved D7 arrived to replace it. By this time, all models, except the D1, sported swinging-arm rear suspension. The D7 continued in production until 1966, the long-running D1 having finally been axed in 1963.

Next, for 1966, came the D10 and D10-4 Sports, the '4' denoting an extra gear ratio. Another D10 was the Bushman, best described as an early example of a trail bike, a concept that would be marketed so successfully during the 1970s by the Japanese.

The final Bantam models were the D14/4 and D175, the last examples of which were built in 1971. Later that year came the demise of BSA itself.

1949 BSA Star Twin, 495cc, overhead-valve, pre-unit twin, 62x82mm bore and stroke, telescopic forks, plunger rear suspension.
£3,000–3,300 S

1949 BSA M21, 596cc, side-valve single, unrestored.
£1,000–1,200 MAY

1949 BSA B33, 499cc, overhead-valve single, 85x88mm bore and stroke, telescopic forks, plunger frame.
£2,500–2,750 VER

Big brother of the B31, the B33 was built between 1947 and 1960.

◄ **1951 BSA ZB32A,** 348cc, overhead-valve, single-cylinder engine, high-level exhaust, telescopic front forks, plunger frame, 800 miles from new, original, unrestored, excellent condition.
£3,500–4,000 VMCC

This particular machine is a rare competition version of the ZB32 and is equipped with an all-alloy engine. When new, it cost £153.0s.9d.

► **1951 BSA A10 Golden Flash,** 646cc, overhead-valve twin, 70x84mm bore and stroke.
£1,500–1,650 PS

In October 1949, BSA announced a new, larger-capacity twin, the A10. Although very similar in appearance to the early A7, it had a new engine design, but incorporated many of the original basic features.

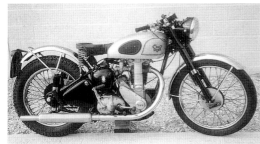

1951 BSA B34 Competition, 499cc, overhead-valve single, plunger frame.
£3,700–4,000 BLM

This all-alloy competition model was often referred to as a Gold Star.

1954 BSA B31, 348cc, overhead-valve single.
£1,200–1,350 PS

B31 and B33 models first appeared with the swinging-arm frame (originally for export only) in 1954.

1955 BSA C11, 249cc, overhead-valve single, 63x80mm bore and stroke, plunger frame, original, unrestored.
£700–750 CStC

1955 BSA B33, 499cc, overhead-valve single, telescopic forks, swinging-arm frame, headlamp nacelle, dualseat.
£2,000–2,250 AT

1955 BSA A7, 497cc, overhead-valve twin, 66x72.6mm bore and stroke, swinging-arm frame, 8in front brake, standard specification, unrestored.
£1,750–1,875 CotC

1956 BSA B31, 348cc, magneto/dynamo, swinging-arm frame, full-width Ariel brake hubs, valanced mudguards.
£1,500–1,650 PS

1955 BSA CB34 Gold Star, 348cc, overhead-valve single, restored, excellent condition.
£6,300–7,000 BKS

Nineteen-fifty-two saw the introduction of the now famous duplex Goldie frame, which was largely a result of the efforts made by Bill Nicholson. The all-welded frame used Girling oil-damped rear shocks to control the swinging arm. Initially, the frame was fitted with the existing engine, but in 1954, a new engine was introduced for the clubman's and racing variants, known as the CB. The crankshaft material became EN36, and eccentric rocker spindles replaced the earlier adjusters. However, the most striking change was to the exterior of the engine, greatly increased finning identifying the new version. This example is in full Clubman's trim, complete with RT2 gearbox and 'twittering' silencer.

1956 BSA B31, 348cc, overhead-valve single, swinging-arm frame, Ariel full-width hubs.
£1,700–1,900 BLM

The B31 was the reliable workhorse of the BSA range.

1956 BSA CB32 Gold Star Catalina Special, 348cc, overhead-valve single, US-export specification, smaller Amal GP carburettor with matchbox float chamber, small fuel tank, high handlebars, forward footrests.
£5,500–£6,000 BLM

▶ **c1956 BSA Golden Flash A10,** 646cc, overhead-valve, pre-unit twin, iron head, single carburettor, full-width brakes.
£2,500–3,000 BLM

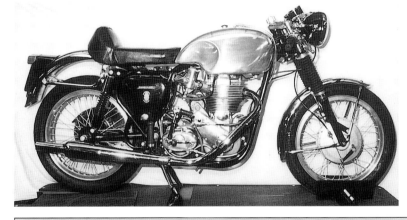

◀ **1958 BSA DBD34 Gold Star Clubman,** 499cc, 1½in Amal GP carburettor, RRT2 gearbox, 5-gallon Lyta alloy fuel tank, Taylor Dow Superleggera fork conversion, 190mm front brake, alloy rims, Feridax racing seat, 30 miles covered since engine rebuilt by John Gleed, concours condition.
£8,500–9,300 GBF

Miller's
Motorcycle Milestones

BSA Gold Star 499cc (British 1938)
Price range: £3,000–8,000
Few motorcycles can be everything to everyone, but the Gold Star – the famous 'Goldie' – came closer than most: a 100mph lap at Brooklands, clubman's racing, scrambling, trials, street bike; the versatile Goldie could cope with almost anything.

Its origin goes back to 1937 when, on the final day of June, the famous TT rider Wal Handley won a Brooklands Gold Star for lapping the Surrey circuit at over 100mph on a 499cc, iron-engined BSA Empire Star, specially prepared by Jack Arnott and Len Crisp to run on dope. This outstanding performance resulted in the Empire Star title being dropped in favour of Gold Star for 1938.

Three versions were offered: standard, competition and pure racing. Light alloy was used for the barrel and head with screw-in valve seats, and the pushrod tower was an integral part of the castings.

An Amal TT carb was standardised and, most surprising of all, the gearbox shell was cast in magnesium alloy. For the following year, the gearbox shell reverted to aluminium, but there was the advantage of an optional close-ratio cluster.

The 1939 Gold Star was the last for nine years, the war causing BSA to concentrate on production of side-valve M20 military models. After the conflict, the factory began by building the 'cooking' B31 and B33 models, which were fitted with telescopic forks. A competition model – the B32 – with an iron engine was offered for trials.

The post-war Gold Star story really began in 1948 with the advent of high-performance versions of the B31/33 series, rather than direct descendants of the pre-war M24. These were known as the B32 and B34. The series sequence was Z, B, C and finally DBD, but the last was only offered as a 500.

Production of the Gold Star came to an end in 1962.

1958 BSA D5 Bantam, 172cc, 2-stroke single, swinging-arm frame, restored, excellent condition.
£600–700 PS

1958 BSA Shooting Star, 497cc, overhead-valve, pre-unit twin, BSA full-width hubs, non-original seat.
£1,800–2,000 PM

1958 BSA C11G, 249cc, overhead-valve, pre-unit single, 63x80mm bore and stroke, 11bhp at 5,400rpm, full-width brake hubs.
£1,200–1,350 YEST

1959 BSA Gold Star Replica, 499cc, touring trim, excellent condition.
£2,150–2,250 CotC

This machine was built from a B33 frame and some Gold Star components.

c1959 BSA A7/A7SS, 500cc, overhead-valve twin, built from a combination of A7 and A7SS parts.
£2,200–2,600 BLM

▶ **1959 BSA A10 Golden Flash,** 646cc, overhead-valve, parallel twin-cylinder engine, fully-enclosed final drive chain, cast-iron brake hubs, completely original, very good condition.
£2,850–2,950 CotC

This A10 is fitted with the headlamp cowl that was introduced in 1958.

1959 BSA C15, 247cc single, standard specification except for fork gaiters.
£1,000–1,200 MAY

1960 BSA DBD34 Gold Star Clubman, 499cc, 1½in Amal GP carburettor, RRT2 gearbox, 190mm Duetto twin-leading-shoe front brake conversion, alloy rims.
£ 8000+ BMR

1961 BSA A10 Super Rocket, 646cc, overhead-valve twin, fitted later twin-leading-shoe front brake, touring trim with panniers and top box.
£2,400–2,650 PS

1961 BSA D1 Bantam, 123cc, 2-stroke single, 52x58mm bore and stroke, flat silencer, plunger frame, sprung saddle.
£500–900 BLM

The Bantam was built from 1948 to 1963 with very few changes.

◄ **1961 BSA A10,** 646cc, overhead-valve twin, standard specification, but minus headlamp cowl.
£2,000–2,250 CoH

1961 BSA A7, 497cc, overhead-valve, parallel twin, 66x72.6mm bore and stroke, very good condition.
£2,000–2,250 AT

The 1961 A7 was the last of this model to be fitted with an iron cylinder head.

c1961 BSA C15 Star, 247cc, alloy cylinder head, rear-mounted distributor, 15bhp at 7,000rpm, full-width hubs, dualseat.
£900–1,200 BLM

1961 BSA DBD34 Gold Star Clubman, 499cc, overhead-valve single, Amal GP carburettor. RRT2 gearbox, 190mm front brake, alloy rims, concours condition.
£8,000+ WEED

1962 BSA B40, 343cc, overhead-valve, unit-construction single, 21bhp at 7,000rpm, 79x70mm bore and stroke.
£1,000–1,100 HERM

A development of the 250 C15, the B40 ran from 1960 through to 1965. It was used extensively by the British Army.

1962 BSA Bantam D7, 172cc, 2-stroke single, 61.5x58mm bore and stroke, 4.5bhp at 5,000rpm, good condition.
£450–500 PS

The D7 was built between 1959 and 1966.

1962 BSA Rocket Gold Star, 646cc, completely restored by John Gleed.
£5,750–6,250 BKS

Perhaps the most sought-after of the fashionable 1960s café racers, the Rocket Gold Star was introduced in 1962, a top-of-the-range machine representing the last of the traditional pre-unit bikes at a time when BSA was announcing its new unit-construction range. It was relatively short-lived, only 1,800 or so being built over a two-year period.

1963 BSA A50, 499cc, overhead-valve, unit twin, 65.5x74mm bore and stroke, dry-sump lubrication, 28.5bhp at 6,000rpm.
£2,000–2,250 CotC

Announced in January 1962, the A50 and its bigger brother, the 650 A65, were the first of a new range of unit-construction, twin-cylinder BSAs.

1968 BSA D14/4 Bantam, 172cc, 4-speed gearbox, restored, excellent condition.
£550–750 CotC

The D10 Bantam was introduced in 1966 with a more powerful engine, points positioned on the offside of the engine, an alternator with improved output, and a four-plate clutch. The D14 was essentially the same machine, but had a larger-diameter exhaust pipe and improved air filter.

◄ **1964 BSA B40,** 343cc, overhead-valve, unit-construction, single-cylinder engine, 18in wheels, 7in front brake, standard specification, restored, excellent condition.
£700–900 MAY

Nineteen-sixty-four was the last year that this model had its distributor mounted at the rear of the cylinder.

1969 BSA D175 Bantam, 172cc, 2-stroke single, good condition.
£350–450 BMM

The D175 of 1969 was the final Bantam model and had new crankcase castings, a central plug and a needle-race clutch. Production ceased in 1971.

1970 BSA Starfire, 247cc, overhead-valve, unit single, 10:l compression ratio, 25bhp at 8,000rpm, good condition.
£900–950 CotC

Calthorpe *(British 1911–39)*

◄ **1937 Calthorpe Ivory,** 494cc, overhead-valve, single-cylinder engine, high-level exhaust with twin Brooklands silencers, foot-change gearbox, girder forks, rigid frame, sprung saddle, pillion pad, restored, very good condition.
£3,800–4,200 CStC

In 1936, Calthorpe's 348 and 494cc overhead-valve engines were equipped with new top ends, providing total enclosure of the valve gear.

Clement *(French 1897–1935)*

◄ **1920 Clement V-twin,** 540cc, overhead-camshaft, narrow-angle, V-twin engine, disc wheels, pressed-steel frame, leaf-spring front suspension, fully enclosed final drive chain, footboards, restored, very good condition.
£15,000+ TDD

Clyno *(British 1911–24)*

1921 Clyno, 225cc, side-valve, single-cylinder engine, inclined cylinder, belt final drive, restored, very good condition.
£2,600–2,750 CotC

Coventry Eagle *(British 1901–40)*

The Coventry Eagle marque had its origins in the Victorian era, making bicycles and early motorised tricycles. The company always used proprietary components, but its attention to detail, combined with a superior finish for its machines, meant that it survived longer than many similar operations.

During the 1920s, Coventry Eagle introduced the Flying Eight series of big V-twins, using JAP power, which challenged Brough-Superior for style and speed. At the same time, the company offered cheaper utility models, which had pressed-steel frames from the 1928 model year, at the time a feature that was most unusual in a British motorcycle.

By the early 1930s, Coventry Eagle had expanded its range to take in most potential customers' demands, both on price and size. At the lower end of the scale was a quartet of models with Villiers two-stroke engines in duplex, pressed-steel, channel frames. These featured fuel tanks atop the frame rails and pressed-steel front forks.

The remainder of the range featured tubular frames, and several of these employed vertically-mounted JAP engines with rear-mounted magnetos. Other machines were powered by Sturmey-Archer engines. By the late 1930s, Matchless engines were also being fitted, having displacements of 245, 348 and 497cc.

With the outbreak of war in September 1939, Coventry Eagle began to find life extremely difficult. Although the company limped into 1940, the situation did not improve, and the marque failed to survive the hostilities.

1934 Coventry Eagle K6, 245cc, overhead-valve, twin-port JAP engine, 62.5x80mm bore and stroke, high-level exhaust, Albion gearbox with hand-change.
£1,000–1,100 BKS

The K6 was only offered for the 1934 season.

1931 Coventry Eagle D25, 172cc, Villiers 2-stroke engine, good condition.
£300–350 BRIT

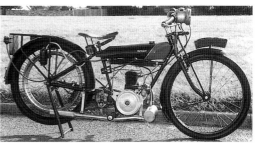

1923 Coventry Eagle S14B, 147cc, 2-stroke single, restored, very good condition.
£550–600 BKS

Six Coventry Eagles were offered for 1923 – all JAP-powered except for a Blackburne-engined 350 – ranging from the formidable 998cc Flying Eight to the diminutive S14. The latter housed JAP's Aza two-stroke engine (claimed by Coventry Eagle as its own) in a simple frame topped with the marque's distinctive, wedge-shaped tank. The standard S14 was a clutchless single-speeder, while the S14A came with a two-speed countershaft gearbox, and the S14B added a clutch to the specification. A kickstart was a £1 option, and all S14s featured chain-cum-belt drive.

Restored Values

The cost of a professional restoration will have an influence on, but no direct relation to, a motorcycle's market value. A restored motorcycle can have a market value lower than the cost of its restoration.

1937 Coventry Eagle N1, 148cc, Villiers 2-stroke engine, 53x67mm bore and stroke.
£750–1,100 AT

1924 Coventry Eagle Flying Eight, 995cc, side-valve JAP V-twin, restored, very good condition.
£10,000–12,000 VMCC

In 1924, the Flying Eight sold for £120.

Dayton *(British 1913–20)*

◄ **1913 Dayton,** 153cc, side-valve, single-cylinder engine, pedals, good condition.
£3,500–3,800 S

Dayton was a bicycle manufacturer that occcasionally built ultra-lightweight motorcycles. This example is one of their earliest models from the first year of manufacture.

Diamond *(British 1910–38)*

1923 Diamond, 275cc, JAP single-cylinder engine, hand gear-change, belt final drive, excellent condition.
£2,950–3,250 VER

DKW *(German 1919–81)*

1938 DKW SB500, 494cc, air-cooled, 2-stroke, twin-cylinder engine, 15bhp, restored, very good condition.
£1,800–2,000 HERM

DMW *(British 1945–71)*

1960 DMW Dolomite, 324cc, 3T Villiers 2-stroke twin, piston-port induction, 4-speed foot-change gearbox, Earles front forks, swinging-arm rear suspension, fully enclosed final drive chain.
£1,200+ PC

Today, the Dolomite is a very rare machine.

Dot *(British 1903–74)*

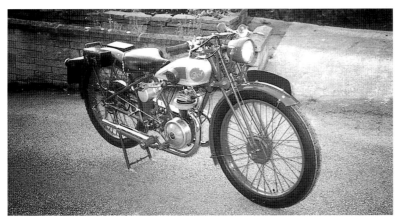

◄ **1929 Dot Super Sports VI,** 172cc, Villiers 2-stroke twin, restored, excellent condition.
£2,300–2,500 BKS

Dot stands for 'Devoid of trouble'. Production at the Manchester factory began in 1903, but ceased between 1932 and 1948. After that, Dots were built until 1977.

Douglas *(British 1906–57)*

1910 Douglas Model C, 350cc twin, 60x60mm bore and stroke, automatic inlet valves, direct belt drive.
£5,000+ YEST

1914 Douglas 2¾hp, fore-and-aft flat-twin, restored, very good condition.
£6,000–7,000 VER

1921 Douglas 2¾hp, some non-original components, otherwise good condition.
£3,000–3,500 ELK

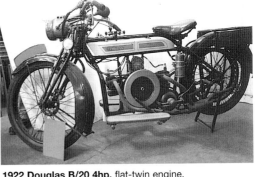

1922 Douglas B/20 4hp, flat-twin engine, older restoration, good condition.
£3,600–4,000 CoH

1923 Douglas B/20 4hp, flat-twin engine, restored, concours condition.
£5,500–6,500 VER

1925 Douglas CW, 350cc, 4-stroke, flat-twin.
£3,300–3,600 BKS

The Douglas CW for 1925 was of typical fore-and-aft engine layout, with an independent gearbox and all-chain drive. The machine appears to have reached the far corners of the British Empire, as *The Motor Cycle* magazine published a report in 1925 of a remarkable journey by a CW of no less than 9,000 miles across Australia, with no punctures and no spare parts being required. However, at one point, the rider had to dismantle his machine and swim it across a river, as there was no other means of crossing.

1929 Douglas SW6, 600cc, flat-twin, competition model, restored, excellent condition.
£11,500–12,500 PM

▶ **1929 Douglas D29,** 350cc, overhead-valve flat-twin, hand-change gearbox, original except for silencer.
£5,000–5,500 VMCC

The Douglas D29 had a hand-change gearbox with the lever mounted low down near the front of the engine. When new, it cost £49.10s.0d. Today, it is a very rare machine.

1930 Douglas S6, 600cc, overhead-valve, flat-twin, very good condition.
£1,600–1,750 BKS

1949 Douglas Mk 4, 348cc, overhead-valve, unit-construction flat-twin, non-standard exhaust, swinging-arm rear suspension with torsion bars, restored, excellent condition.
£3,000–3,500 VER

The Mk 4 Douglas was introduced in 1949.

1953 Douglas Mk 5, 350cc, overhead-valve flat-twin, non-original rear mudguard.
£3,000–3,250 VMCC

When new, the Mk 5 Douglas cost £230.

1956 Douglas Dragonfly, 350cc, overhead-valve, transverse flat-twin, very good condition.
£1,500–1,700 BLM

The Dragonfly was the last of the Douglas flat-twin models.

1956 Douglas Dragonfly, 348cc, overhead-valve, transverse flat-twin, restored to original factory specification.
£2,700–2,950 CotC

Ducati *(Italian 1946–)*

1958 Ducati 175TS, 174cc, in need of restoration, several parts missing, including fuel tank cap, cables and twistgrip.
£600–650 PC

1959 Ducati 175T, 174cc, complete, in need of restoration.
£700–900 MAY

1960 Ducati 125 Aurea, 124cc, complete, original, in need of restoration.
£600–700 DOC

1960 Ducati 125 Aurea, 124cc, overhead-valve, unit-construction single, 4-speed gearbox, non-standard seat, in need of restoration.
£600–650 IVC

1960 Ducati 175 Silverstone Super, 174cc, overhead-camshaft single, completely restored, good condition.
£4,150–4,550 BKS

Ducati concessionaires Kings of Manchester built a small number of specially-tuned 175 Sport models, selling them under the Silverstone Super tag. The specification included a higher-compression piston, a lumpier camshaft and a 25.5mm Dell'Orto SSI racing carburettor. The engine developed 14bhp, and the machine was good for 92mph.

▶ **1961 Ducati 200TS,** 204cc single, bevel-driven overhead camshaft, valve-spring head, 4-speed gearbox, restored.
£2,400–2,600 PC

1961 Ducati Diana, 248cc, 24mm Dell'Orto UBF carburettor, 85mph top speed, completely restored.
£2,500+ PC

The first year of the Ducati 250 single was 1961.

1962 Ducati 125 Bronco, 124cc, overhead-valve, unit-construction single, 4-speed foot-change gearbox, Duplex frame, full-width alloy brake hubs, completely restored.
£900+ PC

1962 Ducati 200GT, 204cc, 67x57.8mm bore and stroke, valanced mudguards, touring specification, unrestored.
£1,500–1,600 DOC

This model has the same style of tank and side panels as the Diana 250 (known as the Daytona in the UK).

1962 Ducati 48 Sport Export, 48cc, 3-speed, twistgrip gear-change, very good condition.
£850–950 MAY

1963 Ducati Daytona, 248cc, original, in need of restoration.
£1,150–1,250 IVC

1963 Ducati Elite, 204cc single, bevel-driven overhead camshaft, non-standard rear suspension units.
£1,700–2,200 MAY

1966 Ducati 160 Monza Junior, 156cc, overhead-camshaft single, 61x52mm bore and stroke, very good condition.
£500–800 PS

This 1966 model was from a batch imported by Bill Hannah of Liverpool in 1968, originally having been destined for the American importers, Berliner of New Jersey. It was first registered in 1971.

1966 Ducati Sebring, 340cc, completely rebuilt to café racer specification with Amal Concentric Mk I carburettor, megaphone silencer, Benelli 2C forks and hubs, alloy rims, specially constructed fuel tank, clip-ons, rearsets, Desmo seat, tachometer, excellent condition.
£2,000+ DOC

1969 Ducati Mk 3D, 248cc, 74x57.8mm bore and stroke, standard but for optional white-faced Veglia tachometer.
£2,800–3,200 PC

The 'D' in this machine's designation stands for 'Desmo'. The Mk 3D was the world's first production roadster to have the desmodromic system of positive valve operation.

◀ **1972 Ducati Scrambler 350,** 340cc, overhead-camshaft single, 5-speed gearbox, wide-case model, 'pancake' air filter, 29mm square-slide VHB carburettor, Silentium silencer, 35mm Marzocchi heavyweight front forks, non-standard rear suspension units, matching speedometer and tachometer, air horns.
£2,000–2,250 VICO

 # Miller's Motorcycle Milestones

Ducati 204cc Elite (Italian 1959)
Price range: £1,600–3,000
In the period immediately after WWII, Ducati Meccanica rose from the ashes of Societa Scientifica Radiobrevetti Ducati, which had been a major producer of radio equipment before the war.

The conflict had caused the virtual destruction of Ducati's Bologna plant. However, an engineer called Aldo Farinelli had created a 48cc four-stroke engine that 'clipped' on to a conventional pedal cycle, which not only saved Ducati from extinction, but also sold in thousands.

A 60cc version of Farinelli's engine powered Ducati's first complete motorcycle in 1950. From this came a series of pushrod lightweights, before Fabio Taglioni joined the company in 1954, heralding an era of great success in the showroom and on the race-track.

The first of Taglioni's new breed of single, the 98cc Gran Sport racer, had its camshaft driven by bevel gears and shafts. It debuted in 1955 and became a class winner in the Milano-Taranto and

Giro d'Italia (Tour of Italy) long-distance road races. The following year saw the twin-cam, 124cc Grand Prix and triple-cam Desmo racers, together with one of Ducati's most important street bikes of all time, the 175 Monoalbero (single camshaft).

The 174.5cc engine, which acted as a stressed member of the frame, had a slightly inclined alloy cylinder with a cast-iron liner. Driven by a pair of bevel shafts and gears on the offside, its overhead-camshaft valve gear had enclosed rockers and hairpin valve springs. The geared primary drive and multi-plate clutch were on the nearside, transmitting power to a four-speed gearbox. A full-circle crank featured a roller big-end bearing, the small-end bush being phosphor bronze. Lubrication was by wet sump with a gear-type oil pump.

The first version, the 175T (Turismo), went on sale in 1957 and was soon followed by Sport and Formula 3 variants. In 1958, the 203.7cc Elite arrived. Thereafter came a vast array of overhead-camshaft bevel singles, culminating with the 436cc in 1969.

Production ceased in late 1974.

1973 Ducati 750GT, 748cc, 90° V-twin, bevel-driven overhead camshaft, valve-spring heads, 80x74.4mm bore and stroke, US export model with leading-axle forks, stainless steel mudguards, high bars and side reflectors, minus side-panel badges and air filters, otherwise standard.
£2,500–3,200 PC

1974 Ducati 350 Mk 3, 340cc single, bevel-driven overhead-camshaft, 76x75mm bore and stroke, 5-speed gearbox, 19in front and 18in rear rims, 1971-style toolboxes, touring handlebars, standard except for direction indicators.
£2,000+ IVC

This model was one of the last Ducatis to be made with steel wheel rims.

1974 Ducati 350 Mk 3, 340cc single, bevel-driven overhead camshaft, valve-spring head, Conti replica silencer, stainless steel mudguards, non-standard Lucas chromed headlamp, tank badges missing.
£1,600–1,700 PC

1974 Ducati 750S, 748cc, 90° V-twin, bevel-driven overhead camshaft, valve-spring heads, 5-speed gearbox, completely restored.
£6,000–6,500 CotC

◀ **1978 Ducati 900GTS,** 864cc, Conti silencers, non-standard fork gaiters, aftermarket rear suspension units, alloy wheel rims, stainless steel mudguards, 860GT Mk 3 dualseat, completely restored, very good condition.
£3,000–3,250 PC

▶ **1978 Ducati 500 Sport Desmo,** 497cc, V-twin engine, chain-driven overhead camshafts, desmodromic valve gear, points ignition, non-standard chromed silencers, triple disc brakes, cast alloy wheels, very good condition.
£1,500–1,650 PC

The 500 Sport Desmo was an underrated motorcycle that looked good and offered plenty of power.

1978 Ducati 500 Sport Desmo, 497cc, overhead-camshaft V-twin, desmodromic valve gear, electric starter, triple Brembo disc brakes, cast alloy wheels, original, concours condition.
£1,800–2,100 PC

The 500 Sport Desmo was styled by Leopoldo Tartarini.

1978 Ducati Darmah SD900, 864cc, Silentium silencers, hydraulic steering damper, stainless steel mudguards, ND clocks, non-standard mirrors, restored, concours condition.
£3,000+ DOC

1979 Ducati Mike Hailwood Replica, 864cc V-twin, restored, excellent condition.
£4,000–5,000 BKS

Mike Hailwood's 1978 Isle of Man TT comeback ride is the stuff of legend. Out of top-flight bike racing for seven years, he beat the Honda team to win the F1 TT at record speed. His mount was a V-twin Ducati, and the factory lost little time in launching a roadgoing replica. Like the race bike, the MHR was based on the production 900SS, but had much more in common with the latter than the former. The most obvious differences were the full fairing, fibreglass tank (containing a steel fuel reservoir) and racing seat. Mechanical changes were confined to lighter wheels and improved Brembo brakes. The MHR's performance was similar to that of the 900SS: around 135mph flat out.

1979 Ducati Mike Hailwood Replica, 864cc V-twin.
£4,500–5,000 IVC

This particular bike was one of the very first Hailwood Replicas to be built.

1982 Ducati 500SL Pantah, 499cc, 90° V-twin, desmodromic valve gear, 52bhp at 9,000rpm, non-standard 2-into-1 exhaust, 5-speed gearbox.
£2,500+ IMOC

This is a late 500SL fitted with a 600SL-type fairing.

Excelsior *(British 1886–1964)*

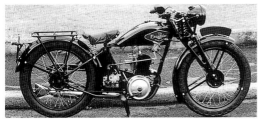

1930 Excelsior Model 4, 196cc Villiers engine, 61x67mm bore and stroke.
£1,500–1,650 PM

In 1930, Excelsior sold its 196cc, Villiers-engined machine as the Model 3 and Model 4. Basically, they were the same, but for minor details.

1948 Excelsior Autobyk, 98cc, Villiers 2-stroke engine.
£450–500 PM

Production of the Autobyk began in 1938.

▶ **1936 Excelsior D9,** 249cc, water-cooled, twin-port, 2-stroke single, 63x80mm bore and stroke, restored, excellent condition.
£1,500–1,650 BKS

For 1934, Excelsior offered two versions of its water-cooled, two-stroke 250. One, the D9, was enclosed at the gearbox and rear of the engine unit. The other had no enclosure.

Francis-Barnett *(British 1919–64)*

1951 Francis-Barnet 58 Falcon, 197cc, Villiers 6E engine, 59x72mm bore and stroke.
£450–500 AT

1959 Francis-Barnett 81 Falcon, 197cc, Villiers 10E engine.
£450–500 PS

Garelli *(Italy 1918–)*

◀ **1977 Garelli KL100,** 79cc, air-cooled, 2-stroke, single-cylinder engine, restored, very good condition.
£170–190 PS

The KL100 was a development of the 49cc Rekord and Tiger Cross models. It was imported into Britain by the Nottingham-based Agrati concern.

Gilera *(Italian 1909–)*

1972 Gilera 50 Trail, 49cc, 2-stroke single, alloy cylinder and radial-fin head, 5-speed gearbox.
£500–600 PC

This ultra-lightweight motorcycle was also built with pedals for use by younger riders.

1989 Gilera 125 OSPI, 124cc, liquid-cooled, 2-stroke single, reed-valve induction, 6-speed gearbox.
£900–1,100 IMOC

Gitan *(Italian 1950–66)*

◄ **1951 Gitan 125 Scirocco,** 124cc, 2-stroke, single-cylinder engine, piston-port induction, blade-type front forks, plunger rear suspension, pillion pad, completely restored, excellent condition.
£2,500–3,000 IMOC

This is an extremely rare machine.

Greeves *(British 1952–78)*

1961 Greeves 25 Sports Twin, 249cc, 2-stroke Villiers 2T twin, 50x63.5mm bore and stroke, restored to original specification, concours condition.
£2,500–2,750 SWS

◀ **1965 Aermacchi Ala Verde,** 246cc, overhead-valve single, horizontal cylinder, wet-sump lubrication, 5-speed gearbox, unit construction, café-racer style with twin-leading-shoe front brake, alloy rims, special tank, seat, front mudguard and megaphone-type silencer, British rear light assembly, Veglia tachometer.
£2,800–3,000 PC

Aermacchi joined with the American Harley-Davidson concern in 1960. The 'marriage' ended in 1972.

▶ **1958 AJS Model 20,** 498cc, overhead-valve twin, 66x72.8mm bore and stroke, original dynamo and magneto, cast primary chaincase, fitted with incorrect seat and Vincent flat bars.
£2,250–2,350 CotC

Girling rear dampers were fitted to the Model 20 for the first time in 1958.

1960 AJS Model 31 De Luxe, 646cc, overhead-valve twin, 72x79.3mm bore and stroke, Amal monobloc carburettor, AMC gearbox, chrome tank panels.
£2,000–2,500 BLM

▶ **1989 Aprilia AFI Replica,** 124.7cc, liquid-cooled, reed-valve, 2-stroke single, 32.8bhp at 10,750rpm, 6-speed gearbox, 320mm front disc, 240mm rear disc, concours condition.
£1,100–1,300 IVC

The AFI Replica was developed as a roadgoing version of Aprilia's GP racing bike.

◀ **1956 Ariel NH Red Hunter,** 346cc, overhead-valve single, 72x85mm bore and stroke, 4-speed, foot-change gearbox.
£1,800–2,200 BLM

Ariel gave the Red Hunter a swinging-arm frame for 1954, providing much improved roadholding. It had been pioneered on the works trials and MX machines.

1938 Brough-Superior SS80, 982cc, Matchless side-valve engine, 85.5x85.5mm bore and stroke, Norton gearbox, rigid frame, concours condition.
£16,000–17,000 VER

Today, the Brough-Superior V-twin is sought after by collectors and enthusiasts alike.

▶ **1933 BSA Blue Star R33,** 348cc, overhead-valve, twin-port single, wet-sump lubrication.
£2,500–3,500 BLM

◀ **1949 BSA B31,** 348cc, overhead-valve, single-cylinder engine, 71x88mm bore and stroke, rigid frame, restored to original specification, excellent condition.
£1,750–1,850 CotC

The B31 was a real workhorse and remained in production from 1945 through to 1959. Essentially, it was a smaller-engined version of the 500 B33.

▶ **1955 BSA A7,** 497cc, Burgess silencers, headlamp nacelle, chrome tank, restored, very good condition.
£2,650–2,950 CotC

Nineteen-fifty-five was the last year of A7 production before the arrival of full-width hubs. It was also the first year that the Amal monobloc carburettor was used on BSA twin-cylinder models.

◄ **1956 BSA C12,** 249cc, overhead-valve single, 63x80mm bore and stroke.
£1,100–1,200 PS

The C12 was manufactured from 1956 to 1958. It used the earlier C11G engine in a swinging-arm frame with damped forks, full-width hubs and a new four-speed gearbox. It was the last of BSA's pre-unit 250 singles and was replaced by the unit-construction C15.

► **1959 BSA C15,** 247cc, overhead-valve unit single, 67x70mm bore and stroke.
£600–700 PM

The C15 was launched in September 1958 and became the basis for an entire family of unit-contruction-engined machines. Features of this early model include a distributor mounted behind the cylinder barrel, 17in wheels and a cowled headlamp.

◄ **1961 BSA A10 Super Rocket,** 646cc twin, Amal monobloc carburettor, 43bhp.
£3,000+ BLM

The A10 Super Rocket was the sporting version of BSA's 1961 twin-cylinder range. During a contemporary road test by *Motor Cycle News*, it returned 52mpg, often cruising at between 70 and 90mph.

► **1962 BSA D1 Bantam,** 123cc, 2-stroke single, restored, very good condition.
£700–1,000 BLM

The long-running Bantam was derived from the German DKW RT125. Launched in 1948 with a rigid frame, it was offered with optional plunger rear suspension for the 1950 model year. The last year of production for the D1 was 1963.

◄ **1964 BSA A65 Star,** 654cc, overhead-valve twin, 75x74mm bore and stroke, 38bhp at 5,800rpm, unit construction.
£2,700–3,000 BLM

The A65 and its smaller 499cc brother, the A50, were announced in the motorcycling Press in January 1962. They replaced the long-running A10 and A7 pre-unit twin-cylinder machines.

▶ **1969 BSA B44 Victor Special,**
441cc, overhead-valve single,
79x90mm bore and stroke,
coil ignition, restored.
£1,500–1,700 BKS

Introduced in 1969, the Victor
Special was an improved version of
the preceding Victor Enduro. It had
a more powerful front brake, the
diameter of which was increased
from 7 to 8in. A full lighting set
was also fitted.

◀ **1971 BSA Royal Star,**
499cc, overhead-valve unit
twin, single carburettor,
rev-counter, twin-leading-
shoe front brake,
completely restored
using original parts.
£3,500+ PC

Introduced in September
1965, the 500 Royal Star
was a very underrated
performer with a much
smoother engine than
the 650.

▶ **1971 BSA 650 Lightning,**
654cc, oil-in-frame model, conical
brake hubs, imported from USA,
original specification.
£2,000–2,500 MAY

This top-of-the-range sports
model was restyled by the
Umberslade Hall team to include
a duplex, oil-containing frame,
exposed-stanchion forks and
new bodywork. But it was all to
no avail, as BSA folded later
that year.

◀ **1986 Cagiva Alazzurra 650 GT,** 649.5cc, Ducati
Pantah desmo 90° V-twin, 82x61.5mm bore and stroke,
66bhp at 9,000rpm, hydraulic clutch, triple Brembo disc
brakes, cast alloy wheels, full fairing.
£1,750–1,950 IVC

In 1983, Cagiva signed an agreement with Ducati to
supply engines. Then, in May 1985, Cagiva purchased
the Ducati company from the Italian government.

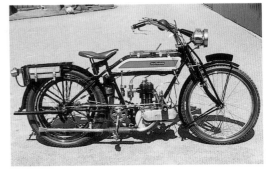

▶ **1912 Campion Single,** 3½hp, inlet-over-exhaust,
single-cylinder engine, completely restored, very good
condition throughout.
£8,000–8,500 VER

This model is now extremely rare.

1937 Coventry Eagle Flying 500 Model P50/1,
498cc, Matchless overhead-valve engine,
megaphone silencer, 4-speed gearbox,
Webb forks, rigid frame, concours condition.
£5,000+ PC

▶ **1951 Douglas 80 Plus,** 348cc, overhead-
valve, horizontally-opposed twin.
£4,000–4,500 BKS

The most sought-after of all the Douglas
post-war flat-twin models are the specially-
tuned, limited-production 80 Plus and 90
Plus. The latter was raced with considerable
success in the Isle of Man Clubman's TT
series during the early 1950s. The '80' and
'90' in their titles referred to their maximum
speeds, but these could usually be bettered,
hence the 'Plus'.

◀ **1958 Ducati 175TS,** 174cc single, bevel-
driven overhead camshaft, wet-sump
lubrication, unit construction, 4-speed
gearbox, concours condition.
£2,400–2,800 INM

Launched on a wave of publicity at the
Milan show in November 1956, the 175
Ducati was the forerunner of a whole family
of singles from the Bologna factory,
culminating in the 450 (436cc) of 1969.

1964 Ducati Daytona, 248cc, completely restored,
concours condition.
£2,750–3,150 IVC

1974 Ducati 250 Desmo, 248cc, 35mm Ceriani forks,
280mm single Brembo disc front brake, drum rear
brake, alloy rims, racing seat, rearsets, clip-ons,
all-chrome Aprilia headlamp, completely restored,
concours condition.
£4,000+ PC

The 1974 250 Desmo was the final version of the long-
running bevel-driven singles line.

◀ **1979 Ducati Mike Hailwood Replica,** 864cc,
90° desmo V-twin, Goldline Brembo brake callipers,
single/dualseat converter, restored, concours condition.
£5,500+ PC

◄ **1954 Francis-Barnett 71 Cruiser,** 224cc, Villiers IH engine, 63x72mm bore and stroke, 4-speed foot-change gearbox, telescopic forks, swinging-arm rear suspension.
£900–1,000 PC

Affectionately known throughout the industry as 'Fanny B', Francis-Barnett made its name with affordable, easily-maintained commuter bikes, of which the Cruiser is a typical example.

► **1963 Honda C77,** 305cc, overhead-camshaft, parallel twin, unit construction, electric start, restored, very good condition.
£2,000–2,500 SWC

When the first Honda motorcycles reached Europe at the beginning of the 1960s, the flag carriers were the C77 tourer and CB77 sports models. Both featured a level of sophistication that was unknown on European models of the period.

1941 Indian 751B, 750cc, side-valve V-twin, ex-WWII dispatch rider's bike.
£5,500–6,000 IMC

1981 Honda CBX 1000B, 1047cc, pro-link rear suspension, fairing, rear panniers.
£2,000–3,500 CBX

With its mighty six-cylinder, across-the-frame engine, the CBX 1000B is an impressive piece of engineering. It was only available in grey in the UK, but was also offered in white in the USA, Canada and mainland Europe.

1964 James M25S Super Swift Sports, 249cc, Villiers 4T 2-stroke twin, restored, concours condition.
£1,500–1,800 BMR

The Super Swift Sports was one of the best-looking British lightweights of its era.

◄ **1984 Kawasaki KR250,** 249.1cc, in-line, 2-stroke twin, rotary- and reed-valve induction, 54x54.4mm bore and stroke, 6-speed gearbox, aluminium frame, air-adjustable and anti-dive forks, Uni-Trak rear suspension, concours condition.
£2,500–2,800 VJMC

Making its debut in 1984, the KR250 was never imported into the UK. It was discontinued at the end of 1987 and today is very rare.

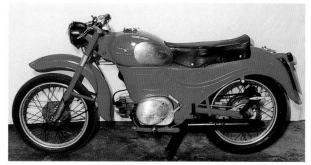

◄ **1957 Moto Guzzi 98 Zigolo Series 1,** 98cc, disc-valve, 2-stroke, single-cylinder engine, 50x50mm bore and stroke.
£1,500–1,750 BKS

Based on the earlier Motoleggera 65, the rotary-valve Zigolo made its debut in 1953. it was one of the very few motorcycles in the world that made a success of enclosure. Later, its capacity was raised to 110cc. Production ceased in 1966.

► **1970 Moto Guzzi Nuovo Falcone,** 498.4cc, overhead-valve single.
£1,750–2,500 IMOC

The Nuovo (New) Falcone was originally designed with police and military contracts in mind. It appeared in prototype form during late 1969 and went on sale in mid-1970, boasting what amounted to virtually a new engine, frame, full-width hubs (a twin-leading-shoe brake at the front) and 12 volt electric starting.

◄ **1981 Moto Morini 500,** 478cc, overhead-valve, 72° V-twin, triple disc brakes, non-standard front mudguard.
£1,500–1,800 OxM

The original 500 Morini was first shown as a pre-production prototype at the Milan show in November 1975. It was a development of the 3½ model, sharing the same 72-degree V-twin format.

► **1983 Moto Morini 500/6 Turismo,** 478.6cc, overhead-valve V-twin, black exhaust system, 6-speed gearbox, triple disc brakes, 7-spoke cast alloy wheels, original.
£1,650–1,850 IVC

Until the end of 1981, the 500 Morini V-twin employed a five-speed gearbox. From the 1982 model year onwards, it was given an extra ratio, making six in all.

◄ **1988 Moto Morini 350 Dart,** 344cc, very good condition.
£2,500+ MOR

Moto Morini was taken over by Cagiva in 1987, that company having already gobbled up Ducati and Husqvarna. Introduced for 1988, the Dart was a clever mix of a Cagiva 125 Freccia chassis and Morini V-twin engine. Later, a 400 version was offered. Production ceased in 1991.

◀ **1974 MV Agusta 750S,** 743cc, double-overhead-camshaft, 4-cylinder engine, 65x56mm bore and stroke, 69bhp at 8,500rpm, 122mph top speed, concours condition.
£15,000+ PC

This is a late 750S with Scarab double disc front brake and higher-specification engine with new camshafts, 10:1 Borgo pistons, larger 31.8mm inlet valves and 27mm square-slide Dell'Orto VHB carburettors. These changes began at engine number 2140418.

▶ **1937 New Imperial Model 46,** 344cc, overhead-valve, twin-port single, unit construction, concours condition.
£3,000–3,500 BKS

During the 1930s, New Imperial was at the forefront of popularising unit-construction engine and gearbox assemblies, which offered a number of benefits. From the rider's point of view, the arrangement removed the need to service the chain that was normally used for the primary drive, while from the manufacturer's point of view, it was more economical to produce.

◀ **1924 Norton 16H,** 490cc, side-valve, single-cylinder engine, 79x100mm bore and stroke, restored, very good condition.
£4,850–5,350 VER

Over 100,000 Norton side-valve singles were built during WWII, most of them the 16H model. Although a heavy machine, it proved very robust and reliable in service.

▶ **1957 Norton International Model 30,** 490cc, overhead-camshaft, single-cylinder engine, 4-speed gearbox, completely restored, concours condition.
£7,500–8,500 VER

The 1957 model was the final version of the famous International line, with Featherbed frame, Roadholder forks and full-width hubs. Alan Shepherd finished third in the 1956 Junior (350cc) Clubman's TT on the smaller-engined International Model 40.

◀ **c1972 Norton 850 Commando Roadster,** 844cc, overhead-valve, pre-unit twin, disc front brake, drum rear brake, unregistered.
£8,000+ OxM

During the late 1960s and early 1970s, the Norton Commando won the *Motor Cycle News* Machine of the Year award several times in succession. This particular example was built from new components by Les Emery of Fair Spares.

Harley-Davidson *(American 1903–)*

The history of Harley-Davidson began in 1903, when it built an inlet-over-exhaust single-cylinder engine that later became known as the F-head. Complete motorcycles were made at the factory in Milwaukee, Wisconsin, until 1972, after which engines only were produced by the plant, then shipped to York, Pennsylvania, for final assembly. From the beginning, the machines were soundly engineered and solidly constructed, ensuring durability, which has contributed to the fanatical following enjoyed by Harley-Davidson products right up to modern times.

The wide open spaces of America, with their many long, straight roads, led to a demand for large, powerful motorcycles, and by 1907 the first prototype V-twin had been built. Once the twin-cylinder layout had been found satisfactory, Harley-Davidson quickly developed a range of powerful and reliable machines, many of which found use with the American War Department during WWI. The experience gained from war production and the level of reliability required for military machines were carried forward into civilian production after the war, allowing the company to improve its products and develop a reputation for sturdy machines that lasts to this day.

1920 Harley-Davidson Model J, 8.68hp, 4-stroke, narrow-angle V-twin, hand-change gearbox.
£7,350–8,000 BKS

Fitted with an 8.68hp V-twin motor, the Model J was chain driven throughout. Engine changes were made to the 1920 models, including new cylinders, inlet pushrods, pushrod spring covers and new flywheels, but otherwise they were substantially the same as the first post-WWI civilian models.

1927 Harley-Davidson Model J, 350cc single, chain final drive, sprung forks, rigid frame.
£4,000–5,000 VER

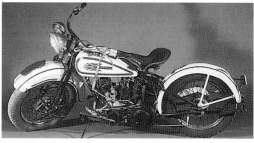

1930 Harley-Davidson V-twin, 750cc, restored, very good condition.
£9,000–10,000 BERN

◄ **1933 Harley-Davidson Model VLE,** 1206cc V-twin, restored, excellent condition.
£13,800–15,000 BKS

Harley-Davidson introduced its new 1206cc, side-valve V-twins in 1929 to replace the long-running F and J models and counter competition from Indian. The bike was all new, with stronger I-beam forks, a lower seat, better brakes and a more powerful engine. Early machines suffered reliability problems, but these were soon overcome, and the model went on to earn a reputation for speed and reliability.

◄ **1974 Harley-Davidson Special,** 1340cc, overhead-valve, 1980 V-twin engine, drag-style exhaust pipes, belt final and primary drives, Kawasaki ZX10 front forks, fully-floating front disc brakes, 1974 Harley-Davidson frame, very good condition.
£5,250–5,500 CotC

1975 Harley-Davidson Electraglide, 1340cc V-twin, big-bore conversion, custom exhaust, Lester alloy wheels, otherwise largely standard.
£5,250–£5,500 CotC

Henderson *(American 1911–31)*

Founded in 1911, the Henderson company produced technically-advanced, four-cylinder motorcycles that were ideal for covering the long distances found in North America. By the early 1920s, the firm had been taken over by cycle manufacturer Schwinn, owners of the American Excelsior brand. Production continued until 1931, when the effects of the depression forced the company to close down.

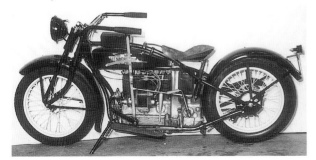

◄ **1922 Henderson De Luxe,** 1340cc, 4-cylinder, in-line engine, chain final drive.
£12,650–13,650 BKS

The side-valve engine fitted to this motorcycle was equipped with a reliable electrical system and produced approximately 30bhp, allowing the machine to attain 80mph. Regarded by many as the finest of the American fours, Hendersons are highly sought after.

Hesketh *(British 1981–)*

The Rt Hon Lord Hesketh KBE developed the exclusive V1000 model on his estate at Easton Neston. His objective was to produce a bespoke motorcycle, essentially British in character, and the handsome V1000 was the result. Launched in April 1980 at the Hesketh family home, the V1000 was demonstrated for the Press by Mike Hailwood, and later that year appeared at Earl's Court. Many applauded the fact that the 'right' sort of British bike was in contention again.

Hesketh Motorcycles Plc elected to hand-assemble their luxury machines at Daventry, and the Hesketh order book was open by the time of the NEC Birmingham show in 1981. At the time, however, the motorcycle industry was under threat from a world recession and faced an uncertain future. Sales figures for August 1981 were down by an alarming 52 per cent on those of the previous boom year.

The first Hesketh motorcycles were delivered in February 1982. More orders followed at the NEC in April, but the prevailing economic climate challenged the wisdom of the initiative and, in August, the company ceased production.

Lord Hesketh and his partner, A G 'Bubbles' Horsley, declared that they had too much faith in the V1000 to let it go, and set out to continue production, under the name Hesleydon, at Easton Neston. By January 1983, the small labour force, including Hesketh engineer Mike Broom, was concentrating its efforts on the export market. Finally, at the Isle of Man TT, the Vampire , a limited-edition touring bike, was announced.

One authority, writing in 1985, suggested that Hesketh would 'come to be more highly regarded than now.' To be sure, the decision to build an expensive, high-quality 'Superbike' for the very top end of the market was amazingly bold, but it demonstrates the role of personalities in the history of the motorcycle. Success may not always be measured by sales and profits, and Alexander Hesketh's contribution as a flag-bearer for the British motorcycle industry has been considerable.

1979/1980 Hesketh V1000, 992cc, double-overhead-camshaft V-twin.
£10,000–11,000 HOC

This machine is the original prototype V1000 and, as such, is unique.

1979/80 Hesketh V1000, 992cc V-twin, only 22 miles from new, completely rebuilt by Mick Broom.
£12,000–13,000 S

This machine is thought to be the first production Hesketh built.

1982 Hesketh V1000, 992cc V-twin, standard specification, but with panniers and rear carrier, finished in black with gold coachlines, very good condition.
£6,000–7,000 HOC

Hewetson *(British 1898–1902)*

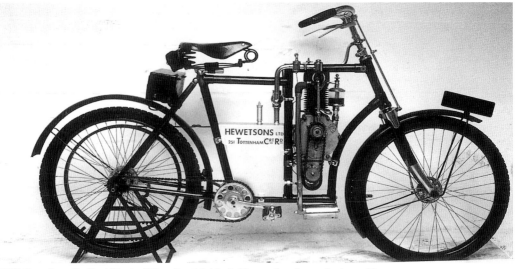

1898 Hewetson Vertical Single, 3½hp, direct flat-belt drive, restored, excellent condition.
£10,000–12,000 VMCC

Sold by Hewetson of Tottenham Court Road, London, under its own name, this machine is actually a Laurin and Klement, imported from Czechoslovakia.

Honda *(Japanese 1946–)*

◄ **1962 Honda C100,** 49cc, overhead-valve single, restored, very good condition.
£450–650 MAY

In many respects, the C100 Cub put Honda on the map. It offered four-stroke reliability and performance, which its rivals simply could not match when it was introduced during the late 1950s.

1975 Honda CB350F, 349cc, 4-cylinder engine, chain-driven overhead camshafts, 4-into-4 exhaust, 5-speed gearbox, single disc front brake, drum rear.
£750–800 IVC

This model was never officially imported into the UK.

1975 Honda CB400F, 408.6cc, overhead-camshaft, 4-cylinder engine, 51x50mm bore and stroke.
£1,100–1,200 CotC

► **1976 Honda CB400F,** 408.6cc, overhead-camshaft, 4-cylinder engine, 4-into-1 exhaust, single disc front brake, non-standard seat.
£950–1,050 IVC

1976 Honda CB750F2, 748cc, non-standard exhaust and paint finish.
£580–640 PS

This model was the last of the single-overhead-camshaft 750s.

1976 Honda 750F2, 748cc, original specification, but for 4-into-1 exhaust.
£750–850 PS

◄ **1978 Honda CBX 1000Z,** 1047cc, double-overhead camshafts, 6 cylinders, 4 valves per cylinder, 64.5x53.4mm bore and stroke, 105bhp, dual disc front brake, standard specification apart from Rickman Brothers crashbars, completely restored, concours condition.
£2,000–5,000 CBX

Launched in 1978 as a range leader, Honda's mighty CBX used the engine as a stressed member of the frame.

1981 Honda CM400 Custom, 395cc, overhead-camshaft, vertical twin, Comstar wheels, stepped seat, aftermarket luggage carriers.
£650–700 PS

1982 Honda CBX 1000C, 1047cc, US specification, Pro-link rear suspension, Comstar wheels, panniers, finished in Pearl Altair (not available in UK).
£2,000–3,500 CBX

◄ **1980's Honda CBX 1000 Moto Martin Tokyo,** 1047cc, double-overhead-camshaft, 4-cylinder engine, 150mph top speed, very good condition.
£3,500–5,500 CBX

Based on the standard CBX 1000Z, this special has a French-built frame. Only a few hundred were built, and of those, about 20 are known to exist in the UK.

Indian *(American 1901–53)*

1940 Indian Sport Scout 75, 750cc, side-valve V-twin, hand gear-change, deeply-valanced mudguards, tank-mounted instruments, footboards.
£13,500–14,750 IMC

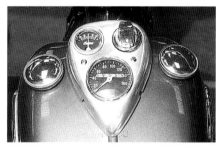

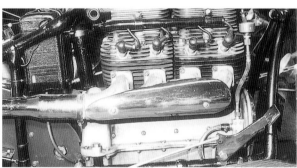

1940 Indian Four, 1265cc, in-line, 4-cylinder engine, tank-mounted instruments, Indian-motif horn.
£19,000+ IMC

◄ **1952 Indian Brave,** 248cc, side-valve, single-cylinder engine, telescopic forks, rigid frame, completely restored, concours condition.
£1,500–1,650 IMC

The Indian Brave was manufactured in the UK by Brockhouse Engineering, of Stockport, for export to the USA. In 1954, a version equipped with a swinging-arm frame was introduced.

Itom *(Italian 1948–68)*

The first Itom was a cyclemotor, which was designed in 1944. Based in Turin, the company soon gained an excellent reputation for its 49cc and, later, 65cc models, all featuring single-cylinder, piston-ported, two-stroke engines.

In the late 1950s, Itom became involved in the 50cc racing boom, which ultimately led to the class being accorded world championship status in 1962. The early 'racing' models had a three-speed gearbox, geared primary drive and a hand-operated, twistgrip gear-change. The Mk 7 had four gears, and the Mk 8, four gears with a foot-change. Although the factory never campaigned works machines, privateer Itom riders made up the majority of the 50cc race grid for several years. Among them was Beryl Swain, who became the first woman to compete in the Isle of Man TT in 1962. She finished 22nd, at an average speed of 48.33mph.

By the mid-1960s, the Itom had become outclassed by later production racers, such as the Honda CR110 and Suzuki TR50, not to mention the full works bikes from Derbi, Kreidler, Suzuki, Honda and Tomos.

1962 Itom Tabor, 65cc, 2-stroke single.
£400–500 VMCC

1960 Itom Mk 8, 49cc, piston-port, 2-stroke single, 4-speed foot-change gearbox, roadgoing trim.
£2,500+ RFC

This bike is an original Mk 8 with a Juller cylinder head.

1964 Itom Mk 8, 49cc, piston-port, 2-stroke single, 18in wheels, Tooley racing tank and seat.
£700–800 VMCC

James *(British 1902–64)*

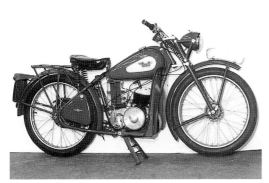

1952 James Comet J10, 98cc, Villiers 1F 2-stroke engine, 2-speed gearbox, girder forks, rigid frame.
£350–400 PS

1959 James Commodore, 249cc AMC 2-stroke engine.
£500–550 PM

JAP *(British 1904–08)*

For many years the dominant supplier of engines to the British motorcycle industry, JAP was founded by John Alfred Prestwich in the closing decade of the 19th century. JAP's arrival on the scene reduced British manufacturers' reliance on Continental power units, but at first the London-based company specialised in the production of scientific instruments, John Prestwich collaborating with William Friese-Green in pioneering the development of the cine-camera. The company built its first motorcycle engine around 1901, and went into production in 1903.

The first engine, a 2½hp, four-stroke single featured 'atmospheric' inlet and side exhaust valves, displaced 293cc (76x70mm bore and stroke) and produced a claimed 2.25bhp at 1,600rpm.

As well as supplying existing manufacturers, JAP also went into motorcycle production, although from 1908, the firm concentrated on engine supply alone. JAP was active in competition right from the start, entering the ACU's 1,000-mile trial in 1903 and supplying the engine for Charlie Collier's winning Matchless in the inaugural Isle of Man TT of 1907.

1904 JAP 2½hp, 4-stroke single-cylinder engine, vertical cylinder, pedals, chain and belt drives, good condition.
£3,100–3,400 BKS

Kawasaki *(Japanese 1962–)*

1968 Kawasaki 650 W1, 624cc, overhead-valve, pre-unit, twin-cylinder engine, 74x72.6mm bore and stroke, no silencers, otherwise in good condition.
£2,000–2,250 CStC

Derived from the earlier Maguro design (itself copied from the BSA A7/A10 series), the Kawasaki 650 W1 ran through the late 1960s, production finally coming to an end in 1971.

1973 Kawasaki Z400, 398cc, overhead-camshaft twin, 5-speed gearbox, disc front brake, drum rear brake, fitted with aftermarket seat.
£500–600 MAY

1974 Kawasaki 500 H1E, 498.8cc, double disc front brake, standard specification.
£1,500+ VICO

1974 Kawasaki Z1B, 903cc, double-overhead-camshaft, 4-cylinder engine, café racer conversion with 4-into-1 exhaust, clip-ons, rearsets, abbreviated mudguards.
£950–1,050 PS

1977 Kawasaki Z650B1, 652cc, double-overhead-camshaft, 4-cylinder engine, 62x54mm bore and stroke, cast alloy wheels, 3,000 miles from new.
£1,100–2,000 CKC

1983 Kawasaki Z1100A, 1089cc, shaft final drive, 5,000 miles from new, good condition.
£1,800–2,000 VICO

Expressly built for touring, the Z1100A is a very comfortable motorcycle, albeit heavy.

Kerry *(British 1902–early 1960s)*

◀ **1904 Kerry,** 3½hp inlet-over-exhaust, single-cylinder engine, completely restored, excellent condition.
£4,800–5,200 VER

This machine was built in Belgium by the Sarolea concern and sold in the UK under the Kerry name by the East London Rubber Company. Only seven examples of this early form of badge engineering are known to survive.

Laverda *(Italian 1949–)*

1980 Laverda Montjuic Series 2, 496.7cc, double-overhead-camshaft twin, 72x61mm bore and stroke, 6-speed gearbox, 2-into-1 exhaust.
£2,500–2,800 PC

The Series 2 Montjuic had revised styling, its fairing being mounted to the frame, rather than the forks.

1974 Laverda 750 SF2, 744cc, overhead-camshaft twin, 4-bearing crank, double front disc brake, drum rear brake, wire wheels, completely restored.
£2,000–2,800 VICO

1982 Laverda Jota 120, 981cc, double-overhead-camshaft, 3-cylinder engine, 120° crankshaft, 8.8:1 compression ratio, rubber engine mounts, 240 watt Denso alternator, left-hand gear-change.
£3,800–4,200 INM

Levis *(British 1911–40)*

◄ **1921 Levis,** 211cc, 2-stroke single.
£2,200–2,400 BKS

Founded in 1911, the British Levis concern concentrated its efforts during the 1920s and 1930s on the production of well-engineered, two-stroke singles, displacing 211cc and 246cc. The reputation of the company's products was enhanced in 1920 when Reg Clark and Gus Kuhn rode Levis machines to first and second places in the 250cc Junior TT.

1925 Levis, 211cc, 2 stroke engine, 2-speed gearbox, restored.
£1,000–1,100 BTS

A little known fact is that Levis exported engines to Germany during the early and mid-1920s to power the first motorcycles built under the well-known Zündapp marque.

Restored Values

The cost of a professional restoration will have an influence on, but no direct relation to, a motorcycle's market value. A restored motorcycle can have a market value lower than the cost of its restoration.

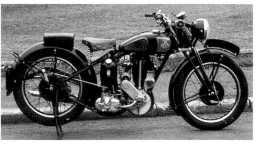

1935 Levis As, 346cc, overhead-valve, single-port single, restored.
£3,250–3,650 PM

The last Levis models were built in 1940, and the company did not survive into the post-war era.

Lube *(Spanish 1949–65)*

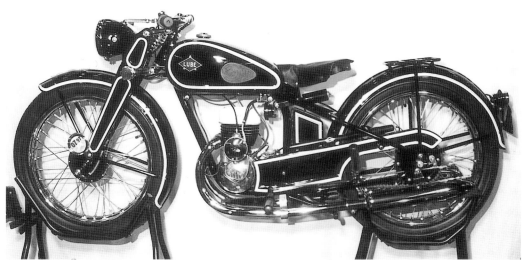

c1950 Lube B25, 124cc, single-cylinder, twin-port 2-stroke, blade-type forks, rigid frame.
£2,000–3,000 SMC

One of Spain's original motorcycle manufacturers, Lube had close associations with the German NSU company for many years. This particular machine is believed to be the only example of its kind outside Spain.

Matchless *(British 1901–69, 1987–)*

1918 Matchless V-twin, 998cc, JAP side-valve engine, 3-speed gearbox, very good condition.
£6,500–7,000 YEST

Very few examples of the Matchless V-twin exist.

1930 Matchless T/5, 497cc, side-valve engine, vertical cylinder, 82.5x93mm bore and stroke.
£3,250–3,550 VER

1937 Matchless Model X, 990cc, side-valve V-twin, completely restored to original specification, finished in black and chrome.
£5,000–5,250 CotC

The Model X was a fast, solo sporting tourer.

1944 Matchless G3L, 348cc, telescopic forks, rigid frame, ex-military machine rebuilt to civilian specification.
£1,700–2,000 BLM

The G3L was a good all-round machine.

1952 Matchless G9, 497cc, overhead-valve twin, megaphone silencers, 'jam pot' rear suspension units, single-sided brakes.
£1,800–2,400 BLM

◄ **1954 Matchless G3LS,** 348cc, very good condition.
£1,750–2,000 BKS

The 1954 season saw improvements incorporated into the AMC heavyweight singles, the most noticeable being full-width alloy hubs. Other changes included a removable clutch cover and auto advance on the 500 models.

1958 Matchless G3LS, 348cc, overhead-valve single, restored, good condition.
£1,550–1,650 BKS

Significant changes in design were made to the 1957 range of Matchless motorcycles. A shock absorber was incorporated into the clutch assembly, and a brand-new AMC-made gearbox replaced the old Burman box. Slim Girling rear suspension units were fitted in place of the famous AMC 'jam pots', and a quickly-detachable rear wheel was incorporated, which was a vast improvement on the previous design. The G3LS was ideal for economical, low-maintenance general use.

1960 Matchless G3, 348cc, overhead-valve, pre-unit single.
£1,500–1,650 PM

1961 Matchless CSR, 646cc, tuned, overhead-valve sports twin, siamesed exhaust, aluminium mudguards, 2 owners from new, restored, excellent condition.
£2,750–3,250 AT

The CSR was probably the most popular Matchless roadster of its era.

1956 Matchless G11, 597cc, megaphone silencers, full-width hubs, pilot lights, original, excellent condition.
£2,500–2,900 BLM

1959 Matchless G9, 497cc, overhead-valve twin, 4-speed foot-change gearbox, alloy primary chaincase.
£1,750–1,850 AT

Minerva (Belgian 1895–1909)

The Belgian Minerva concern was one of the first to offer a viable proprietary engine for motorcycle use. Nominally of 1hp, the 211cc unit was designed to be attached to a bicycle's downtube – a location that became known as the Minerva position – and was of advanced configuration, employing a mechanically-operated inlet valve instead of the automatic type favoured by rival manufacturers. As well as building a complete powered machine of its own, the company also catered for the much larger proprietary engine market, supplying many Continental European manufacturers as well as others in Great Britain, notably Ariel, Matchless, Phoenix, Quadrant, Royal Enfield and Triumph.

The marque achieved many victories in the early days of motorcycle racing, yet despite its commercial and competition successes, Minerva's future plans lay elsewhere. After 1909, the company abandoned two-wheelers to concentrate on automobiles.

1903 Minerva, 211cc, older restoration, good condition.
£5,150–5,650 BKS

Purchased new from Heightons of Peterborough, by Frank Gilbert, this 1903 Minerva is believed to be the city's oldest mechanically-propelled vehicle. After WWII, it was stored for 60 years before being restored in 1986. It successfully completed the Pioneer Run in 1987, 1988 and 1989.

1904 Minerva Single, 211cc, belt and chain drives, restored, very good condition.
£5,000–5,750 VER

> A known continuous history can add value to and enhance the enjoyment of a motorcycle.

Monotrace (French 1926–28)

1925 Monotrace Type MM, 520cc, water-cooled single, chain drive to gearbox and rear wheel, pressed-steel forks and frame, Borlamp electric sidelamps, centre-mounted Luxor acetylene headlamp, original in all major respects.
£4,000–4,500 BKS

The Monotrace was built in France by Morgan-Monotrace and, essentially, was a German Mauser built under licence. Designed like a two-wheeled car, it had tandem seating and two stabilising outrigger wheels that were raised when the vehicle was under way. The horizontal engine was mounted behind the driver, who steered with D-shaped handlebars. Today, this is an exceedingly rare vehicle.

Motobi *(Italian 1951–76)*

1960s Motobi 125, 124cc, overhead-valve, horizontal single, unit construction, full-width alloy brake hubs.
£600–650 IVC

c1959 Motobi Sport, 123.7cc, piston-port, 2-stroke single, horizontal iron cylinder, aluminium head, converted to café racer style, but retaining original roadster tinware, steel wheel rims and kickstarter.
£2,000–3,000 AtMC

Miller's is a price GUIDE not a price LIST

▶ **1971 Motobi 650S,** 643cc, overhead-valve twin, wet-sump lubrication, unit construction, 5-speed gearbox, standard specification apart from clip-on handlebars.
£1,800–2,000 INM

The Motobi 650S was badge engineering at its very best, being a renamed Benelli Tornado.

Moto Guzzi *(Italian 1921–)*

Founded in 1921 at Mandello del Lario, on the shores of Lake Como, Italy, by Giorgio Parodi and Carlo Guzzi, Moto Guzzi has achieved considerable success on both road and track in the eight decades since. Early models were powered by single-cylinder engines with horizontal cylinders; later came twins, triples, fours and even a racing V8, all being of exceptional quality.

The first V-twin model appeared in the mid-1930s, being a 500cc competition-only machine that continued to do well until the early 1950s.

The next V-twin, albeit with the cylinders aligned across the frame, rather than fore and aft, came with the launch of the V7 heavyweight roadster at the Milan show in 1965. Originally intended solely for police and military escort duty, the V7 spawned a whole family of V-twins, culminating in such famous models as the Le Mans, California and Daytona.

As the 21st century dawns, Moto Guzzi is about to launch a new range of singles (with engines having vertical cylinders) and updated versions of its legendary 90-degree V-twin.

◀ **1953 Moto Guzzi Galletto,** 174cc, overhead-valve, horizontal single, 65x53mm bore and stroke.
£750–800 IVC

Shown at the Geneva show in March 1950 as a 150cc prototype, the Galletto (Cockerel) was a cross between a scooter and a motorcycle. It entered production later that year as a 160cc model, the engine size being increased to 175cc in late 1952. It was raised again, to 192cc, in 1954. Production ceased in 1966.

1954 Moto Guzzi Cardellino 65, 64cc, disc-valve
2-stroke, 42x46mm bore and stroke.
£1,300–1,450 NLM

Developed from the earlier Motoleggera 65 (1946–54),
the Cardellino 65 was built from 1954 until 1956.

1960 Moto Guzzi Lodola GT, 235cc, overhead-valve
single, restored excellent condition.
£3,000–3,300 BKS

Carlo Guzzi's final design, the Lodola arrived in 1956
and was powered by an inclined, 175cc overhead-
camshaft engine in a duplex loop frame. A Sport
version followed, and in 1959 the model was enlarged
to 235cc, becoming the Lodola Gran Turismo with
pushrod valve operation producing 11bhp, an output
good enough for a top speed of 70mph. Production
ceased in 1966.

◀ **1962 Moto Guzzi Lodola 235,** 235cc, overhead-
valve, unit-construction, single-cylinder engine,
68x64mm bore and stroke.
£2,000–3,000 SMC

1972 Moto Guzzi Nuovo Falcone, 498.4cc, 88 x 82mm bore and stroke, electric start, original apart from single
silencer instead of dual units.
£2,600–2,850 NLM

The electric starting system used on this bike works by using the dynamo to rotate the engine via a belt.

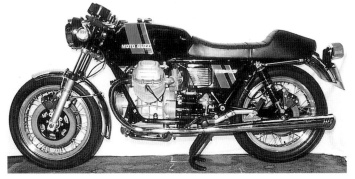

◀ **1975 Moto Guzzi 750S3,** 748cc,
V-twin engine, 5-speed gearbox,
shaft final drive, Lafranconi silencers,
linked brake system with triple
Brembo discs, stainless steel
mudguards, original apart from
chrome-plated rather than black
silencers, completely restored to
concours condition.
£3,000–4,000 IMOC

1977 Moto Guzzi Le Mans 1, 844cc, overhead-valve V-twin, shaft final drive, standard specification apart from production racing Lafranconi exhausts and Minanni rearsets.
£3,500–3,800 PC

1980 Moto Guzzi V35 Series II, 346cc, overhead-valve V-twin, 33bhp at 8,100rpm, shaft final drive, non-standard silencers.
£750–950 MAY

The Series II V35 was launched for 1980, the original electronic ignition of the Series I having been replaced by points to cure a mid-range flat spot in the power curve.

1981 Moto Guzzi 1000SP NT, 948cc, overhead-valve, 90° V-twin, 5-speed gearbox, shaft final drive, crashbars, pannier frames, screen missing, in need of restoration.
£1,500–1,650 PC

1984 Moto Guzzi V35 Imola Mk II, overhead-valve, 90° V-twin, 4-valve cylinder heads, 40bhp at 8,800rpm, 16in wheels, good condition.
£1,200–1,400 BLM

This model was built between 1984 and 1985 only.

1980 Moto Guzzi V50 Series II, 490cc, overhead-valve V-twin, 45bhp at 7,500rpm, 5-speed gearbox, shaft final drive, non-standard handlebar fairing and carrier.
£1,200–1,400 INM

Moto Morini *(Italian 1937–)*

Originally a co-owner of the MM company (a famous motorcycle marque of the inter-war period), Alfonso Morini broke away to set up his own concern in 1937. However, it was not until after WWII that he established the new marque in the two-wheel sector.

The first racing machine was a simple piston-port, single-cylinder two-stroke, which was introduced in 1947. Like the roadster it had been developed from, Morini's two-stroke owed much to the German DKW RT125, sharing the same basic technology with the BSA Bantam and Harley-Davidson Hummer.

During the 1950s, Morini switched its efforts to four-strokes, both on the street and the race track. A landmark machine appeared in 1955 in the shape of the 175 Settebello overhead-valve, sports/racing model. This was one of a trio of 175s, the Briscola, Tressette and Settebello, all named after popular card games in Italy – Trumps, Three Sevens and Seven of Diamonds (Beautiful Seven) respectively.

Then came the more specialised Rebello, from which was developed the Gran Premio (Grand Prix). The latter made a stunning debut at the 1958 Italian GP at Monza. Piloted by Emilio Mendogni, it won the 250cc race. In the 1960s, the ex-FB Mondial and MV star Tarquinio Provini joined the Bologna team and almost took the 250cc world title from Honda in 1963. The Gran Premio was finally retired toward the end of the 1960s.

Upon Alfonso Morini's death in 1969, his daughter, Gabriela, assumed control of the company, and it was under her leadership that the most famous of all Morinis was developed, the 350 V-twin. Built as a prototype during 1971, it was the work of designers Gianni Marchesini and Gianni Franco Lambertini Junior. It was shown to the public for the first time at the Milan Show in November 1971, but production of the 72-degree V-twin did not get under way until early 1973, heralding a new chapter in Morini's history.

Ultimately, 250 and 500 versions joined the original 350, being built in a variety of forms, including roadster, trials, custom and even a pukka ISDT example, which struck 'gold'.

Morini was taken over by Cagiva in 1987 and survived into the 1990s. With the sale of Ducati, the parent company may wish to relaunch the Morini name, much as it did recently with MV Agusta, but only time will tell.

1955 Moto Morini TS125, 123.17cc, piston-port, 2-stroke single, very good condition.
£1,300–1,450 NLM

This model was also made in Sport form, and both types are now quite rare. Like the BSA Bantam, Harley-Davidson Hummer and others, the TS125 was powered by a copy of the DKW engine.

► **1962 Moto Morini Tressette Sprint,** 172cc, overhead-valve, unit-construction single, 60x61mm bore and stroke.
£2,150–2,350 NLM

The Tressette Sprint was part of a family of machines that evolved into the Gran Premio GP racer, through the Settebello, Rebello and others.

1964 Moto Morini Regolarita, 123cc, overhead-valve single, 56x50mm bore and stroke, non-runner, some parts missing.
£600–650 NLM

The Regolarita was similar to the works ISDT bikes and highly regarded in Italy.

1976 Moto Morini 350 Sport Valentini, 344cc, 72° V-twin, uprated engine, double disc front brake, special frame and bodywork.
£5,500–6,000 NLM

Valentini was to Morini what Cooper is to the Mini. The name means 'extra charisma and performance'. Valentini models were the quickest of all the Morini roadster V-twins.

1978 Moto Morini 500/5, 478.6cc, 72° V-twin, 69x64mm bore and stroke, 5-speed gearbox, non-standard black 2-into-1 exhaust, rearset foot controls, clip-ons, otherwise standard.
£1,600–2,000 BLM

The original 500 Morini V-twin appeared in prototype form at the 1975 Milan show, but production did not begin until the 1978 model year.

1975 Morini 350 Strada, 344cc, 72° V-twin, drum brakes front and rear, stainless steel mudguards and chainguard.
£1,250–1,500 MOR

A known continuous history can add value to and enhance the enjoyment of a motorcycle.

1976 Moto Morini 3½ Sport, 344cc.
£2,750–3,000 NLM

Nineteen-seventy-six was the only year in which this model was built with wire wheels and a disc front brake. After that, it had alloy wheels and a disc brake.

1979 Moto Morini 500/5 Tour, 478.6cc, good condition.
£2,000–2,100 NLM

This is an early model with a black frame, a five-speed gearbox and, like the 350 of the same period, stainless steel mudguards and chainguard.

▶ 1980 Moto Morini 500/5 Sport, 478.6cc, 5-speed gearbox, later kinked frame, low mileage, one owner from new, very good condition.
£2,200–2,400 NLM

1981 Moto Morini 500 Camel, 478.6cc, 72° V-twin, high-level exhaust, hydraulic steering damper, long-travel Marzocchi competition front forks, twin-shock rear suspension.
£1,800–2,000 INM

▶ 1981 Moto Morini 350 Sport ES FD, 344cc, 72° V-twin, 62x57mm bore and stroke, 39bhp at 8,500rpm, 108mph top speed, fitted with optional Nisa fairing, black exhaust system.
£1,950–2,150 NLM

'ES FD' stood for 'electric start, three disc brakes'.

◄ **1982 Moto Morini K2 Series 1,** 344cc, 72° V-twin engine, 62x57mm bore and stroke, triple disc brakes, good condition. **£2,000–2,200 NLM**

This model was based on the 350 ES FD with revised styling and details. A later Series 2 (or Export) version was equipped with a tank-mounted fairing.

1981 Moto Morini Camel Series 1, 478.6cc, leading-axle, long-travel front forks, twin-shock rear suspension, non-standard paint scheme. **£2,350–2,600 NLM**

This model was sold as the Sahara in the UK. It was a gold medal winner in the 1981 ISDE.

1984 Moto Morini KJ Kanguro Juniore, 122.69cc, 59x45mm bore and stroke, monoshock chassis. **£1,250–2,400 NLM**

The styling of this model was very similar to the Kanguro V-twin; it had the same engine as the 125H. It sold well in Italy and Spain, but is rare in the UK.

1988 Moto Morini 350 Dart, 344cc, fully-enclosed bodywork, good condition. **£2,500+ NLM**

This model was built after the Cagiva take-over of the Moto Morini marque.

1990 Moto Morini 501 Conguaro, 507cc, overhead-valve, 72° V-twin. **£3,000–3,300 NLM**

Introduced in 1988, the Conguaro was inspired by Honda's Transalp.

◄ **1992 Moto Morini 350 Excalibur,** 344cc, 72° V-twin, electric start, high bars, sculpted seat, very good condition. **£2,000–2,200 NLM**

Very Harley-esque in its styling, the 350 Excalibur was equipped with an efficient braking system and was endowed with good handling.

Motosacoche *(Swiss 1899–1957)*

1910 Motosacoche Single, 211cc, inclined cylinder, belt final drive, sprung forks, flat tank.
£3,500–4,250 **VER**

MV Agusta *(Italian 1945–78)*

◀ **1957 MV Agusta 175CSS,** 174cc, overhead camshaft, single-cylinder engine, magneto ignition, one of three known to survive in completely serviceable condition.
£3,500–4,000 **IMOC**

The 175CSS was a pure-bred sports machine, designed for fast road and competition use. It was built in small numbers between 1955 and 1958.

1967 MV Agusta 600 Four, 591.8cc, double-overhead-camshaft, 4-cylinder engine, 24mm Dell'Orto UBF carburettors, mechanically-operated twin Campagnolo front disc brakes, original specification.
£10,000–11,000 **PC**

1971 MV Agusta 150GT, 149cc, overhead-valve single, unit construction, 5-speed gearbox, in need of cosmetic restoration.
£550–700 **MAY**

1972 MV Agusta 750GT, 743cc, 69bhp at 8,500rpm, touring model with 4-pipe chromed exhaust, drum brakes and dualseat.
£11,000+ PC

Built from 1972 until 1974, the 750GT is one of the rarest of the MV roadster fours.

1973 MV Agusta 350B, 349cc, overhead-valve parallel twin, unit construction, electronic ignition, 12 volt electrics.
£2,250–2,500 IVC

1977 MV Agusta 750S America, 789.7cc, double-overhead-camshaft, 4-cylinder engine, 67x56mm bore and stroke, black one-piece silencers, double Scarab front disc brakes, drum rear brake, wire wheels, optional factory fairing.
£10,500–11,500 COYS

This model was never quite as sought after as the standard 750S or 832 Monza.

1978 MV Agusta Monza 861 Arturo Magni, 862cc, triple Brembo disc brakes, cast alloy wheels, very good condition.
£17,250–19,000 BKS

Developed from MV's multi-cylinder racers, the 750GT tourer and 750S sportster appeared in 1969. The latter's replacement, the 750S America, was launched for 1976, being bored to 789cc and producing 75bhp – good for 100mph in around 13 seconds and a 135mph top speed. Next came an increase to 837cc. Launched in 1977 as the Boxer in the UK, the new model soon reverted to the Monza name, but was short-lived. By 1977, MV was in trouble, and production ceased at the end of 1978. However, ex-works engineer and team manager Arturo Magni had set up on his own to develop and build the MV four. One of his products was an 862cc big-bore kit; while not a factory product, the converted machine was listed by the UK importer as the 861 Arturo Magni.

Neracar *(American/British 1921–26)*

◀ **1921 Neracar 2¼hp,** 285cc, Simplex 2-stroke, single-cylinder engine, friction-drive transmission, hub-centre steering, feet-forward riding position, good condition. **£5,750–6,350 S**

New Imperial *(British 1910–39)*

1926 New Imperial 6.8hp, 680cc, side-valve, JAP V-twin engine, restored, very good condition. **£4,350–4,750 CotC**

1935 New Imperial Model 100, 491cc, overhead-valve, 62.5x80mm bore and stroke, exposed valve gear, enclosed primary chaincase, unit construction, girder forks, rigid frame. **£3,000–3,300 MSW**

◀ **1937 New Imperial 350,** 344cc, overhead-valve engine, inclined cylinder, unit construction, restored, excellent condition. **£3,500–4,250 VER**

Norman *(British 1937–62)*

◀ **1961 Norman B4 Sports,** 249cc, Villiers 2T piston-port, 2-stroke twin, concours condition. **£1,800–2,000 VER**

Formed in 1937, Norman was originally a cycle manufacturer, but it turned to motorcycles on the eve of WWII. Production resumed post-war, and by 1960 no less than nine Norman powered two-wheelers were listed. The B4 was the definitive series, the final year of production being 1962.

Norton *(British 1902–)*

1928 Norton CSI, 490cc, overhead-camshaft single.
£7,600–8,400 BKS

Designed by Walter Moore, the CSI scored a debut victory in the 1927 Senior TT, ridden by Alec Bennett. The production version duly appeared at the 1927 London Motorcycle Show and continued as Norton's top-of-the-range sports model until the introduction of the International.

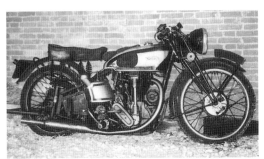

1935 Norton Model 30 International, 490cc, bevel-driven overhead camshaft, single-cylinder engine.
£5,600–6,200 S

Designed by Walter Moore's replacement, Arthur Carroll, the International ran from the early 1930s until production ceased in the early 1960s.

1946 Norton ES2, 490cc, overhead-valve single, girder forks, rigid frame.
£2,800–3,200 BLM

1948 Norton Model 30 International, 490cc, overhead-camshaft single, Brooklands silencer, telescopic forks, plunger rear suspension, pillion pad.
£6,000–6,600 PM

1928 Norton 19, 588cc, overhead-valve single, 79x120mm bore and stroke, very original.
£7,000–8,000 VMCC

Basically a longer-stroke version of the Model 18, the Model 19 cost £66 when new.

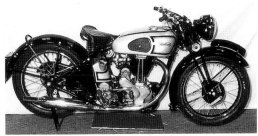

1939 Norton ES2, 490cc, overhead-valve single, girder forks, rigid frame.
£2,400–2,650 PS

The ES2 was one of Norton's longest-running models, spanning nearly four decades.

1949 Norton Model 30 International, 490cc, Clubman's TT model, completely restored, very good condition.
£5,740–6,350 BKS

Norton used the name 'International' for the first time in 1932, applying it to the company's charismatic, top-of-the-range sports roadster, powered by the Arthur Carroll-designed overhead-camshaft engine. The latter was first seen in 1927 and had been developed in the works racers of 1930–31. Although the familiar 79x100mm bore and stroke dimensions were adopted, the engine was all new and proved itself in the Isle of Man. By 1939, four-speed foot-change and plunger rear suspension had been fitted; the 1949 models had telescopic front forks.

1950 Norton ES2, 490cc, overhead-valve single, telescopic forks, plunger rear suspension, sprung saddle, pillion pad, completely restored to original specification.
£2,400+ SWS

The ES2 was the workhorse of the Norton single-cylinder range.

1950 Norton Model 7, 497cc, overhead-valve parallel twin, iron head and barrel, 66x72.6mm bore and stroke.
£2,950–3,250 VER

The Model 7 twin made its debut in November 1948. From the start, it featured telescopic front forks and a plunger frame. From 1953, it gained the Featherbed frame, while other improvements came in succeeding years.

1955 Norton Dominator 88, 497cc, overhead-valve twin.
£4,350–4,800 BKS

Introduced in 1952, the Dominator 88 resulted from marrying the Model 7 engine with the Featherbed frame, which had swept virtually all before it when combined with the Manx engine. The new model was capable of just over 90mph and offered exemplary handling that became the benchmark by which other machines would be judged. For 1955, the Dominator gained a welded subframe with a more enveloping rear mudguard, light-alloy hubs, an alloy head and an Amal Monobloc carburettor.

► **1960 Norton Dominator 99,** 597cc, overhead-valve twin, enclosed rear chain, painted primary cover, converted to twin carburettors, non-standard rear suspension units, headlamp, instrument layout and seat.
£3,500–3,750 CotC

1958 Norton Model 50, 348cc, overhead-valve single, restored, very good condition.
£1,800–2,200 BLM

Essentially, the Model 50 is the same bike as the ES2, but with less power.

Norton Commando 750 (British 1967)
Price range: £2,000–5,000
The Commando project began with the arrival of Doctor Stefan Bauer at the Norton Villiers Group, as director of engineering, on 1 January 1967. His brief was to lead a technical team to develop a new Norton big twin.

In his efforts, Bauer was ably assisted by two British bike engineers, Bernard Hooper and Bob Twigg. This was just as well, as the good doctor had no previous two-wheel experience at all, his background being in nuclear physics, and he had spent the previous 12 years with Rolls-Royce. Even so, his team was successful in creating a very marketable machine, which was launched to much public acclaim at the Earl's Court Motorcycle Show in September of 1967.

The most innovative feature of the newcomer was its frame, the 745cc (73x89mm) Atlas engine and four-speed AMC gearbox being held by rubber mountings in a full-cradle, duplex affair.

There is no doubt that the Commando was a clever *commercial* design, as it appeared to be very different from the machine it replaced, yet most of its components were actually the same.

Even so, it was a success, not only in the showroom, but also in racing. It was voted Machine of the Year by *Motor Cycle News* in 1968, a title it went on to win no less than five years in a row, a feat that has never been equalled since.

An 850 – 829cc (77x89mm) – was introduced in 1973, and by 1975 had been given an electric start and left-hand gear-change. In 1978, the final batch of 30 machines (850s) was built.

1968 Norton P11, 745cc, overhead-valve, twin-cylinder engine, completely restored, excellent condition.
£4,600–5,100 BKS

AMC's final years saw the ailing company launch a bewildering assortment of badge-engineered hybrids. Announced in 1963, the first of these was a street scrambler intended for the USA. The AJS/Matchless-framed machine used the 745cc Norton Atlas engine, and it paved the way for the AJS Model 33 and Matchless G15 roadsters, introduced for 1965, by which time Norton forks and brakes had been standardised throughout the range. The 'mix-and-match' policy continued under Norton Villiers' ownership, when the CSR-framed roadsters were joined by a Norton-badged clone – the N15. While the range contracted, there was one new model for 1967, the Norton P11, another Atlas-engined hybrid, but this time using the Rickman-style frame of the Matchless G85CS scrambler. With the Commando's arrival later that year, the P11's days were numbered, and production ceased at the end of 1968.

1969 Norton Commando 750 Interpol, 745cc, overhead-valve twin, isolastic engine mounting, very good condition.
£1,900–2,100 BRIT

This Commando was originally supplied to the Somerset police force, and it remained in police service until September 1978.

1970 Norton Commando Café Racer, 745cc, overhead-valve twin, 73x89mm bore and stroke, Gus Kuhn exhaust, tank, seat and mudguards.
£2,300–2,550 CStC

1974 Norton Mk II Commando, 828cc, modified with non-standard alloy rims, fork gaiters, headlamp brackets and seat, damaged fuel tank.
£1,800–1,900 PC

1975 Norton Commando 850 Mk III, overhead-valve twin, electric start, 4-speed gearbox, café racer style with swept-back pipes, alloy racing tank, racing seat, alloy rims, clip-ons and alloy front mudguard.
£2,100–2,400 PC

1975 Norton Commando Interstate, 828cc, overhead-valve, twin-cylinder engine, non-electric start model.
£3,600–3,800 BLM

1976 Norton Mk III Commando, 828cc, electric start, front and rear disc brakes.
£2,500–2,750 PM

1976 Norton Mk III Interstate, 828cc, electric start, front and rear disc brakes, standard specification.
£3,250–3,500 CotC

1976 Norton Mk III Interstate, 828cc, electric start, largely original apart from Lester cast alloy wheels and aftermarket touring seat.
£3,000+ PC

1988 Norton Classic, 588cc, Wankel-type rotary engine, 36th of 101 built, very good condition.
£6,300–7,000 S

NSU *(German 1901–67)*

1909 NSU Single, 3½hp, inlet-over-exhaust single, 2-speed epicyclic gears, belt final drive.
£4,600–5,100 BKS

NSU built its first powered two-wheeler in 1900 and, initially, used proprietary engines. However, within a few years, it was making its own power units and was one of the first to fit a two-speed transmission. The marque established a strong presence in the UK prior to WWI.

1950 NSU Fox A1, 98cc, overhead-valve, unit-construction single, 50x50mm bore and stroke.
£800–900 HERM

Designed by Albert Roder, the 98cc, overhead-valve Fox engine was mounted in a pressed-steel chassis with leading-link forks, the latter the subject of a patent taken out by Roder. Production began in 1949. There was a two-stroke version, the Fox 2, which was introduced in 1951.

OEC *(British 1901–54)*

◀ **1922 OEC Blackburne,** 998cc, side-valve V-twin engine.
£13,000–14,000 VMCC

OEC (Osborn Engineering Company) was based in Gosport, Hampshire. When the Blackburne company decided to concentrate on building engines only, in 1920, OEC took over the manufacture of that company's motorcycles. OEC was also famous for breaking records during the 1920s, and in 1925 Claude Temple used one of its machines to set the one-hour world record at over 100mph.

Ossa *(Spanish 1951–80s)*

◀ **1972 Ossa Enduro,** 244cc, 2-stroke, single-cylinder engine, piston-port induction, very good condition.
£750–850 VICO

Ossa was founded by the Spanish industrialist Eduardo Giro. At first, the company manufactured road and racing bikes, but for the late 1960s, like-rivals Bultaco and Montesa, it concentrated on off-road machinery.

Panther *(British 1900–66)*

◄ **1918 Panther P & M,** 499cc, restored, very good condition. **£5,500–7,000 VER**

Known more often as Panther, P & M (Phelan & Moore) was incorporated in 1904. The Panther name was adopted in the 1920s and, at first, applied only to a single model. Later, however, it was common throughout the range. A P & M characteristic was the inclined cylinder.

1935 Panther Red Panther, 249cc, overhead-valve, 60x88mm bore and stroke, very original. **£2,000–2,250 VMCC**

Sold by London dealers Pride and Clarke, the Red Panther cost £29.17s.6d. when new.

1963 Panther Model 120, 645cc, 4-speed foot-change gearbox, full-width brakes, concours condition. **£2,500–3,000 BLM**

Known as the 'Big Pussy', with its massive twin-port, overhead-valve, single-cylinder engine doubling as the frame's front downtube, the Model 120 was seen by many as the ideal sidecar motorcycle of the 1960s.

Praga *(Czechoslovakian 1929–35)*

1928 Praga, 499cc, double-overhead-camshaft, single-cylinder engine, 84x90mm bore and stroke. **£3,850–4,250 YEST**

The Praga's design was ahead of its time, with fully-enclosed valve gear and double overhead camshafts. This particular machine is the roadgoing version, equipped with a Bosch mag/dyno, electric lights, touring handlebars and deeply-valanced mudguards. The sports version had no lights, sporty handlebars, flatter mudguards and lighter wheels. The same engine was used in both versions.

Quadrant *(British 1901–29)*

◄ **1906 Quadrant 3½hp,**
453cc, inlet-over-exhaust,
single-cylinder engine,
completely restored,
very good condition.
£6,200–6,850 S

This machine was built
in 1906 in Birmingham,
prior to the advent of the
financial difficulties that
caused the Quadrant
company to move its
factory to a new location
in Coventry in 1907.

Raleigh *(British 1899–1930s)*

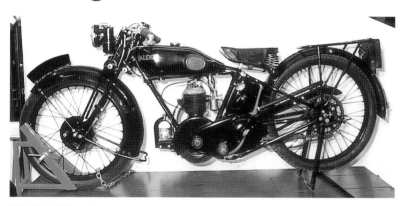

◄ **1928 Raleigh MT30,**
348cc, overhead-valve
single, upright cylinder.
£2,400–2,650 AT

Better known for its
pedal cycles, Raleigh
was involved
intermittently with
motorcyles during the
pioneer and vintage days
until 1934. The company
also supplied engines
and gearboxes, under
the Sturmey-Archer label,
to other manufacturers.

René-Gillet *(French 1898–1957)*

1933 René-Gillet Model J, 1000cc, 4-stroke, V-twin engine, foot-change gearbox, very good condition.
£4,000–5,000 TDD

Royal Enfield *(British 1901–70)*

1914 Royal Enfield, 770cc, inlet-over-exhaust, narrow-angle V-twin, concours condition.
£9,000–10,000 SIP

Today, this model is very rare.

1934 Royal Enfield Model S, 248cc, overhead-valve single, 64x77mm bore and stroke, restored 1996, very good condition.
£2,100–2,300 S

Nineteen-thirty-four was the first year of production for the Model S.

◄ **1935 Royal Enfield Model S,** 248cc, Miliner compression engine, fully enclosed valve gear, 4-speed hand-change gearbox, blade girder forks, duplex frame, original.
£2,800–2,950 VMCC

When new, this model cost £35.14s.0d.

1937 Royal Enfield Model KX, 1140cc, side-valve, V-twin engine, foot-change gearbox, 85.5x99.25mm bore and stroke, completely restored 1993, very good condition.
£5,000–5,750 CotC

In the main, Royal Enfield's KX model was intended for export.

1950 Royal Enfield Model G2, 346cc, overhead-valve single, Albion 4-speed foot-change gearbox.
£1,250–1,400 CotC

The Model G was an improved civilian version of the 350 overhead-valve single supplied to the British armed forces during WWII. There was also the Model J, which had a 500 engine, but otherwise was of a similar specification.

1956 Royal Enfield Clipper, 248cc, overhead-valve single, unfinished restoration project, various parts missing, including alternator, coil, clutch and chains.
£200–250 PS

This is a smaller-engined version of the budget-priced Clipper.

1957 Royal Enfield Clipper, 346cc, overhead-valve single, separate engine and gearbox, completely restored, excellent condition.
£1,150–1,250 COYS

The 350 Clipper was discontinued at the end of 1957.

1957 Royal Enfield Bullet, 499cc, very good condition.
£2,750–3,250 BLM

In 1956, the 350 and 500 Bullets received a new cylinder head, crankcase and frame, together with an alternator and magneto. For 1959, there was a larger cylinder head and dual 7in front brake. This machine has the earlier head and later dual front brake.

◄ **1959 Royal Enfield Clipper Airflow,** 346cc, overhead-valve, single-cylinder engine, restored, very good condition.
£1,150–1,250 PS

This machine is one of only a few to survive with its original Airflow fairing. Manufactured for Royal Enfield by the Bristol Aeroplane Company, the fairing represented one of the first serious attempts at providing full rider protection without making maintenance difficult or reducing the machine's turning circle.

1960 Royal Enfield Crusader Sports, 248cc, overhead-valve single, 70x64.5mm bore and stroke, 4-speed gearbox, café racer style with 1963-type Continental tank, clip-ons and single racing seat, otherwise largely standard.
£800–1,300 MAY

1960 Royal Enfield Bullet, 499cc, unregistered, genuine 12 miles from new, excellent condition.
£3,450–3,800 S

The Airflow fairing was offered on several models, including the Bullet, Constellation and Crusader.

▶ **1970 Royal Enfield Interceptor Series II,** 736cc, overhead-valve twin, 6,000 miles from new.
£5,000–5,500 BKS

The Interceptor Series II sports model was built primarily for export between 1968 and 1970. One version was the so-called Road Scrambler, most examples of which were exported to the USA. The specification remained virtually unchanged for the last few years of Enfield production, and today it stands as an example of what might have been, had the factory continued and been able to develop its potential. This ex-works demonstrator was originally used in Italy for sales promotion work.

Royal Ruby *(British 1909–33)*

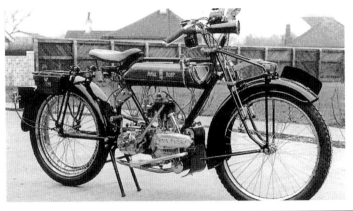

◄ **1918 Royal Ruby Spring Frame,** 3hp, inlet-over-exhaust single, upright cylinder, belt-driven magneto ignition, acetylene lighting, bulb horn.
£6,500–7,150 BKS

This machine features leaf springs front and rear, which was an innovative design at the time of its appearance. Others who used a similar layout were ABC and Indian. Royal Ruby ceased production in 1933, by which time the company was using Villiers two-stroke engines exclusively.

Rudge *(British 1910–40)*

1922 Rudge Multi, 499cc, inlet-over-exhaust single, 85 x 88mm bore and stroke.
£5,800–6,400 YEST

This model is equipped with the famous variable 'Multi' gear, which allows up to 20 gear positions. A Rudge using this feature won the 1914 TT.

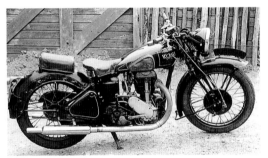

1936 Rudge Special, 499cc, overhead-valve, twin-port single, very original.
£4,000–4,500 VMCC

When new, this model cost £63.10s.

◄ **1938 Rudge Ulster,** 499cc, restored, very good condition.
£6,750–7,450 BKS

Introduced in 1928, the 500cc Ulster was so called in celebration of the Rudge victory in that year's Ulster Grand Prix. It remained the company's range leader during the 1930s, being constantly updated. In 1932, it gained a foot-change, and in 1933 a radial four-valve head, the material changing to aluminium-bronze in 1934. These features would be carried over into 1937, when the machine's valve gear became enclosed.

Rumi *(Italian 1949–late 1950s)*

◄ **1959 Rumi Junior Gentleman,** 124cc, horizontal, 2-stroke, twin-cylinder engine, 42x45mm bore and stroke.
£4,000–4,500 VMCC

Officine Fonderiè Rumi was founded by Donnino Rumi in Bergamo, Italy, just prior to the outbreak of WWI. The company began motorcycle production in 1950, 1959 being the first year of production for the Junior Gentleman model.

Scott *(British 1909–69)*

1928 Scott Flying Squirrel, 597cc, water-cooled, 2-stroke twin, 74.6x68.25mm bore and stroke, partially restored, in need of new radiator, further mechanical work and cosmetic restoration.
£2,000–2,200 SCOT

1929 Scott Squirrel, 299cc, air-cooled, 2-stroke, Scott-built single, iron barrel, aluminium head, 3-speed gearbox, duplex tube frame, Scott telescopic forks.
£1,800–2,000 BLM

Nineteen-twenty-nine was the first year of production for this air-cooled model.

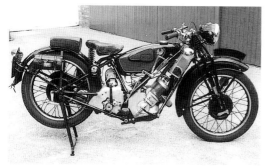

1929 Scott Flying Squirrel Sports, 499cc, water-cooled, 2-stroke, twin-cylinder engine, 68.25x68.25mm bore and stroke, restored, very good condition.
£5,000–6,000 VER

► **1959 Scott Flying-Squirrel,** 596cc, 2-stroke twin, Velocette gearbox, duplex frame, Dowty telescopic forks, full-width hubs.
£3,000–3,300 BLM

1929 Scott Two-Speeder, 596cc, water-cooled, 2-stroke twin, not completely original, good condition.
£4,000–5,000 VER

1957 Scott Flying Squirrel, 596cc.
£3,000–3,300 BKS

Scott production was relocated from Shipley to Birmingham after Matt Holder's Aerco Jig and Tool Company acquired the marque in 1950, but it was not until 1956 that customers could actually buy any of the Birmingham Scotts. However, they featured many long-awaited improvements, including a new duplex chassis with swinging-arm rear suspension and improved brakes.

Singer *(British 1900–15)*

1912 Singer, 300cc, 4-stroke, single-cylinder engine, belt final drive, chain and pedals, flat tank, very good condition.
£8,000–8,500 VER

Sparkbrook *(British 1912–25)*

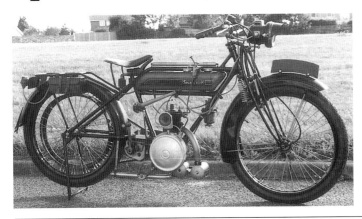

◀ **1921 Sparkbrook 2½hp,** 269cc, Villiers engine, flywheel-magneto ignition, Sturmey-Archer gearbox. **£1,150–1,250 BKS**

A short-lived marque, Sparkbrook began production in Coventry in 1912, offering a range powered by JAP V-twin engines, although after WWI, only single-cylinder machines were made. These were powered by a variety of two-stroke and four-stroke engines, the lightweights all using the reliable Villiers two-stroke. Production ceased in 1925.

Standard *(German/Swiss 1925–50s)*

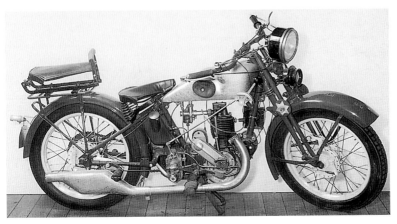

◀ **1930 Standard Ideal Touring,** 348cc, side-valve, MAG single-cylinder engine, restored, very good condition. **£900–1,000 HERM**

Standard was known as a builder of high-quality motorcycles during the inter-war period. However, production petered out after WWII, when the company began concentrating on small cars and agricultural machinery.

Sunbeam *(British 1912–57)*

Sunbeam was at the forefront of bicycle manufacture during the late Victorian/early Edwardian period, offering machines of outstanding quality with advanced features such as 'the little oil bath' chaincase, which improved the life of the drive chain considerably. Therefore, it came as no surprise that when the company began building motorcycles, its products were finished to the same exceptional standard. Introduced in 1911, the first machine broke with convention by adopting a two-speed gearbox and chain final drive, at a time when single-speed, direct belt drives were very much the norm. The benefits of the chain final drive were further enhanced by the adoption of the oil-bath chaincase for motorcycle use. Suddenly, riders were presented with a drive system that was clean and virtually maintenance free.

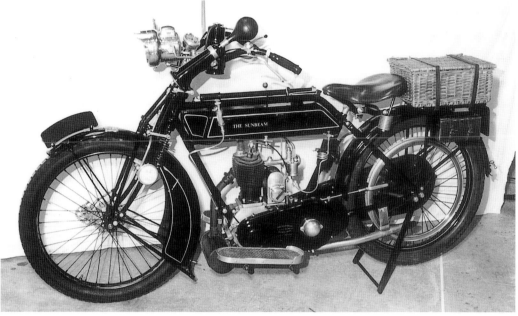

1914 Sunbeam 2¾hp, 4-stroke, single-cylinder engine, restored, excellent condition.
£8,850–9,750 BKS

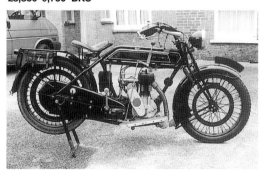

1923 Sunbeam, 491cc, side-valve single.
£4,800–5,200 VER

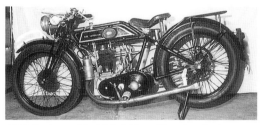

1926 Sunbeam Model 1, 346cc, side-valve single.
£2,750–3,050 BKS

Following restoration, this well-tuned machine took part in the Ormonde Gurr, George Larkin and Edward Lewis One Thousand Mile Round Britain Run, which raised funds for Cancer Research. It has also been a regular competitor in various VMCC events, including the Windmill Rally, which it won, and many Banbury Runs.

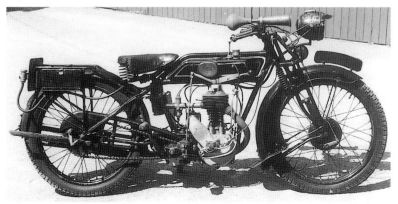

◄ **1927 Sunbeam Model 1,** 346cc, side-valve, single-cylinder engine, 70x90mm bore and stroke, hand gear-change mounted on tank, chain final drive, restored, very good condition.
£3,500–4,500 VER

Sunbeam ensured the quality of its products by doing as much as possible in house, working to the very high standards set by its founder, John Marston.

1927 Sunbeam Model 9, 493cc, overhead-valve single, 80x98mm bore and stroke, 3-speed gearbox, acetylene lighting, completely restored, concours condition.
£6,000–6,600 SUN

The Model 9 continued in production until 1937.

1928 Sunbeam Model 8, 346cc, overhead-valve single, 70x90mm bore and stroke, original specification.
£5,000–5,500 VER

◀ **1934 Sunbeam Li95,** 246cc, overhead-valve, single-cylinder engine, 59x90mm bore and stroke, excellent condition.
£10,000–11,000 PM

This model was only manufactured in 1934, superseding the equally short-lived Li90. As a result, both machines are very rare today.

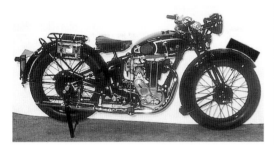

1935 Sunbeam Model 8, 346cc, overhead-valve, twin-port single, 70x90mm bore and stroke, completely restored.
£3,300–3,650 PS

1948 Sunbeam S7, 489cc, overhead-camshaft, in-line twin, 70x63.5mm bore and stroke, shaft final drive.
£2,500–2,800 BLM

◀ **1951 Sunbeam S8,** 489cc, overhead-camshaft, in-line twin, shaft final drive.
£2,350–2,500 CotC

The S8 arrived in 1949. It employed the same engine as the S7, but the forks were standard BSA items, as was the 7in front drum brake. The tyres were of narrower section, too, with a 19in front rim and an 18in rear.

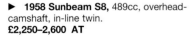

▶ **1958 Sunbeam S8,** 489cc, overhead-camshaft, in-line twin.
£2,250–2,600 AT

Nineteen-fifty-eight was the final year of production for both the S8 and the S7. After that, Sunbeam – by then owned by BSA – produced only scooters, which were actually badge-engineered BSA and Triumph models.

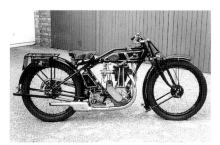

Suzuki *(Japanese 1952–)*

1969 Suzuki AS50, 49.9cc, 2-stroke single, disc-valve induction, 41x37.8mm bore and stroke, 5bhp, 5-speed gearbox, completely restored, concours condition.
£2,000–2,500 VJMC

Now very rare, the AS50 sports model was only built between 1968 and 1970.

1971 Suzuki ASS100, 98.2cc, disc-valve, 2-stroke, single-cylinder engine, 50x50mm bore and stroke, 9.5bhp, 4-speed gearbox.
£200–250 PS

1972 Suzuki GT750J, 739cc, liquid-cooled, 2-stroke, 3-cylinder engine, 70x64mm bore and stroke, 5-speed gearbox, early version with drum front brake, completely restored, concours condition.
£2,600–2,800 SOC

◄ **1973 Suzuki Italia Vallelunga 750/3,** 736cc, expansion-chamber exhaust, Melber alloy wheels, Menani rearsets, clip-ons, special bodywork, one of only 180 built.
£2,750–3,050 NLM

This very rare machine was built by Suzuki Italia, being sold purely through Italian dealers.

1975 Dresda Suzuki GT750 Special, 736cc, water-cooled, 2-stroke, 3-cylinder engine. **£3,000–3,300 SKC**

Built by Dave Degens of Dresda Autos, this GT750 Special has a Dyson-tuned engine with TR750-specification barrels. Of the 50 made, only 4–6 were sold in the UK. Consequently, it is extremely rare.

1976 Suzuki GT750A, 736cc, liquid-cooled, 2-stroke triple, concours condition. **£2,300–2,600 SOC**

1976 Suzuki RE5A, 497cc, oil- and liquid-cooled, single-rotor, Wankel rotary engine. **£3,000+ PC**

The first version of the RE5 (the RE5M) arrived in 1974. It was restyled as the RE5A for 1976. In all, 5,000 RE5s of all versions were built before production came to an end in 1977.

1979 Suzuki GT250 X7, 247cc, air-cooled, 2-stroke twin, alloy cylinder, 6-speed gearbox. **£400–450 PS**

For a time, the X7 was the best-selling 250 in the UK. It was also successful in production racing events, until the arrival of Yamaha's first LC machines.

1983 Suzuki GSX750E, 748cc, double-overhead-camshaft, 16-valve, across-the-frame four, 4-into-2 exhaust, triple disc brakes, twin-shock rear suspension. **£1,500–1,650 IVC**

This machine was imported into the UK from Italy.

◄ **1983 Suzuki GSX1100ES,** 1100cc, double-overhead-camshaft, across-the-frame four, anti-dive front forks, twin-shock rear suspension, triple disc brakes, 6-spoke cast alloy wheels, non-standard 4-into-1 exhaust. **£1,000–1,100 PS**

SUZUKI 97

Terrot *(French 1901–early 1960s)*

1933 Terrot 350, 348cc, side-valve single, magneto ignition, foot-change gearbox, original, unrestored.
£750–850 BKS

Like many marques during the austere days of the late 1920s and early 1930s, Terrot survived by selling cheap, but well engineered, side-valve, single-cylinder machines.

Triumph *(British 1902–)*

1914 Triumph 3½hp Model D TT Replica, 499cc.
£6,500–7,150 BKS

The first Triumph motorcycle of 1902 used a Belgian Minerva engine, but within a few years the Coventry firm was building its own power units. The company soon became involved in racing, and in 1908 Jack Marshall won the Isle of Man TT's single-cylinder class for the company. The resulting publicity greatly stimulated sales. By the outbreak of WWI, the marque's reputation for quality and reliability was well established, leading to substantial orders for 'Trusty Triumphs' for British and Allied forces. The 3½hp model appeared in 1907. Originally of 453cc, its side-valve engine was enlarged to 476cc in 1908, and finally to 499cc in 1910, before being superseded by the 4hp model in 1914. Like rival manufacturers, Triumph was keen to exploit its Isle of Man credentials and added the TT Replica – a stripped-down, single-speed sports roadster – to the range.

1914 Triumph 4hp, 550cc, single-cyllinder engine, 3-speed, Sturmey-Archer hub, pedals, chain, unrestored.
£4,000–4,500 YEST

1921 Triumph 3½hp Model R (Ricardo), 499cc, overhead-valve single, 4-valve cylinder head.
£5,400–5,950 BKS

Triumph's early output was confined to side-valve machines, but in 1921 the firm's first overhead-valve model caused a sensation. Based on the existing SD (spring drive) model, the newcomer sported a four-valve cylinder head designed by Harry Ricardo. Although the 'Riccy' was unsuccessful in the Isle of Man TT, a works bike ridden by Frank Halford broke the world flying-mile record in 1921 with a speed of 83.91mph. The first production models arrived in 1922, equipped with a cast-iron barrel rather than the racer's steel item, but otherwise they were much the same, with paired parallel valves set at 90 degrees in a pent-roof combustion chamber, bifurcated inlet port and separate exhausts. Although Rudge went on to make a success of its four-valve designs, Triumph's were dropped at the end of 1927.

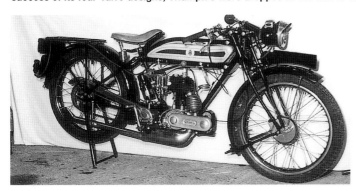

◀ **1927 Triumph Model QA,** 494cc, side-valve single, 3-speed countershaft gearbox, multi-plate clutch, hand gear-change.
£3,350–3,700 BKS

One of the last of Triumph's flat-tank models, the QA was an updated version of the Model P, which was built as a budget machine to combat a difficult sales period.

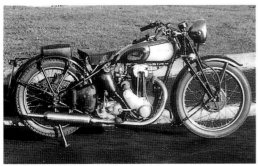

1938 Triumph 100, 499cc, overhead-valve twin, 4-speed foot-change gearbox, 63x80mm bore and stroke, completely restored to original specification, concours condition.
£7,500–8,250 CotC

This machine is the earliest known example of this model, having been registered in October 1938.

1937 Triumph Tiger 70, 249cc, overhead-valve single, 63x80mm bore and stroke, 16bhp at 5,800rpm.
£1,750–1,950 PM

◀ **1946 Triumph 3T,** 349cc, overhead-valve, pre-unit, twin-cylinder engine, iron barrel and head, 55x73.4mm bore and stroke, telescopic forks, rigid frame, restored, very good condition.
£3,000–4,000 VER

Introduced in 1946, the 3T was the smallest of Triumph's immediate post-war twins.

1949 Triumph 6T Thunderbird, 649cc, overhead-valve, pre-unit twin, iron head and barrel, completely restored.
£4,500–5,000 CotC

In September 1949, Triumph launched its first 650 twin, the 6T Thunderbird. To celebrate the event, the company took three bikes to Montlhéry in France for a high-speed reliability test, which the trio passed with flying colours on 29 September.

1949 Triumph TR5 Trophy, 499cc, overhead-valve, pre-unit twin, alloy head and barrel, 63x80mm bore and stroke, very good condition.
£5,750–6,350 CotC

Seen by many as the ultimate enduro bike of its era, the TR5 Trophy featured Triumph's sprung-hub design – an early attempt at providing rear springing, but ultimately it was unsuccessful.

1950 Triumph 5T Speed Twin, 499cc, overhead-valve, pre-unit twin, sprung-hub model with telescopic forks, sprung saddle, headlamp nacelle and tank-top grid, completely restored.
£3,300–3,600 AT

Miller's is a price GUIDE not a price LIST

 # Miller's
Motorcycle Milestones

Triumph Speed Twin 499cc (British 1937)
Price range: £2,000–4,500
Edward Turner won world-wide recognition by penning the Speed Twin shortly after he joined Triumph as chief designer in 1936. The machine would prove a trend-setter, reshaping British motorcycle design in the decades that followed.

Over 20 years earlier, WWI had dashed Triumph's hopes of constructing its first parallel twin, a 600 side-valve job. The company's second effort, designed by Val Page, also failed in 1932. This creation had a semi-unit-construction, 633cc engine with a one-piece crank that ran backwards and a four-speed gearbox with double helical primary gears. Its robustness was proven by Harry Perrey, who used one to win a sidecar Gold Medal in the 1933 ISDT. Its weaknesses were its bulk and the cost of production, which transpired to kill it off after a mere 40 had been built.

Turner had joined Triumph from Ariel, where he had penned the Square Four. On moving to Triumph, he set about designing a parallel twin. His initial idea was for an overhead-camshaft engine, but this was abandoned in favour of a more basic pushrod unit. The latter had the same bore and stroke dimensions (63x80mm) as Triumph's contemporary 250 single, thus maximising production facilities.

An iron cylinder head and barrel were specified, the latter with a six-stud base flange, which was changed to an eight-stud arrangement in 1939 after some had cracked. In prototype form, the engine developed 30bhp, while the early production versions, built in 1937, gave 3–4bhp less, but still enough to reach 90mph.

Compared to other single-cylinder bikes of the period, the Speed Twin was a superb piece of kit, being practical, flexible, quieter and easier to start. Triumph had truly struck gold.

The original Speed Twins were snapped up like hot cakes, and their success encouraged other manufacturers to follow the trend over the next 30 years. In fact, only Honda and its CB750 four, of 1969, really moved the game ahead.

1951 Triumph Tiger 100, 499cc, alloy head and barrel, single carburettor, sprung hub model.
£3,500–3,850 PM

1952 Triumph 5T Speed Twin, 499cc, sprung hub, headlamp nacelle, dualseat, concours condition.
£3,000–3,300 PM

1952 Triumph 6T Thunderbird, 649cc, overhead-valve, parallel twin, sprung-hub model.
£2,750–3,050 CotC

1954/57 Triumph 5T Speed Twin, 499cc, 63x80mm bore and stroke, partial restoration combining parts from more than one model year, swinging-arm frame, headlamp nacelle, spare alloy cylinder head.
£1,500–1,650 OxM

1955 Triumph Thunderbird 6T, 649cc, overhead-valve twin, restored, restored, excellent condition.
£2,850–3,150 BKS

Edward Turner was keen to promote US sales, and turned to native American mythology for the name of his new model. Introduced in 1949, the Thunderbird became one of the most famous of all Triumphs.

◀ **1955 Triumph Tiger 100,** 499cc, overhead-valve twin, restored, excellent condition.
£4,250–4,650 BKS

When tested in *Motor Cycling*, a sprung-hub T100 achieved a maximum speed of 93mph, prompting the magazine to describe the model as 'a sound example of British motorcycle engineering at its best'. For the 1951 season, the model gained an all-alloy engine and benefited from an increase in performance. The next major revision came in 1954 with the adoption of the pivoted-fork frame.

1956 Triumph 5T Speed Twin, 499cc, overhead-valve, pre-unit twin, swinging-arm frame, full-width front hub, original specification, imported from Sri Lanka.
£1,350–1,500 PS

1956 Triumph T100, 499cc, 'barn discovery', completely original, in need of restoration.
£1,900–2,200 AT

◀ **1956 Triumph Tiger 110,** 649cc.
£4,250–4,700 BKS

Introduced in 1954, originally with an iron head and barrel, the T110 brought pivoted-fork rear suspension to the Triumph range. In 1956, it adopted a cast alloy cylinder head, by which time it had established an enviable reputation in production racing, securing a 1-2-3 in the 1955 Thruxton 500, and had met with considerable success in the States. The model led the Triumph range up to 1959, when the T120 Bonneville was announced, and was dropped from the catalogue in 1961.

1956 Triumph T15 Terrier, 149cc, overhead-valve, unit-construction single, 57x58.5mm bore and stroke, 8.3bhp at 6,500rpm, concours condition.
£2,000–2,500 TCTR

Announced in November 1952, on the eve of the Earls Court show, the T15 Terrier was designed by Edward Turner and went on sale in the following year.

▶ **1958 Triumph 6T Thunderbird,** 649cc, standard specification, very good condition.
£2,700–3,300 BLM

1958 Triumph Tiger 100, 500cc, all-alloy engine, single carburettor, full-width front hub, swinging-arm frame.
£4,600–5,000 BLM

1958 Triumph TR6 Trophy, 649cc, overhead-valve, pre-unit twin, high-level exhaust, matching speedometer and tachometer, concours condition.
£7,000–7,700 SWS

1958 Triumph T20 Tiger Cub, 199cc, overhead-valve, unit single, 4-speed gearbox.
£1,000–1,200 MAY

▶ **1959 Triumph 5TA Speed Twin,** 490cc, unit construction, 69x65.5mm bore and stroke.
£2,000–2,200 PM

The 5TA replaced the long-running, pre-unit 5T for the 1959 season. It displayed the same styling as the 3TA Twenty One, which had been introduced a few months earlier.

◀ **1960 Triumph T120R Bonneville,** 649cc, overhead-valve, pre-unit, twin-cylinder engine, twin Amal Monobloc carburettors, restored to concours condition.
£6,000+ PM

To many, the 1960/61 T120R Bonneville is the most desirable of all the Bonneville models. It is certainly one of the most sought after of all Triumph motorcycles.

1961 Triumph 5TA Speed Twin, 490cc, unit construction, distributor ignition, 4-speed gearbox, standard specification with original tinware.
£1,850–2,050 AT

1962 Triumph T20SH Sports Cub, 199cc, overhead-valve, single-cylinder engine, concours condition.
£1,500–1,750 TCTR

The T20SH Sports Cub was introduced in 1962 and featured a two-piece crankpin, a ball-race timing main bearing, a pressed-in timing mainshaft, separate skew and timing gears, increased oil flow, coil ignition and switches mounted under the seat.

Restored Values

The cost of a professional restoration will have an influence on, but no direct relation to, a motorcycle's market value. A restored motorcycle can have a market value lower than the cost of its restoration.

1962 Triumph 5TA Speed Twin, 490cc, overhead-valve, unit-construction twin, completely restored to original condition.
£3,200–3,500 S

The 5TA arrived in time for the 1959 season and basically was a more powerful version of the 3TA Twenty One. Both featured unit-construction engines, 'bathtub' rear enclosure and a deeply-valanced front mudguard.

1963 Triumph Tiger 90, 348cc, concours condition.
£2,400–2,600 CotC

In October 1962, the 3TA was joined by a sports version with a tuned engine, called the Tiger 90. Its specification included a siamesed exhaust, a separate headlamp and partial rear enclosure.

1967 Triumph T20M Mountain Cub, 199cc, overhead-valve, unit single, non-standard exhaust system, concours condition.
£2,250–2,500 TCTR

1963 Triumph T20 Tiger Cub, 199cc, overhead-valve single, Amal 32 carburettor, very good condition.
£1,500–1,750 TCTR

The Tiger Cub was revised for 1963 with contact points in the timing cover, a clutch-cable access hole in the clutch cover, and finned rocker covers.

1966 Triumph TR6C, 649cc, overhead-valve, unit-construction twin.
£3,900–4,300 BKS

Triumph introduced two new C versions of the TR6 for the American market in 1966, both of which were intended for off-road use. They utilised the single-carburettor variant of the 650 twin in a soft state of tune, which endowed the machine with good performance and flexibility. High-level exhausts, a small, quickly-detachable competition headlamp and high, wide handlebars were fitted. Detail differences between the East- and West-coast variants were restricted to colour and mudguards, the latter being chromed on East-coast versions.

1967 Triumph TR6, 649cc, overhead-valve, unit twin, original specification.
£4,500–4,950 PM

Essentially, this model is a single-carburettor version of the T120 Bonneville.

◀ **1967 Triumph T20 S/C Super Cub,** 199cc, overhead-valve, unit-construction, single-cylinder engine, concours condition.
£1,500–2,000 TCTR

This model was the last of the Cub line. It was equipped with a Bantam tank and full-width hubs, and received other minor changes. Production continued into 1968, when it was dropped from the Triumph range.

1969 Triumph TR25W, 247cc, overhead-valve, unit single, 67x70mm bore and stroke, twin-leading-shoe front brake, high-level exhaust, 24bhp at 8,000rpm.
£700–850 CotC

Introduced in 1968, the TR25W was based on the 250 BSA unit-construction engine.

1969 Triumph T120 Bonneville, 649cc, overhead-valve, unit twin, 71x82mm bore and stroke, twin-leading-shoe front brake, 18in wheels front and rear, concours condition.
£4,500–4,950 PM

1972 Triumph T120R Bonneville, 649cc, overhead-valve, unit twin, 5-speed gearbox, non-standard silencer, US export model.
£2.000–2,800 S

1975 Triumph T150 Trident, 740cc, overhead-valve, 3-cylinder engine, 67x70mm bore and stroke, 5-speed gearbox, disc front brake, conical rear hub.
£2,750–3,250 BLM

◄ **1976 Triumph T100R Daytona,**
490cc, overhead-valve, unit-
construction, twin-cylinder engine,
twin carburettors, twin-leading-
shoe front brake, indicators,
one owner, only 770 miles
from new, completely original,
very good condition.
£3,600–3,950 NLM

**The T100R Daytona replaced the
T100T model for 1971.**

1976 Triumph T140V Bonneville, 744cc, overhead-
valve, unit twin, 5-speed gearbox, European export
specification, original.
£3,800–4,000 VER

1979 Triumph T140 Bonneville Special, 744cc,
overhead-valve, unit twin, export specification with
2-into-1 exhaust and cast alloy wheels as standard.
£2,300–2,550 S

The Bonneville Special was introduced in 1979.

◄ **1983 Triumph T140 Bonneville Executive,** 744cc,
overhead-valve, unit twin.
£2,750–3,000 BLM

**The Executive was a limited-edition model that
came with a fairing, panniers and top box as
standard equipment.**

Ultima *(French 1908–58)*

◄ **1921 Ultima Lyon,**
349cc, side-valve, single-
cylinder engine, inclined
cylinder, 70x100mm bore
and stroke, crankshaft-
mounted clutch, direct
belt drive to rear wheel,
handcrank starter,
completely restored,
very good condition.
£4,150–4,550 YEST

**Initially, Ultima made a
range of motorcycles
with a variety of
proprietary engines,
including Zurcher,
Aubier-Dunne and JAP.
Post-WWII, the company
developed a series of
small two-stroke models.**

Velocette *(British 1904–68)*

Percy and Eugene Goodman were the men behind the creation of Velocette. It was Percy's 1913 206cc, two-stroke single that firmly established the marque, although the company was actually called Veloce, and the original use of the Velocette name was for a single model type. Later, it was extended to cover the entire range. The Goodmans saw racing as an effective means of advertising their wares, at first with tuned versions of the two-stroke, and then four-stroke engines.

Sporting success throughout the 1920s and 1930s did much to publicise the Velocette marque, and sales of production roadsters flourished. Models such as the KTS and KSS overhead-camshaft machines were highly respected, while the famous KTT was the over-the-counter version of the factory's race-winning 350. In fact, Velocette had the distinction of being the very first winners of the 350cc World Championship, when Freddie Frith took the title in 1949. Bob Foster repeated the feat in the following year.

During the 1950s, Velocette developed the 349cc Viper and 499cc Venom overhead-valve singles. In 1961, with one of the latter pushrod models, a team of riders averaged over 100mph at the Montlhéry circuit near Paris for 24 hours, setting a new world record. The bike was remarkably standard, the only significant changes being an Avon Dolphin fairing and a megaphone exhaust. The Viper and Venom also did well in production racing. Then, in 1964, Velocette introduced its ultimate sporting roadster, the Thruxton.

Sadly, however, even though its sports singles were revered around the world, the company's management did not always get it right. Notable failures were small-capacity machines such as the Viceroy scooter and Vogue enclosed motorcycle. Even the more successful LE and Valiant models failed to attract customers in the numbers originally anticipated. This, combined with the relatively small sales of the expensive Thruxton, so weakened the Veloce company that it could not recover, and the firm went into liquidation during 1971.

1922 Velocette Model G2, 220cc, 2-stroke, single-cylinder engine, overhung crankshaft, separate magneto, 2-speed gearbox, in need of restoration.
£2,050–2,250 BKS

When Veloce introduced its first two-stroke lightweight in 1913, the company used the Velocette name for the first time, distinguishing the new model from its larger four-stroke siblings.

▶ **1936 Velocette KSS Mk II,** 348cc, overhead-camshaft, single-cylinder engine, 74x81mm bore and stroke, restored to original specification, excellent condition.
£3,500–3,730 CotC

Nineteen-thirty-six saw the introduction of the Mk II version of the KSS, which featured a one-piece alloy cylinder head and camshaft box.

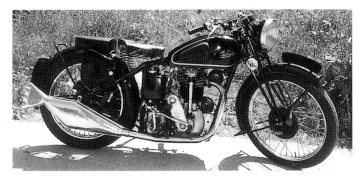

1937 Velocette MOV, 248cc, overhead-valve single, 68x68.25mm bore and stroke.
£1,450–1,500 CotC

The MOV was introduced for 1933.

1948 Velocette KSS Mk II, 348cc, overhead-camshaft, single-cylinder engine, good condition.
£2,650–2,950 BKS

The K-series sporting Velocettes were marketed from the mid-1920s until 1948. This late machine is equipped with Dowty forks, an update for the final year.

1948 Velocette MOV, 248cc, overhead-valve single, Dowty forks, rigid frame.
£1,500–1,600 PM

Nineteen-forty-eight was the final year of production for the MOV.

1948 Velocette LE Mk I Display Engine and Shaft Drive, 149cc, cut away to exhibit inner mechanisms, used by the manufacturers at shows and exhibitions.
£500–550 LVO

1956 Velocette MSS, 499cc, overhead-valve single, 86x86mm bore and stroke, restored to original specification.
£2,700–2,850 CotC

◄ **1956 Velocette MAC,** 349cc, overhead-valve, single-cylinder engine, 68x96mm bore and stroke, complete and running, in need of restoration.
£1,800–2,000 AT

The swinging-arm version of Velocette's MAC was introduced in 1953. Its shock absorber upper mounts could be moved along curved slots to adjust the rear suspension setting.

1956 Velocette Venom, 499cc, overhead-valve single, 86x86mm bore and stroke, updated with Amal Concentric carburettor, alloy rims and Clubman's tank, otherwise standard specification.
£3,000–3,500 BLM

The Venom entered production in 1956.

1959 Velocette Valiant Veeline, 192cc, overhead-valve flat-twin, 50x49mm bore and stroke, shaft final drive, completely restored.
£2,000+ LVO

The Veeline part of this model's name referred to its Dolphin fairing, which was standard equipment in this guise. The Valiant entered production in 1957.

◄ **1957 Velocette MAC,** 349cc, overhead-valve, single-cylinder engine, completely restored, concours condition.
£2,650–2,950 BKS

Production of the MAC began in 1934 and continued until 1960. The model gained an alloy cylinder head and barrel for 1951, as well as Veloce's own telescopic fork in place of the previous Dowty assembly. It was further updated with a swinging-arm frame in 1953.

► **1960 Velocette Viper,** 349cc, overhead-valve, single-cylinder engine, 4-speed foot-change gearbox, full-width hubs, chromed mudguards, restored to original specification, excellent condition.
£3,400–3,700 BLM

The Viper was a traditional British heavyweight 350 that sacrificed outright performance for smoothness, economy and comfort.

◄ **1960 Velocette LE Mk III,** 192cc, water-cooled, overhead-valve flat-twin, shaft final drive, in need of restoration.
£350–450 AT

By the beginning of the 1960s, the LE model had reached Mk III form, having been re-engineered with a foot-change, four-speed gearbox and conventional kickstart.

1960 Velocette Venom, 499cc, very good condition.
£2,500–2,750 BKS

Introduced in 1956 together with the 350cc Viper, the Venom was derived from the touring MSS and was intended to fulfil the sporting role – as was its smaller stablemate – that had been vacant since production of the overhead-camshaft models had ceased. The new model had the MSS frame, but gained a 7⅛in front brake and deeper headlamp shell, which contained the chronometric speedometer. The engine was tuned to improve performance. For 1960, the Venom Special was available with a fibreglass cowling, which enclosed the engine and transmission assembly from the cylinder barrel downward.

1964 Velocette Viper, 349cc, overhead-valve single, alloy rims, larger than standard 4-gallon tank, touring trim.
£2,800–3,200 BLM

◄ **1964 Velocette Vogue,** 192cc, overhead-valve, flat-twin engine, fully enclosed bodywork, fairing, windscreen, panniers, indicators, completely restored, concours condition.
£1,800–2,000 LVO

Only 361 Vogue models were built, and surviving examples are rare. For the period, it featured comprehensive instrumentation.

► **1968 Velocette Thruxton,** 499cc, completely restored in late 1980s by Geoff Dodkin.
£8,000–8,500 CotC

Derived from the Venom, the Thruxton made its debut in 1965. It featured a revised head with a 2in-diameter inlet valve, Amal GP carburettor, close-ratio gearbox, alloy rims, a twin-leading-shoe front brake, swept-back exhaust pipe, oil-tank leaf shield, clip-ons, rearsets, and a special tank and seat.

Victoria *(German 1899–1966)*

1967 Victoria Sport Type 13, 49cc, fan-cooled, 2-stroke, single-cylinder engine, restored, very good condition.
£400–450 HERM

Victoria was part of the Zweirad Union which, from the late 1950s, also included DKW and Express.

Vincent-HRD *(British 1928–56)*

1938 Vicent-HRD Series A, 998cc, overhead-valve
V-twin, siamesed exhaust, dual front brakes, sprung
saddle, pillion pad, original apart from later mudguards.
£18,000–19,000 VMCC

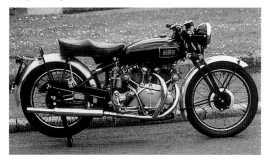

1948 Vincent-HRD Rapide, 998cc, 45bhp at 5,300rpm,
original specification.
£14,000–15,400 PM

Egli Vincent 1332cc (Swiss/British 1971)
Price range: £10,000–17,000
Although production of the British Vincent-HRD 998cc, overhead-valve V-twin ceased during 1955, the engine didn't disappear. Both before and after the company's demise, Vincent engines were used to power a number of record-breaking speed machines. In America, both Rollie Free and Marty Dickinson used the V-twin to set new world and AMA (American Motorcycle Association) records on Bonneville Salt Flats in Utah. In Britain, George Brown (a Vincent dealer and former racer) created first Nero, and then Super Nero to take on and beat the world of drag racing for over two decades.

And so it continued, with Vincent engines finding their way into other peoples' frames, notably the Norton Featherbed to make the Norvin. Finally, the talented Swiss engineer Fritz Egli (with assistance from Englishman Terry Price) employed the Vincent V-twin during the late 1960s and early 1970s as the motivation for a series of street bikes and racers with considerable success.

With his friend and racer Fritz Peier, Egli used Vincent machines to win the Swiss national hillclimb championships on more than one occasion. At first, Egli retained the standard 998cc (84x90mm) Vincent engine displacement, but tuned the V-twin to increase maximum power from 55 to 70bhp. However, by the beginning of the 1970s, even this was not enough to satisfy a power-hungry clientele. As a result, the engine size was increased in stages: first to 1100cc, then 1200cc and finally, in 1971, to a massive 1332cc. This was achieved by enlarging both the bore and stroke dimensions.

However, this was the limit to which the Phil Irving-designed engine could be stretched, and thereafter Fritz Egli switched to Japanese engines, notably the Kawasaki Z1 which, by the late 1980s, had grown to 1428cc and was turbocharged into the bargain!

▶ **1951 Vincent-HRD Series C Comet,** 499cc, overhead-valve single, 84x90mm bore and stroke, 28bhp at 5,800rpm, restored to standard specification.
£4,250–4,500 CotC

The engine of this model was basically one of the big V-twins with its rear cylinder lopped off. In the main, the cycle parts were also the same as the larger bike.

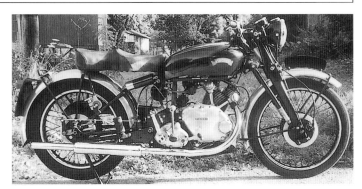

1955 Vincent-HRD Series D 'Open' Black Shadow, 998cc V-twin, rare, but incomplete and in need of restoration.
£10,800–12,800 BKS

The Series D Black Shadow was the last machine produced by the Stevenage factory. While the massive unit-construction V-twin engine and girdraulic forks of previous models were retained, the suspension was altered, with a single shock absorber beneath the saddle. The upper frame oil tank was also modified, and a lifting lever was incorporated to raise the machine on to its centre stand. The D-series was originally designed as an enclosed model, but the original supplier of the fibreglass panels was unable to fulfil its commitment, and Phil Vincent contracted Microplas to manufacture the mouldings for him. Unfortunately, four months passed before fairings of sufficiently high quality could be delivered, so it was decided to produce an 'Open' version of the new series to maintain sales. These machines appeared in March 1955 and were sold until the enclosed models became available.

Yale *(American 1902–15)*

1914 Yale 7-8hp, 950cc, V-twin engine, pedals, completely restored, very good condition.
£11,500–12,650 BKS

The Yale Manufacturing Company of Toledo, Ohio, began manufacturing motorcycles in 1902, but was forced to close in 1915. However, in its final years, the company produced a beautifully designed and built 950cc, inlet-over-exhaust, V-twin machine that featured a two-speed gearbox and all-chain drive. Surviving examples are very rare, particularly in Europe.

Yamaha *(Japanese 1954–)*

1965 Yamaha YDS3C, 246cc, air-cooled, 2-stroke twin, piston-port induction, magneto ignition, Autolube (pump) oil system, 28bhp at 8,000rpm, 5-speed gearbox, concours condition.
£2,000–3,000 SMC

The street-scrambler styling of the YDS3C was aimed primarily at the American market.

▶ **1980 Yamaha RD125DX,** 124cc, air-cooled, 2-stroke twin, reed-valve induction, original specification.
£500–550 PS

'DX' signified that this model had a disc front brake.

Dirt Bikes

Trials and scrambles machines built by major British manufacturers during motorcycling's 'golden era' (1947–65) are popularly known as comp bikes, and among the most desirable of such machines are those built for the International Six Days Trial (ISDT). British manufacturers took that annual Blue Riband contest very seriously, and their competition departments would build a few specially modified bikes by hand for their works riders. Some factories based ISDT machines on their listed scramblers, adding wide-ratio gears, silencers, lights and so on. Others took the sportiest road machine in their range and modified it accordingly. Genuine ex-works ISDT machines occasionally surface at sales and, if still complete with their original quickly-detachable parts, can prove a fulfilling purchase.

Comp bikes have always had more charisma than their roadster siblings and, although representing no more than 2–3 per cent of total factory output (and despite a spartan specification), were usually sold at a premium. Theoretically, and due to their rarity, this should be reflected in current pricing. It is interesting to recall that poseurs were discouraged from buying certain early post-war comp bikes unless the potential purchaser's Competition Licence, supported by a suitable note from his club secretary, was shown to the supplying dealer.

Until the late 1950s, healthy factories could sell every road model built, and production managers were reluctant to incorporate too many non-standard parts into disruptive runs of comp bikes, but market forces dictated that their off-the-shelf trials/scrambles models were at least fitted with smaller fuel tanks, alloy mudguards, gears of suitable ratio, raised exhaust systems, 21in front wheels and motors that had been tuned for their intended purpose. Even so, the finished item still required additional work by its purchaser to make it competitive, which explains why so few comp bikes today conform precisely to their original specification. Owner/competitors were simply compelled to alter unsuitable footrests and improve mudguard clearance. Likewise, lights, toolboxes and centre-stands were promptly dispensed with.

Only three firms bucked this trend between 1949 and 1962, their standard trialers being suitable for riding straight from the showroom to an event, subject only to waterproofing. Any of these three machines converted a mediocre rider into an instant award winner. Norton's 500T (1949) was the first; then came Ariel's HT5 (1956); followed by the 24TES model Greeves in 1962.

Identical criteria apply to the majority of catalogue-model scramblers, with the exception of duplex-framed BSA Gold Stars (1954 onwards) and the MDS and Challenger (post 1962) from Greeves.

Racing, of course, thrives on improvement and modification, and original models are clearly too precious to come under 'starter's orders' in today's vigorous pre-'65 scene. However, thanks to the wide availability of replica hardware, these unique, original comp bikes are justifiably targeted by discerning collectors. May they rest in peace...

Michael Jackson

1934 Panther Stroud Trials, 348cc, overhead-valve single, 71x88mm bore and stroke.
£1,800–2,000 BKS

For 1932, Panther introduced a 250cc, overhead-valve four-stroke with a conventional frame, rather than using the cylinder as the front downtube, which was a characteristic of the marque. A 350 was introduced for 1933, and in 1934, Stroud trials variants appeared. The latter had slimmer mudguards, trials tyres, a small fuel tank, crankcase shield, single-port cylinder head and raised exhaust. Few were built pre-war and today they are rare.

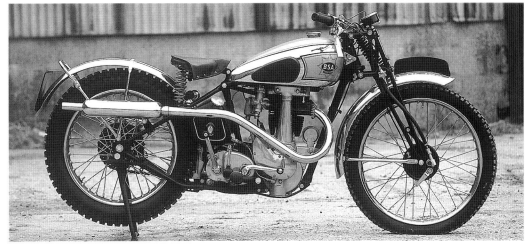

1937 BSA B25 Competition, 348cc, overhead-valve, single-cylinder engine, restored, excellent condition.
£2,450–2,700 BKS

During the 1930s, BSA concentrated on producing a range of dependable, well-made, competitively-priced motorcycles. The firm's single-cylinder range was redesigned by Val Page for 1937, the engines featuring dry-sump lubrication and a rear-mounted magneto, which they retained into the post-war era. There was a quartet of new 350s, the side-valve B23, the overhead-valve B25 Empire Star and B26 Star, and the B25 Competition, which came equipped for trials use.

c1938 Norton Model 18 Scrambler, 490cc, overhead-valve single, restored, very good condition.
£2,600–2,850 BKS

Introduced for 1923, the Model 18 was Norton's first overhead-valve production machine, and it quickly established a reputation for speed and reliability when a standard engine was used to set a host of records. Improvements resulting from the racing programme were regularly incorporated into the production bikes, yet the Model 18 retained its essentially vintage characteristics until extensively redesigned in 1931. That year, Norton's side- and overhead-valve singles adopted the rear-mounted magneto, already seen on the ES2, and switched to dry-sump lubrication. Norton continued to fit Sturmey-Archer gearboxes, and all models, with the exception of the ES2, had an open-diamond frame. Changes between 1931 and 1939 included an additional drive-side main bearing, revised cam gears, the adoption of Norton's own gearbox and, in 1938, a new cylinder head with enclosed valve gear.

1950 Panther Stroud Trials Mk I, 249cc, overhead-valve single, 60x80mm bore and stroke.
£2,750–3,050 BKS

P & M revived the Stroud name for its Panther 250 and 350 trials models in 1949, the duo having debuted in the previous year. Unlike the classic big Panther roadster, the off-roaders eschewed the stressed-member sloping engine in favour of an upright engine in a conventional tubular frame. The overhead-valve engine had an oil reservoir within the crankcase and was unusual in employing plain-bush main bearings. A Dowty Oleomatic front fork was fitted, while the frame was rigid. A mildly revised Stroud, featuring an alloy cylinder head and a low-level exhaust system, was introduced for 1951, and the model gained a strengthened frame in the following year. Produced until 1953, the Stroud sold in small numbers and made very little impact on the national trials scene: the steering geometry was all wrong for trials, and the 250 in particular was far too heavy. This is the rarest of all post-war British four-stroke trials machines.

◀ **1950 Triumph TR5 Trophy,** 499cc, overhead-valve twin, excellent condition.
£4,950–5,450 BKS

Success in the 1948 ISDT prompted Triumph to introduce a production version of the works riders' mounts, the new model being given the name Trophy. Its engine was based on the Speed Twin's, but with a light-alloy barrel and head instead of cast-iron components. A compact, short-wheelbase frame helped offset the handicap of the bulky twin-cylinder motor and made the Trophy competitive, for a time at least, in one-day trials. However, its true forte was scrambles and the ISDT, where the power of the tunable engine worked to its advantage.

1951 Ariel VCH Trials, 497cc, overhead-valve single.
£2,100–2,300 BKS

Ariel restarted civilian production in 1945 with a similar range to that of 1939. However, a telescopic front fork soon replaced the pre-war girder type on the sporting Red Hunter, and in 1948 an experimental trials version of that machine appeared, equipped with an all-alloy engine. Production of the new, alloy-engined competition Hunter, coded VCH, began in time for the 1950 season, the model being offered in trials and scrambles form, both with a rigid frame. Weight was reduced to 300lb, and the motor turned out 25bhp. The VCH proved more successful in scrambles than in trials, where its 56in wheelbase was a handicap, although that shortcoming was addressed for 1953 with a 54in-wheelbase frame. Major one-day trials success continued to elude Ariel, however, the result being separate models for trials (HT) and scrambles (HS) in 1954.

1950 Norton 500T Trials, 490cc, overhead-valve single.
£3,650–4,050 BKS

Norton's post-WWII trials campaign got off to a false start in 1947, the combination of the iron-barrelled, overhead-valve Model 18 engine in a Roadholder-forked WD 16H frame producing a machine that was too long, too heavy and endowed with insufficient ground clearance. Extensive modification and experimentation resulted in the appearance, late in 1948, of an entirely different machine, the legendary 500T. Shortened rear frame stays and a modified lower fork yoke reduced the wheelbase to a more manageable 53in, while an alloy cylinder head and barrel helped reduce weight to around 300lb. Numerous works and privateer competition successes soon confirmed that Norton had produced a machine as good as, if not better than, any other rigid-framed trials iron of the period. However, no sprung-frame development appeared to carry on the line, and the 500T was dropped in 1954.

1954 BSA BB32 Competition, 348cc, overhead-valve, single-cylinder engine, very good condition.
£2,100–2,300 PC

This particular machine is an ex-works competition model and was used by the Royal Artillery Display Team.

1954 Matchless G3LC Trials, 348cc, overhead-valve single, 69x93mm bore and stroke.
£3,900–4,300 BKS

AMC announced its post-war range of AJS and Matchless heavyweight 350 singles in June 1945, coded Model 16 and G3L respectively. Housed in a rigid frame with a teledraulic front fork, the rugged, overhead-valve engine drove through a four-speed gearbox. Hairpin valve springs were adopted for 1949, as was a swinging-arm frame for export models, athough this became available in the UK from 1950. Machines so equipped were suffixed 'S'.

◄ **1955 Dot TDH KAP,** 197cc, Villiers 8E, 2-stroke, single-cylinder engine, 4-speed gearbox, pivoted Earles-style front forks, 21in front wheel, hydraulic rear suspension, direct lighting, completely restored, excellent condition.
£1,500–2,000 VMCC

The swinging-arm front suspension used on this model was introduced for the 1955 season. When new, the bike cost £142.16s.0d.

1955 Royal Enfield Bullet Replica, 348cc, overhead-valve single, trials conversion with Amal Monobloc carburettor, high-level exhaust, Ceriani forks, and alloy tank and mudguards.
£1,150–1,250 PS

1957 Ariel HT5, 499cc, overhead-valve single, 81.8x95mm bore and stroke, telescopic forks, swinging-arm frame, alloy fuel tank.
£4,000–4,500 VER

1958 Ariel HT5, 499cc, overhead-valve single.
£1,950–2,150 BKS

The post-war competition Ariel HT was revised prior to the 1956 season in an attempt to make it more competitive in trials. It had a new pivoted-fork frame, developed from experience with the works machines. In its new form, the model became known as the HT5 and was made famous by Sammy Miller and Ron Langston.

1957 Tandon Trials Model, 197cc, Villiers 8E engine, never registered, rebuilt for show purposes.
£500–550 PS

Tandon motorcycles were built at Watford until November 1955. Apparently, 16 trials bikes were assembled from the remaining spare parts in the factory under the instructions of the official receiver, and this machine is believed to be the only survivor of that batch.

1958 Ariel HT5, 499cc, overhead-valve single, restored to original ISDT trim, concours condition.
£5,050–5,550 BKS

Between 1924 and 1953, the UK won the International Six Days Trial competition on 15 occasions, but by the mid-1950s, British domination of the event was a thing of the past. The succeeding decades would be the preserve of state-supported, East European teams equipped, in the main, with lightweight two-strokes. However, the British motorcycle industry's concentration on large-capacity four-strokes meant that most British ISDT competitors continued to be mounted on such machines. This HT5 is the actual works bike ridden by Ron Langston in the Vase A Team for the 1958 event. Although the efforts of Britain's Trophy and Vase Teams were scuppered by machine failures, there were some notable individual performances, among them Langston's, who finished with no marks lost and a coveted Gold Medal.

1958 Greeves Scottish, 197cc, Villiers 2-stroke, single-cylinder engine, very good condition.
£900–950 CotC

The Greeves Scottish model was probably the best British two-stroke trials bike of its era.

1959 Royal Enfield Bullet Trials, 346cc,
overhead-valve single.
£1,950–2,150 BKS

From the mid-1950s, Royal Enfield enjoyed outstanding success with its works 350 trials machines, especially when ridden by Johnny Brittain. This resulted in a substantial demand from privateers for similar machines. As a result, in 1958, the factory offered a works replica trials model, which had the advantage over the standard production trials model of an aluminium head and cylinder. The compression ratio was 7.25:1, and a heavier flywheel was fitted to improve low-speed performance. Modifications were also made to the frame to duplicate the works machine.

1959 Greeves Hawkstone, 246cc, Villiers 2-stroke engine, original specification, concours condition.
£1,500–1,800 PC

c1960 Francis-Barnett Model 85 Trials, 249cc, AMC 2-stroke engine, excellent condition.
£1,700–1,900 BKS

Francis-Barnett became part of AMC in 1947, being joined by James in 1951. The two marques' ranges became progressively similar until the transfer of Francis-Barnett production to the James factory in 1962 ushered in an era of badge engineering. Francis-Barnett concentrated on the production of lightweight two-strokes, powered by Villiers engines at first, although from 1957, many models used AMC's own engine. Trials and scrambles machines were added to the range in the early 1950s. Initially, they used Villiers 6E and 7E engines and had rigid frames, but by the end of the 1950s, they sported swinging-arm frames and the AMC engine. The latter continued to be fitted to F-B roadsters until the end of production in 1966, but before then, the trials and scrambles models had reverted to Villiers power.

1959 Triumph Cub Trials Conversion, 199cc,
overhead-valve single, non-standard.
£1,000+ TCTR

Restored Values

The cost of a professional restoration will have an influence on, but no direct relation to, a motorcycle's market value. A restored motorcycle can have a market value lower than the cost of its restoration.

1962 Velocette MSS Scrambler, 499cc, overhead-valve, single-cylinder engine, restored, very good condition.
£4,100–4,500 BKS

The third of Veloce's overhead-valve singles, the MSS, was announced in 1935. It disappeared from the range in 1948, but returned in 1954 with a new swinging-arm frame and the company's own telescopic front fork. The engine was updated, gaining square bore and stroke dimensions of 86x86mm, along with an alloy cylinder barrel and head. Much engine work was carried out in the scrambles programme, Velocette having gone off-road after withdrawing its road-racing overhead-camshaft models in 1952. Released in 1954, the first production scramblers were handicapped by excess weight and wayward handling, and although these problems were eventually sorted out and the engine developed into one of the best, the company lacked the resources to compete on level terms with the likes of BSA and AMC. Production petered out in the mid-1960s. This MSS scrambler exemplifies the model in virtually its ultimate form, with Valiant fuel tank and lighter rear subframe, but lacking the cast-iron cylinder barrel of the final version.

1962 BSA Catalina Scrambler, 499cc, overhead-valve single, concours condition.
£7,650–8,450 S

The Catalina Scrambler was designed for the enthusiast who wanted the very finest specification. Between 1959 and 1963, 800 were built for the North American market.

1964 Dot Demon, 246cc, Villiers 32A, all alloy, 2-stroke engine, square barrel, alloy fuel tank.
£900–950 CotC

1963 Triumph T20 Cub Trials, 199cc.
£3,350–3,700 BKS

Originally registered by Triumph themselves, this particular machine was loaned to the British Army Team for the 1963 Scottish Six Days Trial, where it was ridden by Vic Noyce. Years later it was restored by well-known trials rider and author Don Morley.

1969 Greeves Challenger, 246cc, short-stroke engine.
£1,800–2,000 BKS

Introduced in 1964, the Challenger scrambler was built in 246cc and later 362cc capacities. The engine was carried in typical Greeves cycle parts, comprising a cast alloy beam frame and leading-link forks, the latter of the 'banana' type from 1965. A short-stroke 250 motor was introduced for 1969.

◀ **1972 BSA B50 MX Victor,** 499cc, overhead-valve, unit-construction engine, modified with Interspan ignition system, special American gear cluster and CCM footrest assembly. **£2,000–2,500 BLM**

This machine is based on the multi-World Championship winner campaigned by scrambling legend Jeff Smith.

1974 AJS Stormer, 250cc, piston-port, 2-stroke, single-cylinder engine, 4-speed gearbox. **£850–950 CotC**

The engine in the Stormer was based on the earlier Villiers Starmaker unit. Updated versions are still being built by Fluff Brown of Andover.

A known continuous history can add value to and enhance the enjoyment of a motorcycle.

1975 Rickman Metisse Mk 4, 349cc. **£2,750–3,050 BKS**

This example of the off-road Metisse was originally fitted with a BSA unit single engine during the 1970s. In the 1980s, it was rebuilt by Metisse specialist Pat French, receiving a new frame and subsequently being fitted with a mildly tuned Triumph 3TA engine with 22mm Amal Concentric Mk 1 carburettor and electronic ignition.

c1979 CCM Motocross, 499cc, overhead-valve, unit-construction, single-cylinder engine, very good condition. **£3,200–3,500 BKS**

Clews Competition Motorcycles was formed in 1972, when Alan Clews bought the stock of BSA's defunct competitions department. He had already gained plenty of experience in developing his own BSA-based scramblers, and the acquisition allowed him to offer complete machines for sale. As well as the last batch of B50 scramblers, Clews obtained tools, jigs, drawings and raw materials. Development continued, frame builder Mike Eatough looking after the chassis, while Clews concentrated on the engine, which adopted new slimline cases, and came to look progressively less like a BSA. The result was a more powerful machine in 500cc form, weighing around 200lb while churning out 45bhp. Clews finally abandoned the BSA-based design in the early 1980s, merging his company with Armstrong and switching to Rotax powerplants.

▶ **1949 Royal Enfield Model G,** 346cc, overhead-valve single, 70x90 mm bore and stroke, iron head and barrel, telescopic forks, rigid frame, very good condition.
£1,100–1,200 PS

Royal Enfield announced a three-model range in November 1945: a two-stroke and a pair of four-stroke singles – the 350 G and 500 J. The Model G saw very little change during its career, which ended in 1954.

◀ **1954 Royal Enfield Bullet,** 346cc, overhead-valve, semi-unit-construction engine, completely restored.
£3,250–3,500 BKS

The first prototypes of the new Bullet made their debut at the 1948 Colmore Cup Trial, ridden by a trio of works riders. They caused a sensation with their swinging-arm rear suspension, which at the time was unheard of in trials circles. The road version entered production in 1949.

c1955 Royal Enfield 500, 496cc, overhead-valve twin, 70x64.5mm bore and stroke, full-width brake hubs, 19in wheels, dualseat.
£2,000–2,500 OxM

1962 Royal Enfield Crusader, 248cc, overhead-valve, unit-construction engine, 4-speed gearbox.
£600–800 OxM

▶ **1959 Royal Enfield Bullet 500,** 499cc, restored, good condition.
£1,500–2,000 BLM

This Bullet has one of the big heads fitted to the 500 from the 1959 model year. The Bullet lives on today, thanks to a licensing agreement with the Indian company Enfield India, which dates from the 1950s.

1939 Rudge Ulster, 499cc, overhead-valve, twin-port single, bronze semi-radial 4-valve cylinder head, 85x88mm bore and stroke, completely restored to original specification.
£6,500–7,000 SWS

◀ **1928 Scott Sprint Special,** 596cc, water-cooled, 2-stroke twin, competition tuned, Amal twin-float carburettor, BTH competition magneto, 3-speed close-ratio gearbox, Andre steering damper, Webb forks.
£8,500–9,500 SCOT

Bradford-born Alfred Scott's experiments with two-stroke motorcycle engines began in the closing years of the 19th century and continued unabated until his death in 1923.

▶ **1925 Sunbeam 2¾hp,** single-cylinder engine, restored, very good condition.
£3,750–4,250 BKS

Sunbeam introduced the 2¾hp model in 1923, having not manufactured a similar sized machine since 1914. Although considered fairly ordinary, the side-valve design acted as the basis for all of Sunbeam's overhead-valve road and race bikes right into the 1930s. After WWII, Sunbeam was taken over by the BSA Group.

1948 Sunbeam S7, 489cc, overhead-camshaft, in-line twin-cylinder engine, shaft final drive, plunger rear suspension, sprung saddle, pillion pad, restored, very good condition.
£2,000–2,500 CotC

◀ **1955 Sunbeam S8,** 489cc, restored, good condition throughout.
£2,000–2,500 PS

Sunbeam was the first British marque post-war to produce a really innovative design in the S7, followed a few months later by the S8. The concept of one large casting combining the engine and gearbox (united by a car-type clutch) was conceived by designer Erling Poppe. A feature of the S7 (but not incorporated in the S8) were the 4.00x16 balloon tyres.

1912 Triumph Touring, 499cc, side-valve single, double-barrel carburettor, forward-mounted magneto, belt final drive, flat tank, pedals, restored, good condition.
£5,500–6,000 VER

1940 Triumph Speed Twin, 498.76cc, overhead-valve twin, 63x80mm bore and stroke, 26bhp at 6,000rpm, 4-speed foot-change gearbox, original specification.
£4,500+ PC

◄ **1955 Triumph T20 Cub,** 199cc, plunger rear suspension, restored, concours condition.
£2,000–2,500 TCTR

This machine is one of the earliest versions of the Tiger Cub, which was developed from the T15 Terrier.

1958 Triumph Tiger 100, 499cc, overhead-valve, pre-unit twin, all-alloy engine, swinging-arm frame, full-width front hub.
£2,800–2,950 CotC

► **1961 Triumph 5TA Speed Twin,** 490cc, overhead-valve, unit-construction twin, rear-mounted distributor, original cycle parts.
£2,000–2,250 CotC

◄ **1964 Triumph Tiger 90,** 349cc, overhead-valve unit twin, restored to original specification, very good condition.
£2,500–2,650 CotC

Making its debut in 1963, the Tiger 90 was developed from the touring 3TA machine. Nineteen-sixty-four was the first year that the model had an exposed rear end and twin silencers.

▶ **1967 Triumph T100SS,** 490cc, overhead-valve unit twin, 69x65.5mm bore and stroke, 26mm Amal 626 carburettor, concours condition.
£2,500–2,750 CotC

In 1967, the T100SS received a new frame from the twin-carburettor, high-performance T100T model. Production of the T100SS came to an end in 1970.

1976 Triumph T140V Bonneville, 744cc, overhead-valve twin, 76x82mm bore and stroke, 5-speed gearbox, left-hand gear-change, front and rear disc brakes.
£2,300–2,500 CStC

c1977 Triumph Tiger 750, 740cc, overhead-valve, parallel twin, 67x70mm bore and stroke, 5-speed gearbox, left-hand gear-change, European specification, concours condition.
£3,000+ OxM

c1978 Triumph T160 Trident, 740cc, overhead-valve, 3-cylinder engine, front and rear disc brakes, electric and kickstart, high bars, export specification.
£3,000–3,500 OxM

1962 Velocette Venom Clubman, 499cc, overhead-valve single, 86 x 86mm bore and stroke, Clubman version with 4-gallon fuel tank, raised exhaust system, rearset foot controls, alloy wheel rims and Smiths tachometer.
£5,500–6,000 BKS

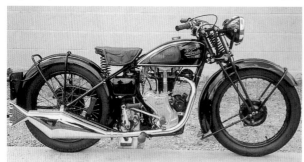

◀ **1936 Velocette MAC,** 349cc, overhead-valve single, foot-change gearbox, restored.
£3,000–3,500 BLM

Introduced for the 1934 season, the MAC was created by extending the stroke of the 250 MOV to 96mm, copying the dimensions of an experimental, long-stroke KTT factory prototype. The last MACs were built in 1960, making it one of Velocette's longest-running models.

▶ **1952 Vincent Series C Rapide,** 998cc, overhead-valve V-twin.
£12,000–14,000 VER

Vincent's Series C Rapide was built in far greater numbers than any of the other Stevenage V-twins. This example is largely original and is fitted with the rare 150mph speedometer. Production of the Vincent V-twin ceased in 1955.

1966 Matchless G85CS, 497cc, good condition.
£4,800–5,300 **BKS**

Along with the single-cylinder roadsters, AMC's production scramblers featured a new swinging-arm frame for 1949, a luxury the works team had enjoyed since 1948. The trials model, though, kept a rigid back end until 1956. The scrambles engine went all-alloy for 1950 and subsequently received different camshafts and larger valves before being redesigned with short-stroke dimensions for 1955. A new duplex frame appeared for 1960, with further engine improvements. AMC dropped the AJS badging from its scrambles range in 1965, at the same time introducing the Matchless G85CS. The latter featured a new frame modelled on the highly successful Rickman Metisse, but despite a significant reduction in weight and an engine developing an impressive 41bhp, the heavyweight four-stroke stood no chance against the latest two-strokes. Production ceased in 1969.

1930 Rudge DT Speedway Bike, 499cc, overhead-valve single, 4-valve, twin-port head, 85x88mm bore and stroke.
£2,500–2,750 **BKS**

The compact, lightweight Rudge, with its four-valve, single-cylinder engine, had established itself as the most effective speedway iron by 1930, the early version being notable for its extra frame bracing struts, although these were soon discarded.

1968 Jawa 500 Ice Speedway Bike, 492cc, roadster-type telescopic forks, shallow steering-head angle, front tyre protective cage, long rear mudguard.
£1,900–2,100 **BKS**

A cold-climate offshoot of conventional speedway, ice racing is immensely popular in Scandinavia. With their spiked tyres, ice-racers are capable of cornering at seemingly impossible angles of lean, and this example embodies many of the special adaptations typical of the breed.

1959 Maico 250 Motocross Bike, 247cc, piston-port, 2-stroke single, 67x70mm bore and stroke, 4-speed gearbox, concours condition.
£2,600+ **MOC**

This machine is similar to the bike that won the 1957 European Moto Cross Championship.

1968 Maico Puissant Motocross Bike, 360cc, expansion-chamber exhaust, original specification, one of only five made, concours condition.
£2,500+ **MOC**

c1960 Hagan 350 Grass Track Bike, 349cc, overhead-valve, long-stroke, 5-stud JAP engine.
£1,500–1,650 **PM**

1977 Rotrax Speedway Bike, 499cc, JAP engine, Neil Street double-overhead-camshaft, 4-valve head.
£5,000–5,500 **BKS**

Despite its great age, the venerable JAP engine retained its devotees well into the 1970s, gaining a boost from the four-valve conversions that appeared in the wake of the successful Weslake engine. This model is fitted with a Neil Street conversion.

◀ **1929 AJS Model M7,** 349cc, overhead-camshaft engine, Amal carburettor, Lucas magneto, hand gear-change.
£6,900–7,600 BKS

The AJS range for 1929 embraced no fewer than 12 different models, ranging from the 250cc lightweight single to the 996cc twins. However, within the range was the sporting, overhead-camshaft M7, a race-bred machine, developed from factory racing experience and using the 'cammy' engine first introduced in 1927. The overhead-camshaft, single-port engine was also offered in 500cc guise as the M10, both machines offering similar performance, although the lighter bike handled slightly better.

▶ **1930 AJS R10,** 495cc, chain-driven overhead camshaft, restored.
£12,000–13,500 BKS

This example of the rare AJS R10 was purchased by well-known ex-racer and journalist Phil Heath in 1956, and used by him for VMCC races, hillclimbs and sprints until 1969. In 1988, he recalled that the machine had a non-standard engine incorporating a lengthened con-rod, cylinder barrel, and camshaft drive case. It transpired that the engine had been built for the Nigel Spring/Bert Denly partnership for their racing and record-breaking attempts at pre-war Brooklands.

◀ **1934 New Imperial Grand Prix,** 344cc, overhead-valve single, dry-sump lubrication, Burman 4-speed foot-change gearbox, oil reservoir in 'pistol-grip' fuel tank.
£6,500–6,100 BKS

Builder of the last British machine to win the Lightweight 250 TT, New Imperial was unsurpassed for innovation during the 1930s, with models featuring pivoted-fork rear suspension and unit construction of engine and gearbox. Introduced for 1934 were the 250 (Model 50) and 350 (Model 60) Grand Prix machines, replicas of the preceding year's works bikes. They were intended for racing and fast road work.

▶ **1950 Vincent Grey Flash,** 499cc, overhead-valve single, Albion racing gearbox, works-type large-capacity fuel tank, dual front brake.
£23,500–25,000 BKS

Development work by George Brown resulted in the Vincent Grey Flash, a tuned version of the Series C Comet single with a power output of 35bhp and a top speed, in racing trim, of 115mph. The Flash retained the overall look of the Comet roadster, with Vincent's distinctive Girdraulic front fork and cantilever rear suspension, but featured an Amal TT carburettor, Elektron magnesium-alloy brake plates and an eye-catching pale grey colour scheme.

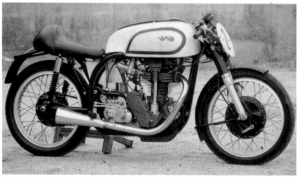

◀ **1952 Norton Manx 40M,** 348cc, double-overhead-camshaft single.
£10,350–11,500 BKS

This machine is an early version of the production Manx Norton with Featherbed frame – introduced on the works bikes in 1950 and a year later on the 'over-the-counter' privateer machines. The last Manx models were built in 1962.

1956/57 FB Mondial Ex-Works 250 Gran Premio, 249.16cc, gear-driven, double-overhead-camshaft, single-cylinder engine, 75x56.4mm bore and stroke, choice of 5, 6 or 7 speeds, 135mph.
£45,000+ IMOC

1959 Matchless G50, 496cc, chain-driven overhead camshaft, 4-speed AMC gearbox, drum brakes, restored, excellent condition.
£14,300–15,300 BKS

c1973 Suzuki TR500, 493cc, piston-port, 2-stroke, twin-cylinder engine, 70x64mm bore and stroke, 5-speed gearbox, twin-disc front brake, single rear disc, restored, unused for four years, in need of recommissioning, otherwise excellent condition.
£3,500–3,800 BKS

1981 Yamaha OW48R, liquid-cooled, 4-cylinder 2-stroke, concours condition.
£75,000 CLR

Originally supplied to the 1976 and 1977 500cc World Champion, Barry Sheene, for the 1981 Grand Prix season, this bike was subsequently raced by Dutchman Boet Van Dulman, and later Steve Parrish until 1985.

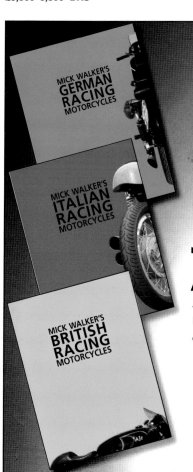

◀ **1923 Monet-Goyon GZA-3 Tricycle,** 298cc, central-spring front forks, chain final drive.
£2,500–2,750 HERM

1958 Norton ES2 and Sidecar, 490cc, overhead-valve, single-cylinder engine, very good condition.
£2,500–3,000 RAC

RAC road patrols used the Norton ES2 outfit from 1958 to 1960.

1950s Triton Stan Cooper Replica, 498cc, Triumph GP engine, Norton frame, replica Manx front brake, short-circuit Lyta alloy tank, concours condition.
£5,500–6,000 IVC

1968 Rickman/Triumph Special, 649cc, Triumph T120R Bonneville unit engine, Rickman chassis, Lockheed front disc, BSA rear hub, café racer trim.
£3,300–3,600 PS

◀ An AA Brands Hatch enamel sign, 1950s.
£50-100 BLM

A British Motor Cycle Racing Club brass plaque, 1920/30s, 7in (17.5cm) diam.
£100-200 BLM

▶ An *Autocycles and Cyclemotors* booklet, third edition, 1957.
£9–10 OM

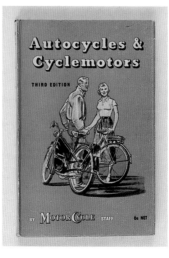

Challenge Motor Oil 1 gallon tin, 1930, 12in (30cm) high.
£50–55 BLM

Military Motorcycles

1915 Triumph Model H, 550cc, side-valve single, originally supplied to the Royal Flying Corps.
£3,500–4,500 VER

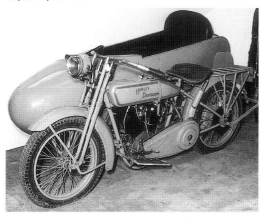

1918 Harley-Davidson Model 18F with Sidecar,
8.68hp, side-valve V-twin.
£7,950–8,750 BKS

The American War Department placed orders with Harley-Davidson totalling 26,486 machines during the period between the USA's entry into WWI and the Armistice. Other examples had been supplied to the allies prior to America's involvement in the war. The machines supplied for service use were the same as the civilian models, confirming their inherent robustness. Harley offered three versions of its 8.68hp twin during 1918: the 18E with a single-speed direct drive, and a pair of three-speed models, the 18F and 18J.

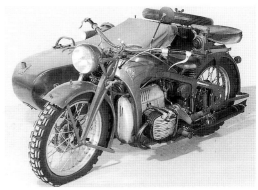

1934 Zündapp K800W with Sidecar, 791cc, side-valve flat-4, 62x66.6mm bore and stroke, 22bhp at 4,300rpm, restored, very good condition.
£3,700–4,100 HERM

1941 BMW KS600W with Sidecar, 597cc, overhead-valve flat-twin, 75x67.6mm bore and stroke.
£2,500–2,750 HERM

Introduced in 1938, the KS600W was adopted by the German armed forces that year.

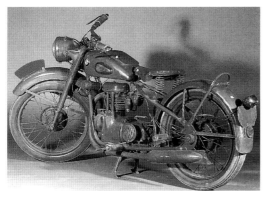

◄ **1939 BMW R23,** 247cc, overhead-valve single, 68x68mm bore and stroke, 4-speed foot-change gearbox, shaft final drive.
£900–1,000 BERN

In all, 9,021 R23s were manufactured between 1938 and 1940.

1939 BMW R12 with Sidecar, 745cc, side-valve flat-twin, 78x78mm bore and stroke, shaft final drive, pressed-steel chassis.
£3,000–3,300 HERM

c1940 Triumph WD Model 3HW, 342cc, overhead-valve single, 70x89mm bore and stroke, 17bhp, chain final drive, girder forks, rigid frame.
£1,500–1,800 BLM

Miller's is a price GUIDE not a price LIST

1944 NSU HK101 Kettenkrad, 1478cc, water-cooled, 4-cylinder, Opel car engine.
£9,650–10,650 HERM

Half motorcycle and half tracked vehicle, the Kettenkrad was one of the weirdest machines of WWII.

1941 Indian 741B, 744cc, side-valve V-twin, 73x88.9mm bore and stroke, 24bhp, chain final drive.
£4,500–4,950 IMC

The Indian 741B was widely used by American and Allied forces during WWII. This particular example was discovered in a bar at the Montlhéry Autodrome, where it had been retired from service many years ago.

▶ **1942 Royal Enfield Model C,** 346cc, side-valve, single-cylinder engine, 70x90mm bore and stroke, 4-speed foot-change gearbox.
£1,500–1,700 PM

1942 BMW R75, 745cc, overhead-valve flat-twin, 78x78mm bore and stroke, 26bhp, 4 forward speeds and reverse gear, shaft final drive, complete, in need of cosmetic attention.
£4,850–5,350 S

More often than not, the R75 was used in conjunction with a sidecar, which had a special drive to its wheel.

1943 BMW R75 with Sidecar, 745cc, overhead-valve flat-twin, restored with full military equipment.
£7,500–8,500 HERM

1940s BSA M20, 496cc, side-valve single, 82x94mm bore and stroke, restored with correct accessories.
£2,000–2,200 MVT

1971 Moto Guzzi Nuovo Falcone, 498cc, overhead-valve, unit-construction, horizontal, single-cylinder engine, 88x82mm bore and stroke, 26bhp, 4-speed gearbox, chain final drive, dual silencer.
£2,000–2,200 VICO

This model was used by the Italian and Yugoslav Armies.

1964 Triumph TRW, 498cc, side-valve parallel twin, 63x80mm bore and stroke, siamesed exhaust, 17bhp, chain final drive, telescopic forks, rigid tubular frame.
£1,900–2,000 CotC

► **1974 Condor Military,** 340cc, Ducati wide-case, overhead-camshaft single, 5-speed gearbox, purpose-built frame, Marzocchi 35mm front forks, Grimeca full-width brake hubs, 12 volt electrics, dualseat, panniers, rear carrier.
£1,300–1,450 TGA

Monkey Bikes

1964 Honda CZ100, 49cc, overhead-valve single, 40x39mm bore and stroke, 3-speed gearbox, 5in wheels, completely restored, concours condition.
£2,500–3,000 VJMC

The machine that started the monkey-bike trend, the Honda CZ100 was built between 1960 and 1967.

1971 Honda Z50A, 49.5cc, overhead-camshaft, horizontal single, 41.4x49.5mm bore and stroke, 2.5bhp at 6,000rpm.
£1,850–2,050 BKS

1974 Honda ST70, 71.8cc, overhead-camshaft, horizontal, single-cylinder engine, restored, very good condition.
£300–400 CARS

The ST70 was a grown-up monkey bike with a larger engine, but it was built to the same basic formula.

◄ 1972 Honda Z50, 49cc, overhead-camshaft, single-cylinder engine, completely restored, excellent condition.
£1,100–1,200 RIM

1979 Rajoot GTS, 173cc, 2-stroke, single-cylinder engine, trailing-link front forks, swinging-arm rear suspension, 28km from new, very good condition.
£700–770 S

1981 Honda Z50J Gorilla, 49.5cc, overhead-camshaft, single-cylinder engine, excellent condition.
£2,100–2,300 S

A known continuous history can add value to and enhance the enjoyment of a motorcycle.

◀ **1976 Suzuki RV90,** 88.4cc, reed-valve 2-stroke, single-cylinder engine, flywheel magneto ignition, 4-speed gearbox, 10in wheels, rear carrier, completely restored, very good condition.
£1,500–1,650 PM

1981 Honda Z50 Gorilla, 49.5cc, overhead-camshaft, horizontal single, completely restored.
£3,450–3,800 BKS

The Gorilla variant of the Z50 Monkey Bike was equipped with a larger-capacity fuel tank, a front carrier incorporating a headlight guard, and a rear carrier. These machines found favour with more adventurous riders thanks to their longer range. This example of the limited-edition chrome model is believed to be one of only five in the UK.

Mopeds

1955 Zündapp Combinette Type 408, 48cc, 2-stroke single, 39x41.8mm bore and stroke, 26in wheels, completely restored.
£300–330 BKS

The original Combimot engine was introduced in 1953 as a clip-on unit for conventional pedal cycles. From 1954, however, Zündapp used the engine in its Combinette moped series. Tested by *Motor Cycling*, the Combinette was described as 'an exceptionally handsome cyclemotor with a useful reserve of power and gentlemanly manners', proving capable of cruising at 25–30mph. Standard equipment included a comprehensive toolkit, 45mph speedometer, lights, carrier and skirtguard. The machine sold for £67.16s.0d.

▶ **1956 TWN FIP3,** 49cc, Sachs 2-stroke, completely restored, concours condition.
£1,500–1,650 SWS

Now very rare, the German Triumph sold in the UK and Commonwealth countries under the TWN label.

1955 Zündapp Combinette De Luxe, 49cc 2-stroke, 2-speed gearbox, 23in wheels, completely restored.
£500–550 BKS

1956 Zündapp Combinette De Luxe, 49cc, 2-stroke, single-cylinder engine, 2-speed gearbox, complete mechanical and cosmetic restoration in 1991, excellent condition throughout.
£500–550 BKS

▶ **1959 NSU Quickly Moped,** 49cc, 2-stroke single, original, in need of restoration.
£140–175 AT

Over 1.1 million Quicklys were sold in the course of a decade, following the start of production in 1953.

1960 Lambretta Lambrettino, 39cc, 2-stroke single, 2-speed gearbox, sprung forks, swinging-arm suspension, in need of restoration.
£300–400 MAY

1962 Ducati Brisk, 48cc, 2-stroke, single-cylinder engine, 3-speed, twistgrip gear-change, swinging-arm rear suspension, built-in rear carrier.
£350–390 MAY

1962 Norman Nippy, 49cc, German Sachs 2-stroke engine, in need of restoration.
£100–150 MAY

1964 Raleigh Runabout, 49cc, 2-stroke, fuel tank mounted above rear mudguard.
£120–130 GAZE

1976 AJW Collie, 49cc, 2-stroke Minerelli engine, pressed-steel disc wheels, front and rear carriers.
£160–180 PS

1975 Giulietta Sports Moped, 49cc Minerelli engine.
£600–700 VMCC

This machine was sold in the UK under the AJW banner during the mid-1970s.

1979 Carnielli Graziella, 49cc, 2-stroke single.
£700–750 NLM

The Graziella could be folded up for easy carriage.

Police Bikes

As the popularity of motor vehicles grew in the early 20th century, it was natural that they began to be used by criminals, forcing the police to follow suit. The increase in traffic also led the Metropolitan Force in London to form traffic patrols in 1919. (Interestingly, the Flying Squad used motorcycles first, several years before the Traffic Department.)

Other forces followed suit, which eventually led to stringent standards being set for police motorcycles by the Home Office. As a result, over the years, only a few machines have been used as marked police bikes in the UK. Initially, however, bikes from Douglas, BSA, Matchless and other factories were chosen. The situation settled down in the 1930s, when Triumph became the main supplier of traffic machines. Later, Velocette supplied the famous LE, or 'Noddy', beat bike, so named because constables had to nod to senior officers rather than salute, which could have led to an accident.

When Triumph got into financial difficulties, Norton, itself on rocky ground, made a last-ditch attempt to supply machines, but failed, leaving the way open for BMW. The German firm dominated the market from the mid-1970s to the early 1990s, when Honda provided a viable alternative in the Pan European.

Other firms, such as Rickman, Moto Guzzi and Harley-Davidson, have tried to gain a foothold in this lucrative market, but have only sold small numbers of bikes to some constabularies.

When machines reach the end of their service life, they are sold at auction, being stripped of their radios, blue lights, etc. Many are minus their livery, too, although some forces simply remove the crests and the word 'Police'. As there is no reserve on them, many are sold well below the price of similar civilian machines.

The vast majority will be converted to civilian specification by their new owners, but some are restored to police specification. For the latter, however, the major problem lies in obtaining the correct equipment and markings, as police forces are reluctant to release such items in case somebody uses the vehicle on the road. Invariably, the owners of such bikes will have given an undertaking not to do so unless the police livery is masked.

There is a thriving club for the owners of fully marked bikes, who are often invited to official police events to show off their machines. In these official parades, the owners may be given the chance to ride on the road under escort, where they can use the lights and horns and get a real feel for the machine. The club also provides the best means of obtaining a bike other than at auction, as many restored examples change hands privately.

A growing number of dealers import American and Italian machines, Guzzis, Cagivas, Harley-Davidsons and Kawasakis (CHiPs-style) particularly springing to mind.

The highest price will always be for a bike in full police regalia, even though it cannot be used as daily transport. For these, expect to pay from £2,000 upwards. Rare machines can fetch over £5,000.

Buyers looking for bikes for transport or touring will be looking at early BMW Boxer twins at around £1,000, with some early high-mileage K-series bikes in the same bracket. Newer bikes will be twice as expensive, and the early Honda Pan Europeans are nearer £3,000.

Dealer prices for imported bikes start at around £1,500 depending on type and model. From time to time, they do have older bikes, but these are normally snapped up very quickly.

Always try to obtain the service history and buy a bike that has had only one rider. Like any machine, it is bound to have been looked after better than one that has had dozens of riders.

Ian Kerr

1952 Triumph TRW, 498cc, side-valve twin, siamesed exhaust, telescopic forks, rigid frame, RAF Police livery.
£1,700–2,200 BLM

1960 Triumph 6T Thunderbird, 649cc, overhead-valve, pre-unit, twin-cylinder engine, very good condition.
£4,300–4,750 BKS

Many of these machines were used by police forces around the world. This particular example was originally supplied to the Home Office and used as a police training machine.

1971 Moto Guzzi Nuovo Falcone, 498.4cc, overhead-valve, unit-construction single, electric start, panniers, radio carrier, finished in Italian Carabinieri livery.
£2,400–2,500 NLM

1982 Moto Guzzi 850T3 PA, 844cc, overhead-valve V-twin, 5-speed gearbox, shaft final drive, fairing, panniers, carrier, front and rear crashbars, single seat, cast alloy wheels, formerly used by the Carabinieri of Bologna, Italy.
£2,500–3,000 HPM

▶ **1997 Harley-Davidson Road King,** 1340cc, overhead-valve, V-twin, evolution-type engine, 5-speed gearbox, concours condition.
£10,500 HPM

1972 Norton Commando Interpol, 745cc, overhead-valve, pre-unit twin, fairing, panniers, radio and carrier, single seat, completely restored.
£1,800–2,300 HPM

1985 Moto Guzzi V35II Police, 346cc, overhead-valve V-twin, formerly used by the Italian Vigili Urbani (local police service).
£1,050–1,150 NLM

Racing Bikes

1905-10 NSU Renn Maschine, 905cc, inlet-over-exhaust V-twin, 80x90mm bore and stroke, 12bhp, pedals and chain, 70mph top speed, completely restored, excellent condition.
£6,500–7,150 BERN

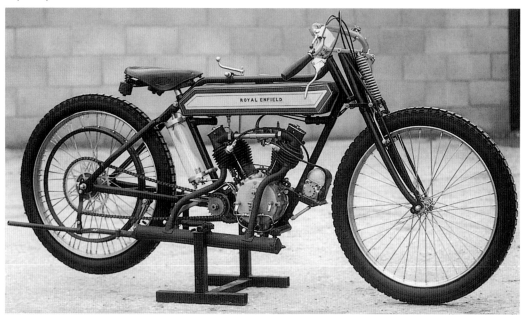

1914 Royal Enfield Ex-Works Racer, 349cc, inlet-over-exhaust, V-twin engine, excellent condition.
£18,400–20,200 BKS

Royal Enfield began manufacturing tri-cars, quadricycles, and motorcycles in 1900, but production of the latter was dropped in 1904, resuming in 1910. The new machine was a Motosacoche-engined lightweight V-twin of 2¼hp, a similar model with a two-speed gear and all-chain drive being introduced soon after. Enfield's famous JAP V-twin-engined 7hp sidecar outfit appeared for 1912, and the firm continued the V-twin theme with a new 3hp, 425cc solo for 1913. The latter's engine featured inlet-over-exhaust valve gear and dry-sump lubrication; in 347cc form, it achieved success at Brooklands and the Isle of Man TT. At the latter event, in 1914, one of the eight works machines entered finished third. Production of the 3hp model continued after WWI, but ceased before the end of 1919. Believed to be one of the 1914 works machines raced at Brooklands by Harry Greaves, this Royal Enfield is thought to be the only survivor of its type.

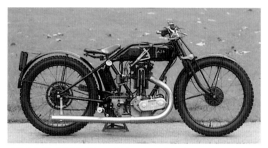

1923 AJS B3 Big Port, 349cc, overhead-valve single.
£6,700—7,400 BKS

AJS' overhead-valve 350 racer scored a memorable double in 1921, Tom Sheard winning the Junior race, and Howard Davies the Senior – the first time such a feat had been achieved on a 350. The production version appeared in 1922 and was destined to achieve countless successes in the hands of privateers. Later known as the Big Port, it changed only in detail before being replaced for 1929.

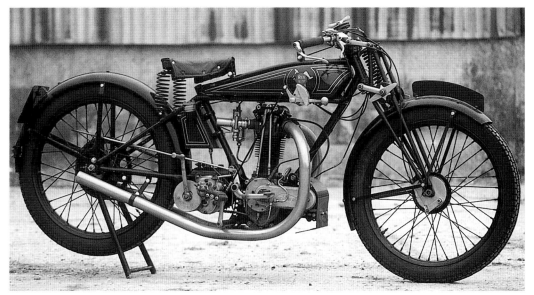

1926 Rex-Acme, 350cc, overhead-valve, twin-port, Blackburne single-cylinder engine, outside flywheel.
£8,250–9,100 BKS

Rex demonstrated its first motorcycle in 1900 and was soon active in competition, including the inaugural 1907 Isle of Man TT, where Billy Heaton's springer-forked Rex finished second in the twin-cylinder class. In 1923, the firm signed rising star Walter Handley, a move that would set Rex-Acme (renamed after the take-over of Coventry Acme) on the road to racing success. Handley had won the 250cc Belgian and Ulster Grands Prix by the end of his debut season, and in 1925 became the first rider to win two TTs in a week – the 350 Junior and 175 Ultra-Lightweight. The latter was to prove Rex-Acme's swansong TT victory, for despite its race-track successes, the firm became a casualty of the Depression and was gone for good by 1933.

1924 Norton Model 18, 490cc, overhead-valve single.
£6,800–7,500 BKS

Norton relied on the side-valve engine until the 1920s, when the well-tried 490cc unit became the basis for the firm's first overhead-valve design. First seen in prototype form in 1922, it made little impact in that year's Senior TT, but at Brooklands D R O'Donovan raised the world 500cc kilometre record to over 89mph using the new motor. A roadgoing version – the Model 18 – was listed for 1923, quickly establishing a reputation for speed and reliability. The Model 18 gained Webb forks and better brakes for 1925, but retained its vintage characteristics until 1931, when the range was redesigned.

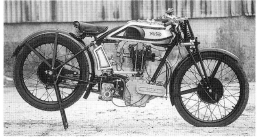

1927 Norton Model 25 TT Replica, 490cc, overhead-valve single, completely restored, very good condition.
£12,350–13,600 BKS

TT victory eluded the overhead-valve Norton until 1924, when Alec Bennett won the Senior race, and George Tucker the sidecar event. Stanley Woods took the Island's premier class for the company in 1926, but by then the overhead-valve Norton was nearing the end of its life as a racing machine. Before the spotlight switched to the overhead-camshaft models, Norton capitalised on the overhead-valve machine's success by introducing the TT Replica – basically a stripped-down Model 18 equipped with a twin-filler, racing fuel tank, lighter mudguards and an open exhaust.

◀ **1928 Dot,** 349cc, overhead-valve, twin-port single.
£9,800–10,800 BKS

Dot's founder, Harry Reed, won the Isle of Man TT's twin-cylinder class on his Dot-Peugeot in 1908. That would be Dot's first and last TT victory, although the firm continued to contest the races during the 1920s with Blackburne-, Bradshaw- and JAP-engined bikes. The most successful year was 1928, when the Twemlow brothers – Ken and Eddie – finished second and third respectively in the Lightweight race, while Ken came third in the Junior.

1928 Sunbeam Model 80 Works TT, no. UK 5232, 347cc, overhead-valve, twin-port single, excellent condition.
£17,250–19,000 BKS

By the mid-1920s, the overhead-valve Sunbeam had become one of the most formidable racing motorcycles of the vintage era, the 500cc Model 90 in particular being a match for anything in its class by the decade's end. Despite the failure of the works 350s in the 1928 Isle of Man Junior TT, Sunbeam came good in the Senior event, Charles Dodson winning after crashing and remounting, while seventh and 15th places went to team-mates Francesco Franconi and Luigi Arcangeli, gaining Sunbeam the Team Prize. Sunbeam's works entry for the 1928 Junior TT comprised four Model 80s, registered UK 5231 to UK 5234 and ridden by Dodson, Franconi, Arcangeli and Frank Major, all of whom suffered lubrication problems with the exception of Arcangeli, who crashed on lap five.

◄ **1928 AJS Model K7,** 349cc, overhead-camshaft single, Amal carburettor, hand gear-change, Druid forks, Andre steering damper, wired-on tyres, restored 1980s.
£7,600–8,400 BKS

The overhead-camshaft AJS engines appeared in 1927 for the 1928 season, the factory having set its sights on a TT victory, which to date had eluded them. The race-bred K7 'cammy' AJS of 1928 was one of the last flat-tank machines.

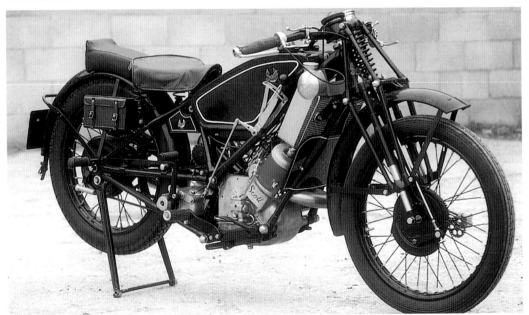

1929 Scott TT Replica, 596cc, watercooled, 2-stroke twin, Bonniksen 'Time and Speed' speedometer.
£8,150–8,950 BKS

The first complete Scott motorcycle appeared in 1908, its twin-cylinder engine, two-speed foot-change gearbox and all-chain drive being advanced features for the day. From the outset, light weight, ample power and sure-footed handling, thanks to a low centre of gravity, were Scott virtues. Introduced toward the end of 1928, the TT model was a replica of the bike ridden to third place in that year's Senior event by Tommy Hatch. It had a long-stroke engine featuring cylinder-wall lubrication, and was available in 498 and 596cc capacities.

1929 Excelsior TT Replica, 250cc, JAP bronze-head, twin-port single, some parts missing, in need of restoration.
£2,550–2,800 BKS

Acquired by R Walker & Sons in 1919, Excelsior moved from Coventry to Birmingham. The Walkers believed in the value of racing for development and publicity, and the revitalised company soon made its mark in competition. Early successes included a number of world records set at Brooklands by Tony Worters on 250 and 350 JAP-engined machines in 1926. Its relatively small size meant that Excelsior could not compete with the likes of Rudge and Norton in the Junior and Senior classes, but in the Lightweight division the marque was a force to be reckoned with throughout the 1930s. Its first Isle of Man TT victory came in 1929, Syd Crabtree winning the Lightweight event, and the firm lost no time in marketing a TT Replica.

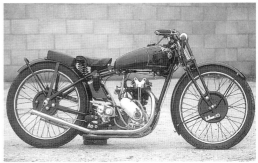

1932 Rudge TT Replica, 245cc, overhead-valve, twin-port, single-cylinder engine, very good condition.
£5,750–6,350 BKS

Rudge employed a four-valves-per-cylinder engine layout for the first time on a 250 in 1931, its previous offerings in the class having used JAP engines. The contemporary 350's fully-radial valve arrangement was chosen. The Rudge 250 was unusual for its day in having coil ignition, although a magneto became optional later, being standard issue on the works racers and TT Replica. New for 1932, the latter was based on the 1931 works bikes, which had gained first, second and fourth places in the Lightweight TT on their Isle of Man debut, and bagged the first three places at the 1931 Ulster Grand Prix.

▶ **1932 Norton International,** 490cc, overhead-camshaft single.
£6,200–6,850 BKS

The first overhead-camshaft Nortons appeared in the hands of works riders Stanley Woods and Alec Bennett during 1927, marking the beginning of two decades that constitute one of the most glorious phases in Norton's long and illustrious history. During this period, the machines gained an astonishing record in competition at both national and international level.

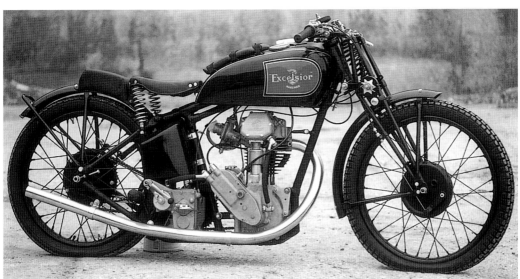

1935 Excelsior Manxman, 249cc, overhead-camshaft, single-cylinder engine, restored, excellent condition.
£7,700–8,500 BKS

Although it had proved fast enough to win the 1933 Lightweight TT, Excelsior's twin-cam, radial four-valve Mechanical Marvel was a disappointment thereafter, and at the end of the 1934 season, the firm opted for a simpler design – the Manxman. Like the Marvel, the Manxman had a Blackburne engine, but increasing friction with its engine supplier forced Excelsior to take over production themselves early in 1936. A single-overhead-camshaft, two-valve design, the Manxman was built in 250, 350 and 500cc capacities. Road and race versions were offered, but the 500 was only marketed as a sports roadster. Although it never won a TT, the Manxman enjoyed considerable success in international racing and the Manx Grand Prix, Denis Parkinson winning the Lightweight race three times on the trot between 1936 and 1938.

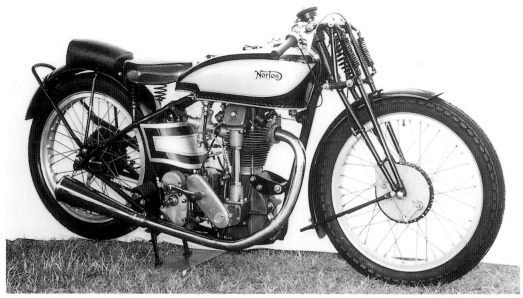

1935 Norton Works Racer, 348cc single, bevel-driven overhead camshaft, magnesium crankcases, magnesium rocker-box, bronze cylinder head, hairpin valve springs, racing magneto, Amal TT carburettor, close-ratio 4-speed gearbox, bolt-through fuel tank, narrow racing forks, straight fork check springs, Dunlop-type light-alloy wheel rims, low cradle frame, completely restored, excellent condition.
£10,000–11,000 YEST

◄ **c1937 Cotton,** 249cc, overhead-valve JAP single, missing some parts, in need of restoration.
£3,100–3,400 BKS

Cotton made its name with a string of racing successes in the 1920s, thanks to an innovative frame. This featured four straight tubes that ran from the steering head to the rear wheel spindle, augmented by straight stays to support the gearbox and engine. The result was a stiff, lightweight chassis. Cotton relied on proprietary engines, but such was the advantage conferred by its frame that the machine had little trouble in seeing off similarly-powered rivals.

1938 Velocette KTT Mk VII Racing Motorcycle, frame no 7TT15, engine no KTT720, overhead-camshaft single, Amal RN9 carburettor, BTH magneto, 21in front and 20in rear rims, Andre steering damper, Smiths tachometer.
£8,600–9,450 BKS

Following the construction of the last Mk V KTT in October 1935, Veloce's commitment to the development of the pushrod-engined M-series meant that there would be no more production KTT racers until the Mk VII of 1938. The few Mk VI bikes were built as works machines only, the last – with a large, square-finned cylinder head and enclosed valve gear – forming the basis for the production Mk VII. Although the works bikes had featured rear springing for the previous two seasons, the Mk VII entered production in 1938 with a rigid frame. Improvements to the cycle parts included a front fork with revised spring mountings, and sturdier brakes equipped with stiffer magnesium-alloy brake plates and wider shoes. Only 37 Mk VIIs were made before the introduction of the spring-framed Mk VIII for 1939, making it the rarest of production KTTs. This example was raced by Jim Garnett in the 1939 Junior TT.

1948 AJS 7R Rolling Chassis, minus engine and gearbox.
£4,600–5,100 BKS

Nineteen-forty-eight was the first year of production for the 7R.

1951 Norton Manx, 499cc, double-overhead-camshaft, single-cylinder engine, excellent condition.
£8,050–8,850 BKS

Norton used the Manx Grand Prix model name for its over-the-counter racer in 1939. When production resumed post-war, what would become the best-known racing motorcycle of all time had become simply the Manx. The 1946 bikes were much as their pre-war counterparts, with overhead-camshaft engine, square cylinder head finning, upright gearbox and plunger-suspended 'garden gate' frames. Only the presence of the Roadholder telescopic front fork distinguished them from the 1939 machines. In 1949, the Manx gained a double-overhead-camshaft cylinder head, like that fitted to the works bikes for many years, but the major change came in 1951 with the Featherbed frame. The works' adoption of the duplex-loop, swinging-arm chassis in the previous year had given the Nortons a new lease of life in GP racing, and Geoff Duke duly took both the 350 and 500cc world titles in 1951.

1949 Vincent-HRD Black Lightning, 998cc, overhead-valve V-twin, Black Shadow frame.
£26,450–29,100 BKS

Rollie Free's capture of the world production motorcycle record in 1948, on a tuned Black Shadow, led Vincent to market a similar racer – the Black Lightning. Free's engine had been boosted from 55 to around 70bhp by such features as raised compression, Mk II cams, Amal TT carburettors and 2in-diameter, straight-through exhausts, all of which appeared on the Lightning. First shown in 1948, it came with alloy wheel rims, Elektron brake plates, a rev-counter and a gearbox modified for quick changes.

1953 EMC-Puch, 124cc, air-cooled, 2-stroke split single.
£2,750–3,050 BKS

Austrian Dr Josef Ehrlich set up EMC – Ehrlich Motorcycle Company – in Britain in 1946. His first machine, a 350 split single, was launched in 1947. Despite respectable speed, economy and pricing, it did not find favour in the conservative motorcycling world. Nevertheless, Ehrlich soon became involved in racing, and collaboration with Puch led to a 125 racer powered by that firm's unit-construction, air-cooled split-single, which featured a four-speed gearbox, twin carburettors and twin megaphone exhausts.

1958 AJS 7R, 349cc, chain-driven overhead camshaft, magnesium engine parts including drive cover, AMC gearbox.
£8,800–9,700 COYS

1957 Itom Competizione, 49cc, single cylinder, 2-stroke engine with piston port induction, 3-speed twistgrip gear-change, full-width brake hubs, duplex frame, Dell'Orto UBF caburettor.
£1,600–2,000 RFC

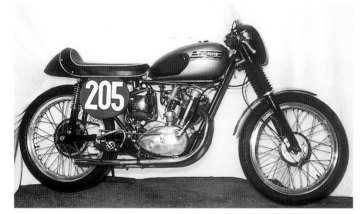

◀ **1958 Triumph Cub,** 199cc, overhead-valve, unit-construction single, tuned engine, Amal Monobloc carburettor, straight-through exhaust, close-ratio gears, alloy rims, rev-counter.
£1,500–1,800 TCTR

During the late 1950s, 200cc class racing was popular on British short circuits. Then, in the mid/late 1960s, Formula Cub events rivalled Bantam racing as a cheap way of getting on to the circuit.

1958 Maserati/Itom GSB Special, 49cc, Mk 5 Itom 2-stroke engine and 3-speed gearbox, Maserati chassis, twistgrip gear-change, expansion-chamber exhaust, alloy rims.
£1,800–2,000 RFC

It is worth recording that during the 1950s, the famous Maserati automobile company also produced spark plugs and motorcycles. The latter came in both two- and four-stroke versions.

1959 Norton Manx 30M, 499cc, double-overhead-camshaft single, matching engine and frame, later disc front brake, race fairing, one owner since 1967, restored, excellent condition.
£12,650–13,950 BKS

There can be no doubt that the Manx Norton was the ultimate racing motorcycle of its era. The long association with the TT and Manx races has forever ensured a place in motorcycle racing legend. The association of this particular machine with the finest traditions of privateer racing is also a high achievement. It was raced by Don Grant between 1967 and 1975, achieving notable success as a privateer and acquiring two silver TT replicas, three bronze TT replicas and a Manx silver in the process. In 1973, Grant achieved a creditable 15th place in the Senior TT, against top riders and more advanced machinery. It is thought that this Manx clocked some 18,000 racing miles during its competitive career.

1959 Norton Manx 40M, 348cc single, good condition.
£8,750–9,650 BKS

The frame of this Manx originates from a machine prepared by Joe Potts, and ridden by Bob McIntyre and Alastair King. With the latter riding, the bike was involved in an accident at Scarborough. King was lucky to survive, and the machine was returned to Potts for a rebuild, using a new frame. Later, it was sold to Alastair Copland, who raced it at all the British short circuits prior to a foray in the Manx Grand Prix. During this event, thought to be in 1964, the machine caught fire. Returned again to Joe Potts, the bike emerged with another new frame, while the fire-damaged frame eventually became the basis for this bike. It was fitted with a 350cc 40M engine, supplied by Colin Seeley and rebuilt by Phil Kettle.

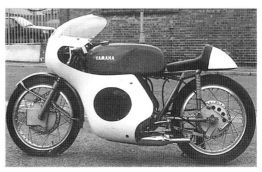

1962 Yamaha TD1, 246cc, air-cooled twin, four transfer ports, 56x50mm bore and stroke, twin 28mm Mikuni carburettors, 32bhp at 9,500rpm.
£6,650--7,350 BKS

The TD1 is arguably the most significant, and was also the least successful, of Yamaha's production racing machines. It marked the company's first attempt at an 'over-the-counter' racer, thus paving the way for the TRs and TZs that dominated the 250 and 350cc classes during the 1970s. This machine was displayed at the 1962 British Motorcycle Show, where it was purchased by Geoff Monty. The TD1 is the rarest of all the Yamaha twin-cylinder, two-stroke production racers, and this example was the sixth machine manufactured.

1964 Honda Works 250 Four, 249.3cc, double-overhead-camshaft, across-the-frame, 4-cylinder engine, 44x41mm bore and stroke, 46bhp at 14,000rpm, 6-speed gearbox, completely restored, concours condition.
£250,000+ WEED

Jim Redman won the 1964 Isle of Man Lightweight (250cc) TT with this machine, at an average speed of 97.45mph for the six-lap, 226.5-mile race.

1966 Ducati 250 Racer, 248cc, bevel-driven overhead camshaft, converted roadster with narrow-case engine, Amal Monobloc carburettor, 5-speed gearbox and 31.5mm enclosed forks.
£1,700–1,900 PC

1967 Itom Mk 9, 49cc, piston-port, 2-stroke single, 4-speed foot-change gearbox.
£2,500+ RFC

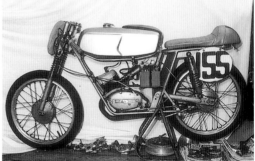

1969 Heldun Hawk, 49cc, piston-port, 2-stroke single, inclined Dell'Orto carburettor, duplex frame.
£850–950 RIM

1971 Kreidler Works Replica, 49cc, 2-stroke horizontal single, roadster-based engine, works-type frame, tank, seat and fairing, fitted with Japanese front brake, very good condition.
£3,000+ RFC

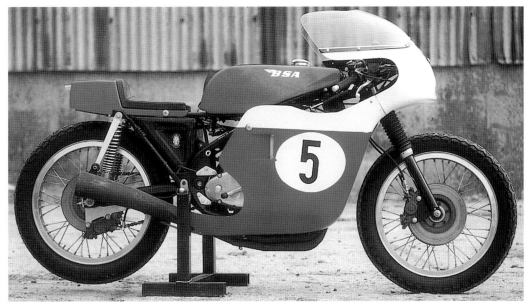

c1972 BSA 'Rob North' Rocket 3, 740cc, 'Mk 2' or 'lowboy' frame, 19in Akront alloy rims, Dunlop TT100 tyres, 'letterbox' fairing, period Krober rev-counter.
£6,450–7,100 BKS

The Triumph and BSA 750 triples were launched in the UK in 1969, just in time to be upstaged by Honda's CB750 four. Faced with increasing foreign competition, the triple did not excel in the showroom, but success on the race-track ensured a place in motorcycling history. BSA-Triumph's chief engineer, Doug Hele, spearheaded engine development throughout 1969, while frame builder Rob North devised a chassis that would stand the test of time. The team narrowly missed victory at the 1970 Daytona 200, Gene Romero finishing second on a Triumph. A revised frame, twin front disc brakes and 'letterbox' fairing were all new for 1971, a year in which the model would become one of the most formidable racing motorcycles ever. Dick Mann won at Daytona, and John Cooper at Mallory Park's Race of the Year, beating Giacomo Agostini and his four-cylinder MV. Both rode BSAs. Percy Tait and Ray Pickrell had won the 24-hour Bol d'Or in the preceding week on another triple, and Cooper wrapped up a memorable season for BSA-Triumph with victory in the 250-mile race at Ontario Motor Speedway. The company's financial difficulties prevented a works effort in 1972, but privateers continued to win with the triple for many years. Today, it remains a force in classic racing.

1972 Minerelli Racer, 50cc, 2-stroke single, piston-port induction, 6-speed gearbox, Honda CB72/77 twin-leading-shoe front brake.
£2,000–2,500 RFC

1972 Gilera Racing Special, 49cc, piston-port, 2-stroke single, tuned engine, 12bhp, Scatacco tank by Pat Townsend.
£2,000–2,200 IMOC

▶ **1976 Kawasaki Works KR750 Model 602L,** 748.2cc, piston-port, 2-stroke, 3-cylinder engine, 71x63mm bore and stroke, 120bhp, 6-speed gearbox, 180mph top speed.
£35,000–38,500 CLR

This bike was ridden by Mick Grant during 1976 and 1977, both years in which he finished second to Barry Sheene in the MCN British Superbike Championships. He also used it to win the 1977 Isle of Man Classic TT, setting new lap (112mph) and race records in the process.

1980 Kreidler 50 GP, 49.8cc, liquid-cooled, disc-valve,
2-stroke, horizontal single, 6-speed gearbox,
40x39.7mm bore and stroke, front and rear disc
brakes, concours condition.
£10,000+ RFC

This machine is an ex-works Grand Prix team bike.

▶ **1980s SGN Polini Special,** 49cc, 2-stroke, water-
cooled, single-cylinder Polini engine, 6-speed gearbox,
front and rear disc brakes, alloy tank and seat.
£1,800–1,900 RFC

c1982 Norton-Cosworth Challenge, 749cc, liquid-cooled, double-overhead-camshaft, parallel twin, anti-dive Ceriani
front forks, rear monoshock swinging arm with underslung coil spring/damper unit.
£11,500–12,650 BKS

The need to replace its ageing Commando prompted NVT to commission a new engine from Cosworth
Engineering. First shown in 1975, the Challenge borrowed heavily from Cosworth's DFV V8, yet despite a
claimed output of 115-120bhp, the racer's few outings were disappointing and, with NVT on the point of
collapse, the project was shelved in 1976. Writing in *Classic Bike*, Alan Cathcart recorded that of the four
bikes made, two went to the USA, while the others were bought by a German entrepreneur. The latter sold
'two engines and enough chassis bits to make a complete bike' to Ian Sutherland, the machine being ridden
by Cathcart at Donington Park's 50th Anniversary meeting in 1981. That machine had Norton's own leading-
axle front fork and cast-aluminium, twin-shock swinging arm. Sutherland continued development and, ridden
by Rob Sewell, an updated version, with Harris cycle parts, came close to a 100mph lap in the Isle of Man TT.
The design's full potential would not be realised until 1988, however, when Roger Marshall won Daytona's Pro
Twins race on the Challenge-based Quantel. This bike is believed to be the ex-Sutherland machine.

Scooters

1919 ABC Skootamota, 125cc, inlet-over-exhaust, horizontal 4-stroke single, 60x44mm bore and stroke, 16in wheels, good condition.
£900–1,400 VER

Designed by Granville Bradshaw, better known for his 400cc, flat-twin ABC motorcycle, the Skootamota was produced from 1919 until 1923. 'ABC' stood for All British Cycle.

1947 Corgi Runabout, 98cc, 2-stroke single, 50x50mm bore and stroke, 2.1bhp at 3,500rpm.
£1,250–1,400 S

This machine was made by Brockhouse Engineering, of Southport, and was developed from the wartime Excelsior Welbike.

◀ **1951 Douglas Vespa 'Rod Model',** 124cc, fan-cooled, 2-stroke single, 56.5x49.8mm bore and stroke, 4bhp at 4,500rpm, in need of restoration.
£500–550 VVC

The Douglas Vespa was announced at the 1949 London Motorcycle Show. Subsequently nicknamed the 'Rod Model', it was a British-built version of the Piaggio Vespa, which had been launched in Italy in 1946.

1953 Lambretta LC125, 123cc, fan-cooled, 2-stroke single, 52x58mm bore and stroke, 4.3bhp at 4,200rpm, twistgrip gear-change, 8in wheels, original specification.
£1,000–1,200 MAY

NSU in Germany bought the rights to manufacture this model under licence, originally badging it as the NSU Lambretta. When the licence expired, further changes were made to produce the NSU Prima.

1954 Lambretta Model D, 148cc, air-cooled, 2-stroke single, 57x58mm bore and stroke, 6bhp at 4,750rpm, in need of restoration.
£600–650 IVC

Miller's is a price GUIDE not a price LIST

c1953 Lambretta Model F, 124cc, original, in need of restoration.
£450–650 MAY

1955 Vespa 42L2, 124cc, 2-stroke single, 56.5x49.8mm bore and stroke, in need of complete restoration.
£200–300 MAY

In February 1955, Douglas announced its 42L2 model Vespa, following Piaggio's lead in mounting the headlamp on the handlebars. The cooling cut-out in the engine side-cover was revamped with simple louvres, and a hydraulic damper was added to the front suspension.

c1955 Messerschmitt Vespa VS150, 145.5cc, fan-cooled, 2-stroke single, 57x57mm bore and stroke.
£1,500–2,000 MAY

This particular machine was built under licence by the German Messerschmitt company, which switched to building scooters and bubble cars instead of aviation products in the immediate post-war era.

1956 Victoria Peggy, 197cc, near-horizontal, 2-stroke single with Elektron castings, 65x60mm bore and stroke, 9.5bhp, 4-speed gearbox.
£450–500 BERN

The Peggy's unconventional power unit, 'live' rear axle and push-button gear-change was the same arrangement that had been used in the company's **KR21 Swing** motorcycle and was unique to the German Victoria marque. The engine and transmission were mounted rigidly to an internally-ribbed, cast-iron strut that carried the rear wheel.

1957 Vespa 42C2, 148cc, fan-cooled, 2-stroke single, fitted with optional spare wheel.
£750–950 MAY

This machine was sold only as a 125 in the UK, this particular example being an Italian-market model.

1957 Lambretta LD150, 148cc, 2-stroke single, completely restored, concours condition.
£1,200–1,500 MAY

1958 Maico Maicoletta M250, 247cc, air-cooled, 2-stroke single, 67x70mm bore and stroke, 4-speed gearbox.
£1,250–1,400 MOC

Designed in great secrecy by the German engineers Tetzlaft and Pohl, the Maicoletta was considered by many to be the 'Rolls-Royce' of the scooter world. It was available in three engine sizes: 175, 247 and 277cc.

1958 Heinkel Tourist, 174cc, overhead-valve, single-cylinder engine, 4-speed gearbox.
£650–750 HERM

Together with Dornier, Junkers and Messerschmitt, Heinkel was one of Germany's leading aircraft manufacturers during the 1930s and WWII. The cessation of hostilities brought a ban on aircraft manufacture, leaving Heinkel to find another means of survival. It chose to build mopeds, microcars and scooters. The famous Tourist was offered from 1953 with, at first, a 149cc engine, and later with a 174cc unit. Both were overhead-valve four-strokes.

1957 Lambretta TV Series 1, 170cc, 2-stroke, single-cylinder engine, twistgrip gear-change, good condition.
£2,000–2,500 MAY

When launched in 1957, the original 170cc TV175 proved under-developed, remaining in production only 16 months before being replaced in 1959 by the 175cc TV Series 2, which was much more successful, production continuing until 1962. It can be identified by its handlebar-mounted headlamp. However, from a collector's viewpoint, the Series 1 is much more valuable.

1959 Dayton Albatros Twin, 249cc, air-cooled, Villiers 2T 2-stroke twin, minus rear panels, in need of complete restoration.
£450–500 MAY

1959 Lambretta TV175 Series 2, 175cc, 2-stroke, single-cylinder engine, 62x58mm bore and stroke.
£800–900 COYS

Innocenti, the makers of Lambretta scooters, moved quickly to replace the TV Series 1 with the much-improved Series 2 in 1959.

1959 Heinkel Tourist, 174cc, overhead-valve, single-cylinder engine, electric start, good condition.
£750–900 MAY

In all, 100,000 examples of the luxurious Tourist scooter had been built when production ended in 1965.

◄ **1959 Vespa GS150,** 145cc, 2-stroke single, 57x57mm bore and stroke, 4-speed gearbox with twistgrip gear-change, good condition.
£680–750 VICO

1960 **Vespa Sportique,** 148cc, fan-cooled, 2-stroke single, twistgrip gear-change, handlebar-mounted headlamp. £900–1,200 **MAY**

1962 **Lambretta Li150 Series 2,** 148cc, completely restored, concours condition. £1,400–1,600 **MAY**

The Series 1 Li150 had a legshield-mounted headlamp; the Series 2 had its headlamp on the handlebars.

◄ 1961 **Dürkopp Diana,** 194cc, fan-cooled, 2-stroke single, 64x61mm bore and stroke, 9.5bhp at 5,500rpm electric and kickstart. £600–650 **PS**

The German Dürkopp concern made many products, including bearings, bicycles, mopeds, motorcycles and scooters. The Diana was considered one of the best machines of its era, originally being offered in the late 1950s with a 175cc engine, then for 1960 with a 194cc unit. Only the larger model was exported.

1962 **Vespa Sportique,** 145cc, fan-cooled, 2-stroke single, 57x57mm bore and stroke, twistgrip gear-change, original specification, 4,000 miles from new. £1,500–1,650 **VVC**

1964 **Vespa GS160 Series 2,** 159cc, piston-port, 2-stroke single, completely restored as a Grimstead Hurricane replica, concours condition. £2,500–2,700 **VVC**

1966 Lambretta Li150 Series 3, 148cc, fan-cooled, 2-stroke, single-cylinder engine, original specification, fitted with optional spare wheel.
£1,500–1,750 VMCC

c1966 Lambretta SX200, 198cc, 2-stroke single, 66x58mm bore and stroke.
£1,900–2,100 BMM

The SX200 was developed from the visually identical TV175 Series 3.

1967 Lambretta TV200, fitted with big-bore 225cc kit, customised with chromed panels and aftermarket accessories.
£1,250–1,400 BRIT

1968 Vespa Sprint, 145.5cc, fan-cooled, 2-stroke single, imported to UK from Italy, in need of restoration.
£350–400 MAY

1969 Vespa SS180, 180cc, resprayed, fitted with non-standard seat.
£1,000–1,400 MAY

Restored Values

The cost of a professional restoration will have an influence on, but no direct relation to, a motorcycle's market value. A restored motorcycle can have a market value lower than the cost of its restoration.

▶ **1980 Lambretta Jet 200,** 198cc, 2-stroke single, 205km from new.
£750–800 VICO

Sidecars

Once the motorcycle had become established, the next question was, 'How many people could it carry?' The earliest examples of the sidecar arrived just after the turn of the century, and by 1903 a couple of firms were offering them for sale. At the time, most sidecar bodies were of wickerwork to reduce weight.

Following WWI, there was an urgent need to provide the family with motorised transport. As a result, not only did many specialised sidecar manufacturers spring up, but several early motorcycle makers also entered the field. The latter included BSA, Ariel, Douglas, Dunelt, Matchless, Panther, Royal Enfield, Raleigh, Sunbeam and Triumph. Of the many Continental European manufacturers, without doubt the two most important were German – BMW and Steib. The former built sidecars alongside its motorcycles for many years, while the latter only made 'chairs'.

In 1936, there were half a million motorcycles on British roads, of which no less than a quarter hauled sidecars. By 1939, there were three sidecars to every ten solos.

But the chair's heyday was the immediate post-war period. With the ending of WWII, established sidecar builders resumed production with new energy. Increased demand led to many new firms joining the established names such as Swallow, Watsonian, Blacknell, BSA, Garrard and Panther.

However, as the 1960s dawned, sidecar sales began the slump from which they never recovered. There were two reasons: ever more sporting motorcycles, many with frames that were unsuitable for a third wheel; and the Mini, which brought affordable four-wheel motoring to even the most economy-minded family.

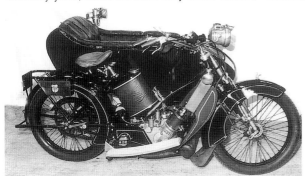

◄ **1919 Scott Squirrel with Sidecar,** 534cc, water-cooled 2-stroke, acetylene lighting, completely restored, very good condition. **£6,300–6,950 BKS**

From the beginning, Scott machines were fitted with a twin-cylinder, water-cooled engine with all-chain drive, and this format continued throughout production. This immediate post-WWI example is one of the first of the long-running Squirrel models.

1914 Zenith Gradua with Sidecar, 550cc, JAP side-valve V-twin engine, completely restored, excellent condition. **£12,650–13,950 C**

During the first years of the 20th century, Freddie Barnes began building Zenith motorcycles, introducing his ingenious Gradua variable gearing in 1909. With an approximate range of 3:1–7:1 being instantly available, the Gradua mechanism gave riders such an advantage that promotors of hillclimbs and other speed events began to ban Zenith Gradua motorcycles. Barnes turned this situation to his advantage, using the advertising slogan, 'Zenith barred'. This particular machine is believed to be the only surviving Zenith Gradua with the countershaft box mounted ahead of the engine, a feature that was introduced for 1914.

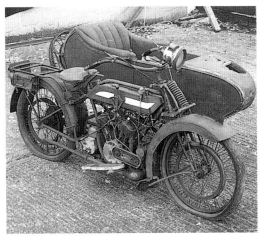

1921 BSA Model E with Sidecar, 770cc, side-valve V-twin engine, chain-driven magneto, 3-speed hand-change gearbox, tubular diamond frame, flat tank, in need of complete restoration.
£3,800–4,200 S

▶ **1922 James 7 with Sidecar,** 750cc, side-valve V-twin, 3-speed hand-change gearbox, chain final drive, restored.
£8,950–9,850 YEST

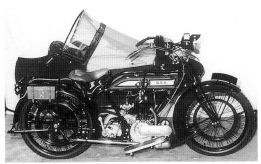

1921 BSA Model K2 with BSA Model No 3 Sidecar, 557cc, 4.25hp, completely restored in 1997, concours condition.
£6,000–6,600 BKS

1923 Triumph Model SD with Watsonian Sidecar, 550cc, fitted 1924 front fork, hub front brake in place of original caliper type.
£4,850–5,350 BKS

The first Triumph motorcycle of 1902 had a Belgian Minerva engine, but within a few years the firm was building its own power units. By the outbreak of WWI, the marque's reputation for quality and reliability was well-established, leading to substantial orders from the military. Equipped with a three-speed Sturmey-Archer gearbox, it was the 4hp Model H that did such sterling service in WWI, some 30,000 'Trusty Triumphs' seeing action with Allied forces. Updated with chain final drive for 1920, it became known as the SD (Spring Drive) because of its clutch-mounted, coil-spring shock absorber, and formed the basis of the later four-valve Ricardo model.

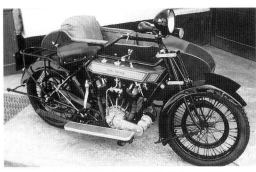

1924 Royal Enfield Model 180 with Sidecar, 976cc, 2-speed gearbox, Lucas electric lighting, MDI Lucas mag-dyno, coachbuilt sidecar on Royal Enfield chassis.
£7,600–8,400 BKS

1927 AJS H2 with Sidecar, 7.99hp, acetylene lighting.
£6,900–7,600 BKS

AJS produced a long line of custom-built, large-capacity, V-twin motorcycle combinations with engines and gearboxes of their own design which, until the mid 1920s, were limited to 7hp. However, for 1927, the company announced a larger-capacity H-series combination of 7.99hp. Two versions were offered: the deluxe H1 and standard H2. These outfits were well proven, being finished in black with gold lining and tank transfers. They were offered with a choice of electric or acetylene lighting.

◄ **1928 Ariel Model A with Sidecar,** 557cc, side-valve single, 86.4x95mm bore and stroke, concours condition. **£3,900–4,300 S**

Production of the Model A came to an end during 1930.

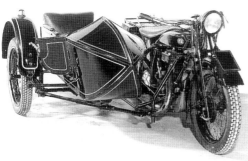

1930 NSU 501T with Sidecar, 494cc.
£5,000–5,500 HERM

Based in Neckarsulm, NSU was a pioneer in production-line techniques in Germany. In 1929, the leading British designer Walter Moore left Norton and joined the company.

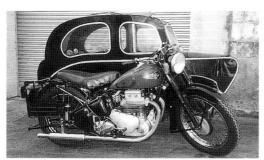

1951 Ariel 4G with Sidecar, 995cc, overhead-valve square-4, 65x75mm bore and stroke, 2-pipe exhaust, telescopic forks, plunger rear suspension.
£3,250–3,500 CotC

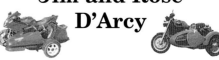

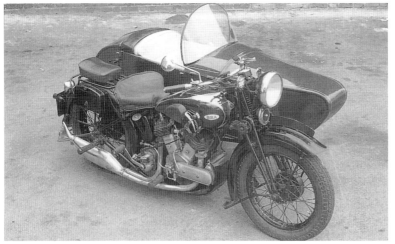

◀ **1936 BSA G14 with Sidecar**, 986cc, side-valve V-twin engine, 80x98mm bore and stroke, single-seater sidecar, restored, very good condition.
£5,300–5,850 BKS

The epitome of the large-capacity, late-1930s workhorse, the Model 14 had evolved from a lineage that had begun in 1919 with the launch of the Model E, a 770cc, overhead-valve, 50-degree V-twin.

1951 Sunbeam S8 with Sidecar, 487cc, overhead-camshaft, in-line twin, shaft final drive, telescopic forks, plunger rear suspension, Avon handlebar fairing and single-seat sidecar.
£1,600–1,800 PS

1955 Ariel VH with Watsonian Sidecar, 497cc, overhead-valve, single-cylinder engine, 4-speed gearbox, single-seater sidecar, very good condition.
£2,950–3,250 PM

1959 Panther Model 120 with Double-Adult Busmar Sidecar, 645cc, 88x106mm bore and stroke.
£2,400–3,000 VER

Introduced for 1959, the Model 120, with its 645cc version of the long-running overhead-valve, twin-port Panther single supplemented the existing 594cc Model 100.

1972 Moto Guzzi 850GT with Squire Sidecar, 844cc, 5-speed gearbox, shaft final drive, screen, alloy rims, chrome mudguards.
£4,000+ BLM

1972 BMW R75/5 with Sidecar, 745cc, 4-speed gearbox with kickstart, twin-leading-shoe front brake, Cossack military sidecar.
£1,500–2,000 OxM

◀ **1985 Yamaha VMX 1200 with Hedingham XL Sidecar**, 1200cc, Lazer exhaust, leading-link forks, Koni 'dial-a-ride' rear shocks, American Corbin seat, imported to UK from Canada.
£3,000+ LSC

Specials

1934 Velocette KTT/KSS Special, 348cc, overhead-camshaft single, 4-speed constant-mesh gearbox.
£2,600–2,900 BKS

This KTT Mk IV has been fitted with the cylinder head from a Mk II KSS engine, an innovation tried by Veloce itself when developing the works-only Mk VI KTT. Launched in 1935, the Mk II KSS represented a major redesign of the overhead-camshaft roadster single, a new aluminium cylinder head with enclosed valve gear replacing the old cast-iron head with exposed springs.

1950s Triton Stan Cooper Replica, 649cc, Triumph pre-unit Bonneville engine, Norton chassis, Dominator front hub, Triumph conical rear hub, concours condition.
£4,000–4,400 PC

Boston rider/tuner Stan Cooper built a number of interesting specials during the late 1950s and early 1960s.

1956 Triton Special, 649cc, pre-unit T120 Bonneville engine, twin Amal Concentric carburettors, Triumph gearbox, slimline Norton frame, twin-leading-shoe front brake, alloy rims, central oil tank, alloy fuel tank, racing seat.
£1,800–2,000 PM

c1959 Tribsa Special, 649cc, Triumph T120 pre-unit engine, iron Tiger 110 cylinder head, twin carburettors, Triumph Bonneville 4-speed gearbox, BSA B31 swinging-arm frame, Norton Roadholder forks, concours condition.
£3,800–4,200 BKS

This machine was featured on the cover of the January 1993 issue of *Classic Bike*.

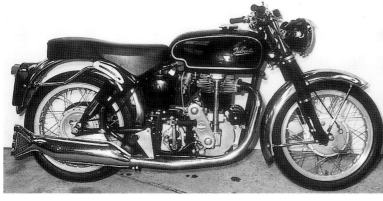

◀ **c1961 Velocette Venom/KSS Special,** 348cc, 1938 overhead-camshaft KSS Mk II engine, 1961 Venom frame, restored, engine rebuilt, hubs overhauled and laced to Borrani alloy wheel rims, stainless steel mudguards, concours condition.
£3,050–3,350 BKS

1970 Triton Special, 498cc, pre-unit Triumph Tiger 100 engine, AMC gearbox, Norton Featherbed frame, Roadholder forks, Dominator hubs, Daytona megaphone exhausts, fibreglass racing tank, seat and front mudguard, central oil tank.
£2,200–2,400 BKS

1967 AJS Cheney Special, 498cc, overhead-valve, parallel twin, AMC Model 20 engine, gearbox and brake hubs, high-level exhaust, Eric Cheney motocross-type frame, alloy tank and mudguards.
£4,000–4,500 BLM

Speedway Bikes

Racing on unsurfaced, or dirt, tracks originated in the USA in the early 1900s, and by the 1920s had established itself in Australia, where the cinder track surface – still in use today – became the norm. Travelling enthusiasts brought word of this exciting sport to the UK, and in 1928 a series of demonstrations was held in Britain, featuring the cream of American and Australian riders. Before they arrived, Britain's first dirt-track meeting had been held that February at High Beech in Epping Forest, attracting a crowd of around 30,000 people. That first meeting had featured converted road machines, ridden by inexperienced competitors, but the overseas contingent brought a new riding technique – broadsiding – and specialised machinery.

The visitors' spectacular displays of daredevil riding fired the public's imagination, and the result was a rapid growth in dirt-track racing in the UK, scarcely a week passing without news of a new venue being opened. In 1929, speedway was established as the 'teams and leagues' sport we know today, leading to the emergence of home-grown stars such as Tommy Farndon, Gus Kuhn, Eric Langton, Wal Phillips, Frank Varey, Arthur Warwick and Colin Watson. Indeed, so quickly did British riders adapt to the new riding techniques that the very first Britain/Australia Test Match Series of 1932 ended in a 3-2 win for the home side.

Before long, almost all major UK manufacturers listed a dirt-track model, the first marque to establish dominance being Douglas, whose flat-twins had benefited from prior development on the Australian long tracks. As shorter tracks became the norm, the Duggie's otherwise excellent handling could not compensate for the handicap of a long wheelbase, and rival manufacturers' single-cylinder models began to assert themselves. By 1930, the four-valve Rudge was the machine to beat. Its supremacy would be short-lived, however, for by 1932, JAP's racing single was well on the way to establishing a dominance in

speedway that would remain unchallenged until the 1960s. As J.A. Prestwich supplied only engines, a cottage industry of independent frame makers arose to satisfy the demand for machines. Of the major manufacturers, only Excelsior, with its JAP-engined model, remained a force in speedway by the end of the 1930s.

The JAP engine's stranglehold loosened in the 1960s with the arrival of the Czech ESO machines. Part of the Jawa-CZ group, ESO specialised in speedway and other off-road competition motorcycles. However, in 1966, the ESO name was dropped, the firm's DT5 speedway model becoming the Jawa 500DT type 680. The Jawa eventually gave best to a more modern design, this time from specialist engine manufacturer Weslake. Harry Weslake had long been a proponent of the four-valves-per-cylinder layout for racing engines, and he incorporated this technology into his new pushrod speedway motor. Introduced in 1975, the Weslake outclassed the two-valve Jawa, the result being a wholesale switch to the British engine, and a rash of aftermarket four-valve conversions for the Czech engine; even Weslake climbed on to that bandwagon. Weslake began building complete speedway machines in 1977, and the firm's dominance of the sport was not challenged until the decade's end, when Jawa introduced a double-overhead-camshaft engine, a move that eventually forced Weslake down the same road.

Although JAP's 'P-N-E-U-M-A-T-I-C-S' letter/year engine code system makes it fairly easy to determine a unit's year of manufacture, this is not necessarily an accurate guide to the age of the machine in which the engine is installed. At any one time, a speedway team was likely to have operated dozens of machines of varying ages, and speedway bikes would undergo many engine swaps and rebuilds before being pensioned off. For example, after a couple of seasons, a 1950 Jackson-Rotrax could have acquired an engine built in 1948 or 1952.

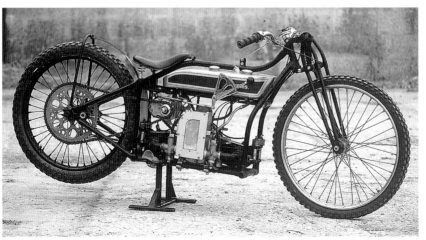

◀ **1928 Douglas DT5,** 499cc, overhead-valve, horizontal (fore-and-aft) twin, 62.25x82mm bore and stroke.
£5,250–5,800 BKS

Bristol-based Douglas was one of the first British manufacturers to build a specialised speedway motorcycle.

1932 Comerford-Wallis-JAP, 499cc, fitted with later 1947 overhead-valve, 5-stud, JAP single-cylinder engine. £2,000–2,200 BKS

The late, great, Wal Phillips assisted in the development of George Wallis' prototype JAP-engined speedway bike, and it proved quick from the very start. Its designer entered into an agreement with Thames Ditton-based motorcycle dealer Comerfords to market the machine. This example is believed to have been ridden by England captain Colin Watson in Test Matches, and to have been presented to him at the conclusion of the Star Championship.

1947 Excelsior Speedway Mk II, 499cc, 1939 overhead-valve, 4-stud JAP engine. £1,500–1,650 BKS

▶ **1950 Excelsior Speedway Mk III,** 499cc, 1947 5-stud JAP engine. £1,550–1,700 BKS

This late-model Excelsior machine was ridden by the former Norwich ace Billy Bales.

1933 Excelsior Speedway Mk 1, 499cc, overhead-valve, 5-stud JAP engine. £1,950–2,150 BKS

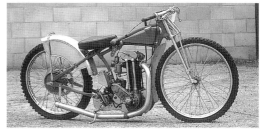

1935 Martin Rudge, overhead-valve JAP engine. £1,900–2,100 BKS

Rudge's reign as the top speedway bike manufacturer was brief, the combination of a JAP powerplant in a proprietary frame having established itself as the winning formula by the mid-1930s. Rights to the Rudge chassis were acquired by JAP employee Victor Martin, who marketed complete machines with JAP engines, Rudge frames and special lightweight forks in place of the original heavy Rudge girder type.

1950 Rotrax-JAP, 499cc, overhead-valve, JAP single-cylinder engine, completely restored, excellent condition. £1,100–1,200 BKS

During the immediate post-war period, Rotrax machines with JAP engines were among the most popular bikes with speedway competitors. This example was taken to South Africa when the Wembley Lions toured that country, and remained there until recently reimported into the UK.

1956 Chipchase-JAP, 499cc, 4-stud JAP engine.
£950–1,050 BKS

Chipchase was yet another frame builder to use JAP power on the shale-track circuit.

1956 Mattingly-JAP,
499cc, overhead-valve,
4-stud JAP engine.
£1,600–1,750 BKS

▶ **1952 Erskine-JAP,** 499cc,
4-stud JAP engine, 1970s Amal
Concentric Mk 1 carburettor.
£1,550–1,700 BKS

The Erskine speedway bike was designed and built in small numbers by rider Mike Erskine.

c1952 Jackson Speedway, 499cc, JAP single.
£1,500–1,650 BKS

Rotrax machines were among the most popular speedway bikes of the immediate post-war era, and this example is fitted with the ubiquitous 4-stud JAP engine.

◀ **c1969 Jawa-
Hagon Grass
Track Bike,** 500cc,
double-overhead-
camshaft, Jawa
speedway engine,
Hagon frame,
conversion by
Neil Street.
£900–1,000 BMM

1967 Jawa 500, 492cc, overhead-valve single, alloy head and barrel, 88x81mm bore and stroke.
£1,550–1,700 BKS

Jawa built the quintessential speedway bike of the late 1960s/early 1970s. It was developed from the ESO, which Jawa took over in the early 1960s.

Memorabilia

An Ariel Motor Cycles enamelled sign, c1900, 19in (47.5cm) square.
£450–500 BRUM

A Rudge-Whitworth agency enamelled sign, 1910, 24in (60cm) diam.
£400–500 BRUM

A Puch domed enamel advertising sign, 1960s, 18in (45cm) diam.
£40–60 BLM

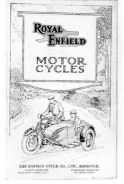

A Royal Enfield Motor Cycles brochure, 1925, 8½x5½in (21.25x13.75cm).
£25–28 DM

▶ A Raleigh brochure, 1933, 7x8½in (17.5x21.25cm).
£20–22 DM

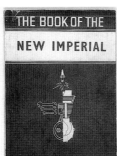

The Book of the New Imperial, Pitman's Motor Cyclist's Library, 1935–40.
£15–17 DM

A BSA Instruction Manual, B31 and B33 models, 1950s, 8½x5½in (21.25x13.75cm).
£6–7 DM

A Corker crash helmet, 1940/50s, good condition.
£38–42 PC

An Avon hand-operated tyre pump, 1920.
£40–44 BLM

A Raleigh mudguard mascot, late 1930s, rare, 2¾in (6.9cm) long.
£35–39 ATF

OSPREY AUTOMOTIVE

FOR THE COLLECTOR AND ENTHUSIAST

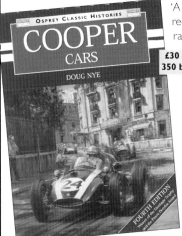

COOPER CARS
OSPREY CLASSIC HISTORIES

DOUG NYE

FOURTH EDITION

'A great read and an essential record for any true blue motor racing follower.' *MotorSport*

£30 • h/c • 400pp • 16 colour, 350 b/w • ISBN 1 85532 919 0

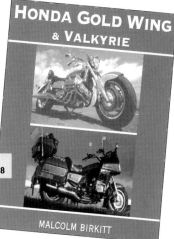

HONDA GOLD WING & VALKYRIE

MALCOLM BIRKITT

A fully updated edition of this best-selling title with an extra 16 pages to include the Valkyrie street machine.

£10.99 • s/c • 144pp • 140 colour; ISBN 1 85532 879 8

BENTLEY
FACTORY CARS 1919-1931
OSPREY CLASSIC HISTORIES
MICHAEL HAY

A limited edition of the most complete analysis ever published. 'An extraordinarily impressive account.' *Classic Cars*

£45 • h/c • 368pp • 40 colour, 350 b/w • ISBN 1 85532 883 6

HERITAGE
FROM THREE-WHEELER TO SUPERBLOWER
SIMON TAYLOR & PETER BURN

£16.99 • s/c • 144pp • 156 colour • ISBN 1 85532 534 9

Birthplace of the mighty Cobra, the oldest independent manufacturer; includes the new Ace and Superblower.

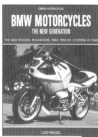

BMW MOTORCYCLES
THE NEW GENERATION

UDO REGEL

Full colour throughout, including design sketches from the company's archives. The BMW bike revolution of the 1990s laid bare.

£12.99 • s/c • 128pp • 120 colour • ISBN 1 85532 933 6

EXPERT HISTORIES New revised editions of classic titles from a best selling series, all written by the world's best known and best loved authors.

MERCEDES-BENZ SL & SLC
OSPREY EXPERT HISTORIES
L J K SETRIGHT

ISBN 1 85532 880 1

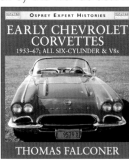

EARLY CHEVROLET CORVETTES
1953–67; ALL SIX-CYLINDER & V8s
OSPREY EXPERT HISTORIES
THOMAS FALCONER

ISBN 1 85532 971 9

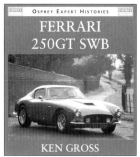

FERRARI 250GT SWB
OSPREY EXPERT HISTORIES
KEN GROSS

ISBN 1 85532 884 4

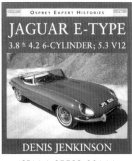

JAGUAR E-TYPE
3.8 & 4.2 6-CYLINDER; 5.3 V12
OSPREY EXPERT HISTORIES
DENIS JENKINSON

ISBN 1 85532 881 X

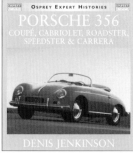

PORSCHE 356
COUPÉ, CABRIOLET, ROADSTER, SPEEDSTER & CARRERA
OSPREY EXPERT HISTORIES
DENIS JENKINSON

ISBN 1 85532 970 0

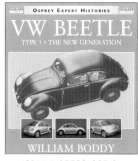

VW BEETLE
TYPE 1 & THE NEW GENERATION
OSPREY EXPERT HISTORIES
WILLIAM BODDY

ISBN 1 85532 885 2

£12.99 • s/c • 144pp • 22 colour, 120 b/w

Available from all good bookshops

or in case of difficulty from Osprey Direct

Tel: 01933 443862   Fax: 01933 443849   E-mail: info@OspreyDirect.co.uk

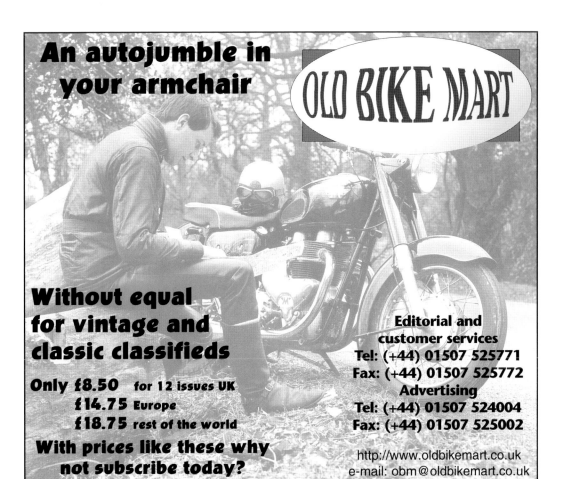

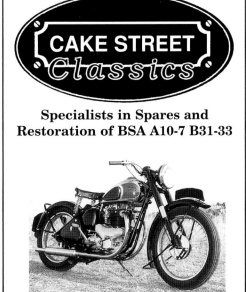
165

Key to Illustrations

Each illustration and descriptive caption is accompanied by a letter code. By referring to the following list of auctioneers (denoted by *), dealers (•), clubs, museums and trusts (§), the source of any item may be immediately determined. Inclusion in this edition no way constitutes or implies a contract or binding offer on the part of any of our contributors to supply or sell the goods illustrated, or similar articles, at the prices stated. Advertisers in this year's directory are denoted by †.

If you require a valuation, it is advisable to check whether the dealer or specialist will carry out this service and if there is a charge. Please mention Miller's when making an enquiry. A valuation by telephone is not possible. Most dealers are willing to help you with your enquiry; however, they are very busy people and consideration of the above points would be welcomed.

AOC/ AOM	§	Ariel Owners Motor Cycle Club, UK Membership Secretary, Andy Hemingway, 80 Pasture Lane, Clayton, Bradford, Yorkshire BD14 6LN Tel: 01274 882141
AT	•†	Andrew Tiernan Vintage & Classic Motorcycles, Old Railway Station, Station Road, Framlingham, Nr Woodbridge, Suffolk IP13 9EE Tel: 01728 724321
ATF	•	A T Fletcher (Enthusiast & Collector), Lancashire
AtMC	•†	Atlantic Motorcycles, 20 Station Road, Twyford, Berkshire RG10 9NT Tel: 0118 9342266
BERN	*	Bernaerts, Verlatstraat 18-22, 2000 Antwerpen/Anvers Tel: +32 (0)3 248 19 21
BKS	*†	Brooks (Auctioneers) Ltd, 81 Westside, London SW4 9AY Tel: 0171 228 8000
BLM	•†	Bill Little Motorcycles, Oak Farm, Braydon, Swindon, Wiltshire SN5 0AG Tel: 01666 860577
BMM	§	Battlesbridge Motorcycle Museum, Muggeridge Farm, Maltings Road, Battlesbridge, Essex SS11 7RF Tel: 01268 769392
BMR	§	British Motorcycle Riders Club, Geoff Ives, PO Box 2, Eynsham, Witney, Oxfordshire OX8 1RW
BMW	§	BMW Club, c/o Mike Cox, 22 Combermere, Thornbury, Bristol, Glos BS35 2ET Tel/Fax: 01454 415358
BRIT	*	British Car Auctions Ltd, Classic & Historic Automobile Division, Auction Centre, Blackbushe Airport, Blackwater, Camberley, Surrey GU17 9LG Tel: 01252 878555
BRUM	•	Fred Brumby Tel: 01487 842999
BTS	§	British Two Stroke Club, 5 Madden Close, Swanscombe, Kent DA16 0DH
C	*	Christie, Manson & Woods Ltd, 8 King Street, St James's, London SW1Y 6QT Tel: 0171 839 9060
CARS	•	C A R S (Classic Automobilia & Regalia Specialists), 4-4a Chapel Terrace Mews, Kemp Town, Brighton, Sussex BN2 1HU Tel: 01273 601960
CBX	§	CBX Riders Club, Mel Watkins, 9 Trem Y Mynydd, Abergele, Clwyd, LL22 9YY Tel: 01745 827026
CKC	§	Classic Kawasaki Club, PO Box 235, Nottingham NG8 6DT
CLR		Classic Racer, PO Box 100, Stamford, Lincolnshire PE9 1XQ Tel: 01780 755131
CoH	*	Cooper Hirst, The Granary Saleroom, Victoria Road, Chelmsford, Essex CM2 6LH Tel: 01245 260535
CotC	•†	Cotswold Classics, Ullenwood Court, Leckhampton, Nr Cheltenham, Glos GL53 9QS Tel: 01242 228622
COYS	*	Coys of Kensington, 2-4 Queens Gate Mews, London SW7 5QJ Tel: 0171 584 7444
CStC	•†	Cake Street Classics, Bellview, Cake Street, Laxfield, Nr Woodbridge, Suffolk IP13 8EW Tel: 01986 798504
DM/ OM	•	Don Mitchell & Company, 132 Saffron Road, Wigston, Leicestershire LE18 4UP Tel: 0116 277 7669
Doc/ DOC	*	David Dockree, Cheadle Hulme Business Centre, Clemence House, Mellor Road, Cheadle Hulme, Cheshire SK7 1BD Tel: 0161 485 1258
ELK	•†	Elk Engineering, The Little Farm, Ashford Road, Ivychurch, Romney Marsh, Kent TN29 0AL Tel: 01797 344277
GAZE	*	Thomas Wm Gaze & Son, 10 Market Hill, Diss, Norfolk IP22 3JZ Tel: 01379 651931
GBF	•	GB Fabrications, Unit 2, Station Goods Yard, Long Buckby, Northampton Tel: 01327 843432
HERM	*	Hermann Historica OHG, Postfach 201009, 80010 Munchen, Germany Tel: 00 49 89 5237296
HOC	§	Hesketh Owners Club, Peter White, 1 Northfield Road, Soham, Cambs CB7 5UE Tel: 01353 720550
HPM	§	Historic Police Motorcycles Tel: 0181 393 4958

IMC	§	Indian Motorcycle Club, c/o John Chatterton (Membership Secretary), 183 Buxton Road, Newtown, Disley, Stockport, Cheshire SK12 2RA Tel: 01663 747106
IMOC	§	Italian Motorcycle Owners Club (GB), John Riches, 12 Wappenham Road, Abthorpe, Towcester, Northants NN12 8QU Tel/Fax: 01327 857703
INM	•†	In Moto, 187 St James Road, Croydon, Surrey CR0 2BZ Tel: 0181 684 1515
IVC	•	The Italian Vintage Company, Lincolnshire Tel: 01673 842825
LEV/ LVO	§	LE Velo Club Ltd, P. Walker, Grantley House, Warwicks Bench, Guildford, Surrey GU1 3SZ
LSC	§	London Sidecar Club, 107 Silverweed Road, Walderslade, Chatham, Kent ME5 0RF Tel: 01634 864298
MAY	•†	Mayfair Motors, PO Box 66, Lymington, Hampshire SO41 0XE Tel: 01590 644476
MOC	§	Maico Owners Club, c/o Phil Hingston, 'No Elms', Goosey, Faringdon, Oxfordshire SN7 8PA Tel: 01367 710408
MOR	§	Morini Owners Club, c/o Kevin Bennett, 1 Glebe Farm Cottages, Sutton Veny, Warminster, Wiltshire BA12 7AS
MSW	*	Marilyn Swain Auctions, The Old Barracks, Sandon Road, Grantham, Lincolnshire NG31 9AS Tel: 01476 568861
MVT	§	Military Vehicle Trust, Simon Johnson, 7 Carter Fold, Mellor, Lancashire BB2 7ER Tel: 01254 812894
NLM	•†	North Leicester Motorcycles, Whitehill Road, Ellistown, Leicestershire LE67 1EL Tel: 01530 263381
OxM	•†	Oxney Motorcycles, Rolvenden, Cranbrook, Kent TN17 4NP Tel/Fax: 01797 270119
PC		Private collection
PM	•†	Pollard's Motorcycles, The Garage, Clarence Street, Dinnington, Sheffield, Yorkshire S25 7NA Tel: 01909 563310
PS	*†	Palmer Snell, 65 Cheap Street, Sherbourne, Dorset DT9 3BA Tel: 01935 812218
RAC	§	Royal Automobile Club, PO Box 700, Bristol, Glos BS99 1RB Tel: 01454 208000
RFC	§	Racing 50 Enthusiasts Club, Chris Alty, 14a Kestrel Park, Ashhurst, Skelmersdale, Lancashire WN8 6TB
RIM	•	Racing & Investment Motorcycles, Warwickshire

S	*†	Sotheby's, 34-35 New Bond Street, London W1A 2AA Tel: 0171 293 5000
SCOT	§	Scott Owners Club, Brian Marshall (Press Officer), Walnut Cottage, Abbey Lane, Aslockton, Nottingham NG13 9AE Tel/Fax: 01949 851027
SIP	•	T Sipma, Rolderstraat 4, 9444 XC Grollod, Holland Tel: 0031 592 501 397
SKC	§	The Kettle Club, Shaun Chandler, 66 Provene Gardens, Waltham Chase, Southampton, Hampshire SO32 2LE
SMC/ SWC	§	Shrivenham Motorcycle Club, 12-14 Townsend Road, Shrivenham, Swindon, Wiltshire SN6 8AS
SOC	§	Suzuki Owners Club, PO Box 7, Egremont, Cumbria CA22 2GE
SUN	§	Sunbeam MCC Ltd, Ian McGill, 13 Victoria Road, Horley, Surrey RH6 9BN A club for all makes pre-1931
SWS	§	South Wales Sunbeam MCC, Kate Baxter, 17 Heol-Glynog, Beddau, Pontypridd, South Wales
TCTR	§	Tiger Cub & Terrier Register, Mike Estall, 24 Main Road, Edingale, Tamworth, Staffordshire B79 9HY Tel: 01827 383415
TDD	§	Tour du Dauphine en Petrolettes, 38550 St Maurice L'Exil, France Tel: 04 74 86 58 54
TGA	•	TGA, Smithy Cottage, Liverpool Road, Blackerstaffe, Lancashire L39 0EF Tel: 01695 423621
VER	•†	Verralls (Handcross) Ltd, Caffyns Row, High Street, Handcross, Haywards Heath, Sussex RH17 6BJ Tel: 01444 400678
VICO	•†	Toni Vico, Reg. Tre Rivi 40, 12040 Monteu Rodero (CN), Piedmont, Italy Tel: 00 39 173 90121
VJMC	§	Vintage Japanese Motorcycle Club, PO Box 515, Dartford, Kent DA1 3RE
VMCC	§†	Vintage Motor Cycle Club, Allen House, Wetmore Road, Burton-on-Trent , Staffordshire DE14 1TR Tel: 01283 540557
VVC	§	Veteran Vespa Club, Ashley Lenton, 3 Vincent Road, Croydon, Surrey CR0 6ED Tel: 0181 656 4953
WEED	•	Weeden Classic Restorations, Unit 5 Atlas Court, Hermitage Ind Estate, Coalville, Leicestershire LE67 3FL. Tel: 01530 811118
YEST	•†	Yesterday's, VOF Yesterday's, Maaseikerweg 202, 6006 AD Weert, The Netherlands. Tel: 0475 531207

Glossary

We have attempted to define some of the terms that you will come across in this book. If there are any other terms or technicalities you would like explained or you feel should be included in future editions, please let us know.

ACU – Auto Cycle Union, which controls a large part of British motorcycle sport.

Advanced ignition – Ignition timing set causing firing before the piston reaches centre top, variation is now automatic.

Air-cooling – Most motorcycle engines rely on air-cooling, their cylinder barrels and heads being finned to dissipate heat.

Air intake – The carburettor port that admits air to mix with fuel from the float chamber.

AMCA – Amateur Motor Cycle Association, promoters of British off-road events.

APMC – The Association of Pioneer Motor Cyclists.

Auto Cycle Club – Formed in 1903, this was the original governing body of motorcycle sport. In 1907, it became the Auto Cycle Union.

Automatic inlet valve – Activated by the engine suction; forerunner of the mechanically-operated valve.

Balloon tyres – Wide-section, low-pressure tyres, fitted to tourers for comfort.

Beaded-edge tyres – Encased rubber beads in channels on wheel rim.

Belt drive – A leather or fabric belt running from the engine or gearbox to the rear wheel.

BHP – A measure of engine output: the amount of power required to lift 33,000lb to a height of 1ft in a minute equals 1bhp.

BMCRC – British Motor Cycle Racing Club, formed in 1909.

BMF – British Motorcycle Federation.

Bore/stroke ratio – The ratio of an engine's cylinder diameter to its piston stroke.

Caliper – A clamping device containing hydraulically-operated pistons that forms part of a disc brake.

Cam – Device for opening and closing a valve.

Camshaft – The mounting shaft for the cam; can be in low, high or overhead position.

Carburettor – Used to produce the air/fuel mixture required by the engine.

Chain drive – Primary form of drive from engine to gearbox and secondary gearbox to rear wheel.

Combustion chamber – Area where the fuel/air mixture is compressed and ignited, between the piston and cylinder head.

Compression ratio – The amount by which the fuel/air mixture is compressed by the piston in the combustion chamber.

Crankcase – The casing enclosing the crankshaft and its attachments.

Crankshaft – The shaft that converts the vertical motion of the piston into a rotary movement.

Cylinder – Contains the piston and is capped by the cylinder head. Upper portion forms the combustion chamber where the fuel/air mixture is compressed and burnt to provide power.

Cylinder head – Caps the top of the cylinder. In a four-stroke engine, it carries the valves and, in some cases, the camshaft(s).

Damper – Fitted to slow the movement in the suspension system, or as crankshaft balance.

Displacement – The engine capacity or amount of volume displaced by the movement of the piston from bottom dead centre to top dead centre.

Distributor – A gear-driven contact that sends high-tension current to the spark plugs.

DOHC – Double overhead camshaft.

Dry sump – An engine lubrication system in which the oil is contained in a separate reservoir and pumped to and from the engine by a pair of pumps.

Earles forks – A front fork design incorporating long leading links connected by a rigid pivot behind the front wheel.

Featherbed – A Norton frame, designed by Rex and Crommie McCandless, of Belfast, used for racing machines from 1950; road machines from 1953.

FIM – Federation Internationale Motorcycliste, controls motorcycle sport world-wide.

Flat-twin – An engine featuring two horizontally-opposed cylinders.

Float – A plastic or brass box that floats upon the fuel in a float chamber and operates the needle valve controlling the fuel flow.

Flywheel – Attached to the crankshaft, this heavy wheel smooths intermittent firing impulses and helps slow running.

Friction drive – An early form of drive using discs in contact instead of chains and gears.

Gearbox – Cased trains of pinion wheels that can be moved to provide alternative ratios.

Gear ratios – Differential rates of speed between sets of pinions to provide faster or slower rotation of the rear wheel in relation to the engine speed.

GP – Grand Prix, an international race to a fixed formula.

High camshaft – Mounted high up in the engine to shorten the pushrods in an ohv arrangement.

IOE – Inlet over exhaust, a common arrangement with an overhead inlet valve and side exhaust valve.

Leaf spring – Metal blades clamped and bolted together, used in early suspension systems.

Magneto – A high-tension dynamo that produces current for the ignition spark; superseded by coil ignition.

Main bearings – Bearings in which the crankshaft runs.

Manifold – Collection of pipes supplying fuel/air mixture or removing exhaust gases.

MCC – The Motor Cycling Club, which runs sporting events; formed in 1902.

Moped – A light motorcycle of under 50cc with pedals attached.

OHC – See Overhead camshaft.

Overhead camshaft – An engine design in which the camshaft (or camshafts) is carried in the cylinder head.

OHV – See Overhead valve.

Overhead valve – A valve mounted in the cylinder head.

Pinking – A distinctive noise produced by an engine with over-advanced ignition or inferior fuel.

Piston – Moves up and down the cylinder, drawing in fuel/air mixture, compressing it, being driven down by combustion and forcing spent gases out.

Post-vintage – A motorcycle made after December 31, 1930, and before January 1, 1945.

Pressure plate – The plate against which the clutch springs react to load the friction plates.

Pushrods – Operating rods for overhead valves, working from cams below the cylinder.

Rotary valve – A valve driven from the camshaft for inlet or exhaust and usually of a disc or cylindrical shape; for either two- or four-stroke engines.

SACU – Scottish Auto Cycle Union, which controls motorcycle sport in Scotland.

SAE – Society of Automotive Engineers. Used in a system of classifying engine oils such as SAE30, I0W/50, etc.

Shock absorber – A damper, used to control vertical movement of suspension, or to cushion a drive train.

Silencer – Device fitted to the exhaust system of an engine in which the pressure of the exhaust gases is reduced to lessen noise.

Swinging arm – Rear suspension by radius arms, which carry the wheel and are attached to the frame at their forward ends.

Torque – Twisting force in a shaft; can be measured to determine at what speed an engine develops most torque.

Index to Advertisers

Antiques Magazine . . . . Back endpaper
Atlantic Motorcycles 111
Len Baker 33
Keith Benton 166
Peter Best Insurance Services . . . . Front endpaper
Boyer Bransden Electronic Ignitions . . . . Front endpaper
Brooks Ltd . . . . Jacket/cover
Cake Street Classics 165
Charnwood Classic Restorations 157
Classic Bike Guide 170
The Classic Motor Cycle 177
Conquest Motorcycles 166
Cotswold Classics 25
Crowmarsh Classics 29
Devitt DA 6
Elk Engineering 41
Finishing Touch 166
Footman James & Co Ltd . . . . Front endpaper
Hughie Hancox Restorations 101
In Moto 73
Bill Little Motorcycles 17
Mayfair Motors 149

Miller's Publications 4
North Leicester Motorcycles 75
Old Bike Mart 165
Osprey Publications Ltd 164
Oxney Motorcycles 35
Palmer Snell 177
Pollard's Motorcycles 81
Pooks Motor Bookshop 163
Quintrans Ltd 166
Redline Books 127
Martyn Rowe, Truro Auction Centre 177
RTS Auctions Ltd . . . . Front endpaper
Peter Smith Motorcycles 65
Sotheby's . . . . Back endpaper
Speedograph Richfield 165
Andy Tiernan Classics 27
Verralls (Handcross) Ltd 95
Toni Vico 153
Vintage Motor Cycle Club 173
Rick & Mick Walker 43
George Yeoman's Motor Cycle Spares 6
Yesterday's 69

Bibliography

Bacon, Roy; *British Motorcycles of the 1930s*,
Osprey, 1986
Bacon, Roy; *Matchless & AJS Restoration*, Osprey 1993
Bacon, Roy; *Norton Twin Restoration*, Osprey, 1993
Bacon, Roy; *Triumph Twins & Triples*, Osprey, 1990
Birkitt, Malcolm; *Harley-Davidson*, Osprey, 1993
Champ, Robert Cordon; *Sunbeam S7/S8 Super Profile*,
Haynes, 1983
Davis, Ivor; *It's a Triumph*, Haynes, 1980
Morley, Don; *Classic Motorcycles: Triumph*, Osprey, 1991
Stuart, Garry, and Carroll, John; *Classic Motorcycles:
Indian*, Osprey, 1994
Tragatsch, Erwin, ed; *The New Illustrated Encyclopedia of
Motorcycles*, Grange Books, 1993

Walker, Mick; *Aermacchi*, Transport Source Books, 1995
Walker, Mick; *Benelli*, Transport Source Books, 1996
Walker, Mick; *British Racing Motorcycles*, Redline
Books, 1998
Walker, Mick, and Carrick, Rob; *British Performance
2-strokes*, Transport Source Books, 1998
Walker, Mick; *Ducati Twins*, Osprey 1998
Walker, Mick; Hamlyn *History of Motorcycling*,
Hamlyn, 1997
Walker, Mick; *Italian Racing Motorcycles*, Redline
Books, 1998
Walker, Mick; *Morini*, Transport Source Books, 1996
Walker, Mick; *MZ*, Transport Source Books, 1996
Woollett, Mick; *Norton*, Osprey, 1992

Classic Bike Guide

takes its readers on a nostalgic journey through
the world of classic motorcycles.

● Well-written features with a friendly personal approach ●

● An essential read for the Classic Biker ●

● Buying or Selling? Hundreds of free readers ads every month ●

Reserve it at your Newsagent or call our
Subscriptions Hotline on 01732 459925

Directory of Museums

ARE Classic Bike Collection
285 Worplesdon Road, Guildford, Surrey GU2 6XN
Tel: 01483 232006
Around 50 mainly British bikes and memorabilia.
Open Monday and Friday 9am–1pm, Tuesday and
Thursday 9am–5pm.

Battlesbridge Motorcycle Museum
Muggeridge Farm, Maltings Road, Battlesbridge, Essex
SS11 7RF Tel: 01268 769392
Classic motorcycles and scooters.
Open Sundays 10.30am–4pm.

Birmingham Museum of Science & Industry
Newhall Street, Birmingham, West Midlands B3 1RZ
Tel: 0121 235 1661
Cars and motorcycles.
Open Monday to Saturday 10am–5pm, Sunday
12.30pm–5pm. Closed December 25–26, and January 1.

Bristol Industrial Museum
Princes Wharf, City Docks, Bristol, Glos BS1 4RN
Tel: 0117 925 1470
Douglas machines, including the only surviving V4 of
1908, and a 1972 Quasar.
Open Tuesday to Sunday 10am–5pm. Closed Thursdays
and Fridays, Good Friday, December 25–27 and January 1.

Brooklands Museum
The Clubhouse, Brooklands Road, Weybridge, Surrey
KT13 0QN Tel: 01932 857381
Collection of motorcycles.
Open daily 10am–5pm summer, 10am–4pm winter.
Closed Mondays, Good Friday and Christmas.

Combe Martin Motorcycle Collection
Cross Street, Combe Martin, Ilfracombe, Devon EX34 0DH
Tel: 01271 882346
Around 100 motorcycles and memorabilia.
Open daily May to October 10am–5pm.

Craven Collection of Classic Motorcycles
Brockfield Villa, Stockton-on-the-Forest, Yorkshire YO3 9UE
Tel: 01904 488461/400493
Over 200 vintage and post-war classic motorcycles.
Open first Sunday of every month and Bank Holiday
Mondays, 10am–4pm. Club visits and private parties.

Foulkes-Halbard of Filching
Filching Manor, Jevington Road, Wannock, Polegate,
Sussex BN26 5QA
Tel: 01323 487838
30 motorcycles, including pre-1940s American bikes
ex-Steve McQueen, 100 cars dating from 1893–1993.
Open Easter to October, Thursday, Friday, Saturday and
Sunday 10am–4pm.

Geeson Bros. Motorcycle Museum and Workshop
South Witham, Grantham, Lincolnshire
Tel: 01572 767280/768195
Collection of over 80 motorcycles.
Open days throughout the year.

Grampian Transport Museum
Main Street, Alford, Aberdeenshire, Scotland AB33 8AD
Tel: 019755 62292
Collection of 30–40 machines ranging from a 1902
Beeston Humber to a Norton F1.
Open March 28–October 31, 10am–5pm.

Haynes Sparkford Motor Museum
Sparkford, Yeovil, Somerset BA22 7LH
Tel: 01963 440804
Collection of around 50 machines from a 1914
BSA onwards.
Open Monday to Sunday summer 9.30am–5.30pm,
winter 10am–4pm. Closed December 25–26 and January 1.

London Motorcycle Museum
Ravenor Farm, 29 Oldfield Lane South, Greenford,
Middlesex UB6 9LB Tel: 0181 579 1248
Collection of around 50 British motorcycles.
Open weekends.

Madog Cars & Motorcycle Museum
Snowdon Street, Porthmadog, Wales LL49 9DF
Tel: 01758 713618
Collection of around 70 motorcycles and memorabilia.
Open May to September, Monday–Saturday 10am–5pm.

Sammy Miller Museum
Bashley Manor, Bashley Cross Roads, New Milton,
Hampshire BH25 6TF Tel: 01425 620777
Collection of motorcycles, artefacts and memorabilia.
A reconstructed workshop of 1925 shows a large display
of the tools used at that time.
Open daily 10am–4pm.

Mouldsworth Motor Museum
Smithy Lane, Mouldsworth, Chester, Cheshire CH3 8AR
Tel: 01928 731781
Collection of over 25 motorcycles, automobilia and
replica 1920s garage.
Open Sundays March to November 12pm–5pm, Bank
Holidays and Wednesdays July to August 1pm–5pm.

Murray's Motorcycle Museum
Bungalow Corner, Mountain Road, Snaefell, Isle of Man
Tel: 01624 861719
Collection of 140 machines, including Mike Hailwood's
250cc Mondial and Honda 125cc.
Open May to September 10am–5pm.

Museum of British Road Transport
St Agnes Lane, Hales Street, Coventry, Warwickshire
CV1 1PN Tel: 01203 832425
Collection includes around 100 motorcycles.
Open daily except December 24–26, 10am–5pm.

Museum of Transport
Kelvin Hall, 1 Bunhouse Road, Glasgow, Scotland G3 8DP
Tel: 0141 357 2656/2720
Motorcycles including Automobile Association BSA
combination. Open Monday to Saturday 10am–5pm,
Sunday 11am–5pm. Closed December 25 and January 1.

Myreton Motor Museum
Aberlady, East Lothian, Scotland EH32 0PZ
Tel: 01875 870288
Motorcycles including 1926 350cc Chater-Lea racer and
Egli Vincent. Open daily 10am–6pm. Closed December 25.

National Motor Museum
Brockenhurst, Beaulieu, Hampshire SO42 7ZN
Tel: 01590 612123/612345
Motorcycle collection, reference and photographic
libraries. Open Easter to September 10am–6pm, October
to Easter 10am–5pm. Closed December 25.

National Motorcycle Museum
Coventry Road, Bickenhill, Solihull, W Midlands B92 0EJ
Tel: 01675 443311
Over 650 machines restored to original specification.
Open daily 10am–6pm. Closed December 25–26.

National Museum of Scotland
The Granton Centre, 242 West Granton Road,
Edinburgh, Scotland EH1 1JF
Tel: 0131 225 7534
Small display of engines and complete machines,
includes the world's first four-cylinder motorcycle, an
1895 Holden. Tours available, book in advance.

Norfolk Motorcycle Museum
Station Approach, North Walsham, Norfolk NR28 0DS
Tel: 01692 406266
Over 100 motorcycles from 1920s to 1960s.
Open daily 10am–4.30pm. Closed Sundays in winter.

Science Museum
Exhibition Road, South Kensington, London SW7 2DD
Tel: 0171 589 3456
Collection of engines and complete machines.
Open Monday to Saturday 10am–6pm, Sunday
11am–6pm. Closed December 24–26.

Stanford Hall Motorcycle Museum
Stanford Hall, Lutterworth, Leicestershire LE17 6DH
Tel: 01788 860250
Collection of older machines and racers.
Open Saturdays, Sundays, Bank Holiday Mondays and
Tuesdays Easter to September, 2.30pm–5.30pm.

Ulster Folk & Transport Museum
Cultra, Holywood, Co. Down, Northern Ireland
Tel: 01232 428428
Includes 70–100 motorcycles at any one time.
Open all year round 10.30am–5/6pm. Sundays
12pm–6pm. Closed Christmas.

Directory of Motorcycle Clubs

If you wish to be included in next year's directory or if you have a change of address or telephone number, please would you inform us by 28 April 2000.

ABC Owners Club, D A Hales, The Hedgerows, Sutton St Nicholas, Hereford HR1 3BU Tel: 01432 880726

Aircooled RD Club, Susan Gregory (Membership Secretary), 6 Baldwin Road, Burnage, Greater Manchester M19 1LY Tel: 0161 286 7539

AJS & Matchless Owners Club, Northants Classic Bike Centre, 25 Victoria Street, Irthlingborough, Northamptonshire NN9 5RG Tel: 01933 652155

AMC Owners Club, c/o Terry Corley, 12 Chilworth Gardens, Sutton, Surrey SM1 3SP

Androd Classics, 70 Broadway, Frome, Somerset BA11 3HE Tel: 01373 471087

Ariel Owners Motor Cycle Club, Andy Hemingway (UK Membership Secretary), 80 Pasture Lane, Clayton, Bradford, Yorkshire BD14 6LN Tel: 01274 882141

Ariel Owners Motorcycle Club Swindon Branch, Paul Hull (Branch Secretary), Turnpike Cottage, Marlborough Road, Wootton Bassett, Wiltshire SN4 7SA

Association of Pioneer Motorcyclists, Mrs J MacBeath (Secretary), Heatherbank, May Close, Headley, Nr Bordon, Hampshire GU35 8LR

Bantam Enthusiasts Club, c/o Vic Salmon, 16 Oakhurst Close, Walderslade, Chatham, Kent ME5 9AN

Benelli Motobi Riders Club, Steve Peace, 43 Sherrington Road, Ipswich, Suffolk IP1 4HT Tel: 01473 461712

Best Feet Forward MCC, Paul Morris (Membership Secretary), 43 Finedon Road, Irthlingborough, Northamptonshire NN9 5TY

BMW Club, c/o Mike Cox, 22 Combermere, Thornbury, Bristol, Gloucestershire BS35 2ET Tel & Fax: 01454 415358

Bristol & Avon Roadrunners Motorcycle Club, 177 Speedwell Road, Speedwell, Bristol, Glos BS5 7SP

Bristol & District Sidecar Club, 158 Fairlyn Drive, Kingswood, Bristol, Gloucestershire BS15 4PZ

Bristol Genesis Motorcycle Club, Burrington, 1a Bampton Close, Headley Park, Bristol, Gloucestershire BS13 7QZ Tel: 0117 978 2584

British Motor Bike Owners Club, c/o Ray Peacock, Crown Inn, Shelfanger, Diss, Norfolk IP22 2DL

British Motorcycle Association, Pete Reed, AMCA, 28 Mill Park, Hawks Green Lane, Cannock, Staffordshire WS11 2XT

British Motorcycle Club of Guernsey, c/o Ron Le Cras, East View, Village De Putron, St Peter Port, Guernsey, Channel Islands GY1

British Motorcycle Owners Club, c/o Phil Coventry, 59 Mackenzie Street, Bolton, Lancashire BL1 6QP

British Motorcycle Riders Club, Geoff Ives, PO Box 2, Eynsham, Witney, Oxfordshire OX8 1RW

British Motorcyclists Federation, Jack Wiley House, 129 Seaforth Avenue, Motspur Park, New Malden, Surrey KT3 6JU

British Two Stroke Club, 5 Madden Close, Swanscombe, Kent DA16 0DH

British Two-Stroke Club, Eric Hathaway, 23 Finch Way, Narborough, Leicester, Leicestershire LE9 5TP

BSA Owners Club, Ray Haynes, PO Box 436, Peterborough, Cambridgeshire PE2 8SF

CBX Riders Club (United Kingdom), Mel Watkins, 9 Trem Y Mynydd, Abergele, Clwyd LL22 9YY Tel: 01745 827026

Christian Motorcyclists Association, PO Box 113, Wokingham, Berkshire RG11 5UB Tel: 0870 606 3610

Classic Kawasaki Club (Formerly The Kawasaki Triples Club), PO Box 235, Nottingham, Notts NG8 6DT

Classic Racing Motorcycle Club Ltd, Ron Key, 6 Cladgate Grove, Wombourne, Wolverhampton, West Midlands WV5 8JS

Cossack Owners Club, Alan Mottram (Membership Secretary), 19 The Villas, West End, Stoke on Trent, Staffordshire ST4 5AQ

Cotton Owners Club, P Turner, Coombehayes, Sidmouth Road, Lyme Regis, Dorset DT7 3EQ

Derbyshire and Staffordshire Classic Motorcycle Club, 51 Westwood Park Newhall, Swadlincote, Derbyshire DE11 0R5 Tel: 01283 214542

Dot Motorcycle Club, c/o Chris Black, 115 Lincoln Avenue, Clayton, Newcastle-under-Lyne ST5 3AR

Edge & District Vintage Motorcycle Club, 10 Long Lane Larkton, Malpas, Cheshire SY14 8LP

Exeter British Motorcycle Club, c/o Bill Jones, 7 Parkens Cross Lane, Pinhoe, Exeter, Devon EX1 3TA

Exeter Classic Motorcycle Club, c/o Martin Hatcher, 11 Newcombe Street, Heavitree, Exeter, Devon EX1 2TG

Federation of Sidecars, Jeff Reynard, 5 Ethel Street, Beechcliffe, Keighley, Yorkshire BD20 6AN

Fellowship of Christian Motorcyclists, Phil Crow, 6 St Anne's Close, Formby, Liverpool L37 7AX

FJ Owners Club, Lee & Mick Beck (Membership Secretary), 1 Glen Crescent , Stamford, Lincs PE9 1SW

Forgotten Racing Club, Mrs Chris Pinches, 73 High Street, Morton, Bourne, Lincolnshire PE10 0NR Tel: 01778 570535

Francis-Barnett Owners Club, John Baker (Hon Sec), Leigh, Durrant Lane, Northam, Bideford, Devon EX39 2RL Tel: 01237 473994

Gilera Network, Pete Fisher, 4 Orton Grove, Penn, Wolverhampton WV4 4JN Tel: 01902 337626

Gold Star Owners Club, Maurice Evans, 211 Station Road, Mickleover, Derby, Derbyshire DE3 5FE

Goldwing Owners Club, 82 Farley Close, Little Stoke, Bristol, Gloucestershire BS12 6HG

Greeves Owners Club, c/o Dave McGregor, 4 Longshaw Close, North Wingfield, Chesterfield, Derbyshire S42 5QR

Greeves Riders Association, Dave & Brenda McGregor, 4 Longshaw Close, North Wingfield, Chesterfield, Derbyshire S42 5QR Tel: 01246 853846

Harley-Davidson Manufacturers Club. Tel: 01280 700101

Harley-Davidson Owners Club, 1 St Johns Road, Clifton, Bristol, Gloucestershire BS8 2ET

Harley-Davidson Riders Club of Great Britain, SAE to Membership Secretary, PO Box 62, Newton Abbott, Devon TQ12 2QE

Harley Owners Group, HOG UK, The Bell Tower, High Street, Brackley, Northamptonshire, NN13 7DT Tel: 01280 700101

Hedingham Sidecar Owners Club, John Dean (Membership Sec), Birchendale Farm, Fole Lane , Stoke-on-Trent, Staffordshire ST10 4HL Tel: 01889 507389

Hesketh Owners Club, Peter White, 1 Northfield Road, Soham, Cambridgeshire CB7 5UE Tel: 01353 720550

Historic Police Motorcycles. Tel: 0181 393 4958

Honda Monkey Club, 28 Newdigate Road, off Red Lane, Coventry, Warwickshire CV6 5ES Tel: 01203 665141

Honda Owners Club (GB), Membership Secretary, 61 Vicarage Road, Ware, Hertfordshire SG12 7BE Tel: 01932 787111

Indian Motorcycle Club, c/o John Chatterton, (Membership Secretary), 183 Buxton Road, Newtown, Disley, Stockport , Cheshire SK12 2RA Tel: 01663 747106

International CBX Owners Association, Mel Watkins, 9 Trem Y Mynydd, Abergele, Clwyd LL22 9YY Tel: 01745 827026

International Laverda Owners Club, c/o Alan Cudipp, 29 Claypath Road, Hetton-le-Hole, Houghton-le-Spring, Tyne & Wear DH5 0EL

International Motorcyclists Tour Club, James Clegg, 238 Methane Road, Netherton, Huddersfield, Yorkshire HD4 7HL Tel: 01484 664868

Italian Motorcycle Owners Club (GB), John Riches, 12 Wappenham Road, Abthorpe, Towcester, Northamptonshire NN12 8QU Tel/Fax: 01327 857703

Jawa-CZ Owners Club, John Blackburn, 39 Bignor Road, Sheffield, Yorkshire S6 IJD

Kawasaki GT Club, D Shucksmith (Club Secretary), Flat K, Lichfield Court, Lichfield Road, Walsall, West Midlands WS4 2DX Tel: 01922 37441

Kawasaki Riders Club, Gemma, Court 1, Concord House, Kirmington, Humberside DN39 6YP

The Kettle Club, Shaun Chandler, 66 Provene Gardens, Waltham Chase, Southampton, Hampshire SO32 2LE

Kickstart Club Torbay, c/o Eddie Hine, 12 Vale Road, Kingskerswell, Newton Abbot, Devon TQ12 5AE

Laverda Owners Club, c/o Ray Sheepwash, 8 Maple Close, Swanley, Kent BR8 7YN

LE Velo Club Ltd, P Walker, Grantley House, Warwicks Bench, Guildford, Surrey GU1 3SZ

Leader and Arrow Club, Stan Davies, 11 Hollins Lane, Tilstock, Whitchurch SY13 3NT

Leominster Classic MCC, Ron Moore, The Yew Tree, Gorsty, Pembridge, Herefordshire HR6 9JF

London Douglas Motorcycle Club, R Dix, 23 Stockhay Lane, Hammerwich, Lichfield, Staffordshire WS7 0JE

London Sidecar Club, 107 Silverweed Road, Walderslade, Chatham, Kent ME5 0RF Tel: 01634 864298

Maico Owners Club, c/o Phil Hingston, No Elms, Goosey, Faringdon, Oxfordshire SN7 8PA Tel: 01367 710408

Marston Sunbeam Register, Ray Jones, 37 Sandhurst Drive, Penn, Wolverhampton, West Midlands WV4 5RJ

Military Vehicle Trust, Simon Johnson, 7 Carter Fold, Mellor, Lancashire BB2 7ER Tel: 01254 812894

Morini Owners Club, c/o Kevin Bennett, 1 Glebe Farm Cottages, Sutton Veny, Warminster, Wiltshire BA12 7AS

Morini Riders Club, c/o Kevin Bennett, 1 Glebe Farm Cottages, Sutton Veny, Warminster, Wiltshire BA12 7AS Tel: 01985 840055

Moto Guzzi Club GB, Polly Foyle (Membership Secretary), 43 Poplar Avenue, Bedworth, Warwickshire CV12 9EW

MV Agusta Owners Club of GB, Liz Cornish, 50 Burlingham Avenue, Evesham, Worcestershire WR11 5EF

National Association of Supertwins, Sue Beneke, 10A Queens Road, Evesham, Worcestershire

National Autocycle & Cyclemotor Club, Rob Harknett, 1 Parkfields, Roydon, Harlow, Essex CM19 5JA

National Sprint Association, Judith Sykes (Secretary), 10 Compton Street, Clifton, York, Yorkshire YO3 6LE

National Trailers Owners Club (NaTo), 47c Uplands Avenue, Rowley, Regis Warley, West Midlands B65 9PU

New Imperial Owners Association, Mrs J E Jarvis, Lyndhurst House, Victoria Road, Hayling Island, Hampshire PO11 0LU Tel: 01705 469098

North Devon British Motorcycle Owners Club, D E Davies (Hon Sec), 47 Old Town, Bideford, Devon EX39 3BH Tel: 01237 472237

Norton Owners Club, Colin Coleman, 110 Skegby Road, Annesley Woodhouse, Nottinghamshire NG17 9FF

Norton Owners Club, c/o Philip Hill (Secretary), 11 Hammond Close, Thatcham, Newbury, Berkshire RG19 4FF

Norton Rotary Enthusiasts Club, Alan Jones, 112 Fairfield Crescent, Newhall, Swadlingcote DE11 0TB

Panther Owners Club, Graham & Julie Dibbins, Oakdene, 22 Oak Street, Netherton, Dudley, West Midlands DY2 9LJ

Preston Vintage Enthusiasts, Lancashire.

Racing 50 Enthusiasts Club, Chris Alty, 14a Kestrel Park, Ashhurst, Skelmersdale, Lancashire WN8 6TB

Raleigh Safety Seven and Early Reliant Owners Club, incorporating Historic Raleigh Motorcycle Club, Mick Sleap, 17 Courtland Avenue, Chingford, London E4 6DU Tel: 0181 524 6310

Rolls-Royce Vintage & Classic Motorcycle Club, Ken Birch, 111 Havenbaulk Lane, Littleover, Derby DE23 7AD

Rotary Owners' Club, c/o David Cameron Dunbar, Ingatestone Rd, Highwood, Chelmsford, Essex CM1 3QU

Royal Enfield Owners Club, Les Power, 18 Redhouse Road, Tettenhall, Wolverhampton, West Midlands WV6 8ST

Rudge Enthusiasts Club Ltd, c/o Colin Kirkwood (General Secretary), 41 Rectory Green, Beckenham, Kent BR3 4HX

Rudge Enthusiasts Club Ltd, 13 Lade Fort Crescent, Lydd-on-Sea, Kent TN29 9YG

Scott Owners Club, Brian Marshall (Press Officer), Walnut Cottage, Abbey Lane, Aslockton, Nottingham NG13 9AE Tel/Fax: 01949 851027

Shrivenham Motorcycle Club, 12–14 Townsend Road, Shrivenham, Swindon, Wiltshire SN6 8AS

Sidecar Register, c/o John Proctor, 112 Briarlyn Road, Birchencliffe, Huddersfield, Yorkshire HD3 3NW

South Wales Sunbeam MCC, Kate Baxter, 17 Heol-Glynog Beddau, Pontypridd, South Wales

Street Specials Motorcycle Club, inc Rickman O/C, Harris O/C & Featherbed O/C, c/o Dominic Dawson, 12 St Mark's Close, Gosport, Hampshire PO12 2DB Tel: 01705 501321

Sunbeam MCC Ltd, Ian McGill, 13 Victoria Road, Horley, Surrey RH6 9BN A club for all makes pre-1931

Sunbeam Owners Club, Stewart Engineering, Church Terrace, Harbury, Leamington Spa, Warwickshire CV33 9HL

Sunbeam Owners Fellowship, c/o Stewart Engineering, Church Terrace, Harbury, Nr Leamington Spa, Warwickshire CV33 9HL

Suzuki Owners Club, PO Box 7, Egremont, Cumbria CA22 2GE

Tamworth & District Classic Motorcycle Club, Roger Steele Tel: Tamworth 281244

Tiger Cub & Terrier Register, Mike Estall, 24 Main Road, Edingale, Tamworth, Staffordshire B79 9HY Tel: 01827 383415

Tour du Dauphine en Petrolettes, 38550 St Maurice l'Exil, France Tel: 04 74 86 58 54

Trail Riders Fellowship, Tony Stuart, Cambrea, Trebetherick, Wadebridge, Cornwall PL27 6SG Tel: 01208 862960

Trident and Rocket 3 Owners Club, John Atkins (Club Secretary), 47 Underhill Road, Benfleet, Essex SS7 1EP

Triumph Motorcycle Club, 6 Hortham Lane, Almondsbury, Bristol, Gloucestershire BS12 4JH

Triumph Owners MCC, M Davies, 5 Wesley Crescent, Shifnal, Shropshire TF11 9AQ

Triumph Triples Club, H J Allen, 50 Sylmond Gardens, Rushden, Northamptonshire NN10 9EJ

Velocette Owners Club, Vic Blackman (Secretary), 1 Mayfair, Tilehurst, Reading, Berkshire RG3 4RA.

Veteran Grass Track Riders Association (VGTRA) Tel: 01622 204745

Veteran Vespa Club, Ashley Lenton, 3 Vincent Road, Croydon, Surrey CR0 6ED Tel: 0181 656 4953

Vincent-HRD Owners Club, c/o John Wilding, Little Wildings, Fairhazel, Piltdown, Uckfield, Sussex TN22 3XB Tel: 01825 763529

Vintage Japanese Motorcycle Club, PO Box 515 , Dartford, Kent DA1 3RE

Vintage Motor Cycle Club, Allen House, Wetmore Road, Burton-on-Trent, Staffordshire DE14 1TR Tel: 01283 540557

Vintage Motor Scooter Club, c/o Ian Harrop, 11 Ivanhoe Avenue, Lowton St Lukes, Nr Warrington, Cheshire WA3 2HX

Virago Owners Club, John Bryning (President), River Green House, Great Sampford, Saffron Walden, Essex CB10 2RS Tel: 01799 586578

Vmax Club, H Doyle, 87 Honiton Road, Wyken, Coventry, Warwickshire CV2 3EF Tel: 01203 442054

Yamaha Riders Club, Alan Cheney, 11 Lodden Road, Farnborough, Hampshire GU14 9NR

Zl Owners Club, c/o Jerry Humpage, 90 Delves Crescent, Walsall, West Midlands WS5 4LT

Index

Italic page numbers denote colour pages; **bold** numbers refer to information and pointer boxes

A

ABC Skootamota (1919) 149
Aermacchi 11, *49*
  Ala Verde (1965) *49*; (1966) 11
  Chimera 175 (1957) 11
  Sprint (1968) 11; (1971) 11
  SX350 (1972) 11
AJS 12–15, *49*, *126*
  7R (1958) 143
  7R Rolling Chassis (1948) 143
  31 De Luxe (1960) 15
  B1 Sporting (1922) 12
  B3 Big Port (1923) 138
  Big Port (1927) 13
  Cheney Special (1967) 159
  H2 with Sidecar (1927) 157
  Model 8 (1960) 15; (1961) 15
  Model 16MC (1952) 13
  Model 16MS (1953) 14; (1958) 14; (1961) 15
  Model 18 (1957) 14
  Model 18S (1959) 14
  Model 20 (1952) 13; (1954) 14; (1955) 14; (1958) *49*
  Model 31 De Luxe (1960) *49*
  Model G8 (1926) 12
  Model K7 (1928) 140
  Model M7 (1929) *126*
  R10 (1930) *126*
  Single (1912) 12
  Sporting Model 5 (1926) 12
  Stormer (1974) 120
  Twin Port (1938) 13
  V-twin (1913) 12
AJW Collie (1976) 135
Alcyon Single (1914) 15
Aprilia *49*
  AF1 Replica (1989) *49*
Ardie 16
  BD176 (1956) 16
Ariel 16–18, *50*, 163
  4F/6.32 (1932) 16
  4G Mk 2 (1949) 17; (1953) 17
  4G with Sidecar (1951) 157
  Arrow (1961) 18
  Colt Model LF (1929) 17
  FH Huntmaster (1955) 17; (1958) 18
  HT5 (1957) 117; (1958) 117
  Leader **18**
  Model A with Sidecar (1928) 157
  NH Red Hunter (1956) *50*; (1957) 18
  VCH Trials (1951) 116
  VH Red Hunter (1954) 17
  VH with Watsonian Sidecar (1955) 158

B

Baker 247cc (1925) 19
Benelli 19
  125 Sport (1963) 19
  250 2C (1973) 19
  654 Turismo (1981) 19
Bianchi 125 Mendola (1957) 20
BMW 20–2, 129–30, 131
  KS600W with Sidecar (1941) 129
  R2 (1933) 20
  R12 with sidecar (1939) 130
  R23 **20**; (1939) 129
  R25/4 (1955) 21
  R27 (1962) 21
  R39 (1932) 20
  R60 (1960) 21
  R67 (1952) 21
  R69S (1964) 21
  R75 (1942) 131
  R75 with Sidecar (1943) 131
  R75/5 with Sidecar (1972) 158
  R100CS (1982) 22
books *128*, 163
Bradbury (1912) 22
Bridgestone GTR 350 (1966) 22
Brough-Superior 23–4, *50*
  11.50 (1939) 24
  680 (1931) 23
  SS80 (1925) 23; (1936) 23; (1937) 24; (1938) *50*
  SS100 (1936) 23; (1937) 24
BSA 25–35, *50–2*, 163
  500 Empire Star Q8 (1936) 26
  650 Lightning (1971) *52*
  A7 (1955) 30, 50; (1961) 33
  A7/A7SS (c1959) 32
  A10 (1961) 33
  A10 Golden Flash (1951) 29; (1959) 32
  A10 Super Rocket (1961) 33, *51*
  A50 (1963) 35
  A65 Star (1964) *51*
  B25 Competition (1937) 115
  B28 (1926) 25
  B31 (1949) 27, *50*; (1954) 29; (1956) 30
  B33 (1949) 28; (1955) 30
  B34 Competition (1951) 29
  B40 (1962) 34; (1964) 35
  B44 Victor Special (1969) *52*
  B50 MX Victor (1972) 120
  Bantam **28**
  BB32 Competition (1954) 116
  Blue Star R33 (1933) 26, *50*
  C10 (1939) 27

C11 (1955) 30
C11G (1958) 32
C12 (1956) *51*
C15 (1959) 33, *51*
C15 Star (c1961) 33
Catalina Scrambler (1962) 119
CB32 Gold Star Catalina Special (1956) 31
CB34 Gold Star (1955) 30
D1 Bantam (1961) 33; (1962) *51*
D5 Bantam 32
D7 (1962) 34
D14/4 Bantam (1968) 35
D175 Bantam (1969) 35
DBD34 Gold Star Clubman (1958) 31; (1960) 33; (1961) 34
E2 DeLuxe (1921) 25
Flat Tank (1924) 25
G14 (1936) 26
G14 with Sidecar (1936) 158
Gold Star **31, 119**
Gold Star Replica (1959) 32
Golden Flash A10 (c1956) 31
M20 (1940s) 131; (1946) 27
M21 (1945) 27; (1949) 28
Model B Round Tank (c1925) 25
Model E with Sidecar (1921) 156
Model K2 with BSA Model No 3 Sidecar (1921) 156
'Rob North' Rocket 3 (c1972) 147
Rocket Gold Star (1962) 34
Royal Star (1971) *52*
Shooting Star (1958) 32
Sloper (1932) 26
Star Twin (1949) 28
Starfire (1970) 35
W35-6 (1935) 26
Y13 (1936) 26
ZB32A (1951) 29

C

Cagiva Alazzurra 650 GT (1986) *52*
Calthorpe Ivory (1937) 36
Campion Single (1912) *52*
Carnielli Graziella (1979) 135
CCM Motocross (c1979) 120
Chipchase-JAP 499cc (1956) 162
Clement V-twin (1920) 36
Clyno 225cc (1921) 36
Comerford-Wallis-JAP (1932) 161
Condor Military (1974) 131
Corgi Runabout (1947) 149
Cotton 249cc (c1937) 142
Coventry Eagle 37–8, *53*

C11 (1955) 30
Eagle D25 (1931) 37
Flying 500 Model P50/1 (1937) *53*
Flying Eight (1924) 38
K6 (1934) 37
N1 (1937) 38
S14B (1923) 37

D

Dayton
  153cc (1913) 38
  Albatros Twin (1959) 152
Diamond 275cc (1923) 38
dirt bikes 114–20, *125*
DKW SB500 (1938) 39
DMW Dolomite (1960) 39
Dot
  349cc (1928) 139
  Demon (1964) 119
  Super Sports VI (1929) 39
  TDH KAP (1955) 116
Douglas 40–1, *53*
  2¾hp (1914) 40; (1921) 40
  80 Plus (1951) *53*
  B/20 4hp (1922) 40; (1923) 40
  CW (1925) 40
  D29 (1929) 40
  Dragonfly (1956) 41
  DT5 (1928) 160
  Mk 4 (1949) 41
  Mk 5 (1953) 41
  Model C (1910) 40
  S6 (1930) 41
  SW6 (1929) 40
  Vespa 'Rod Model' (1951) 149
Ducati 42–6, *53*
  48 Sport Export (1962) 43
  125 Aurea (1960) 42
  125 Bronco (1962) 43
  160 Monza Junior (1966) 44
  175 Silverstone Super (1960) 42
  175T (1959) 42
  175TS (1958) 42, *53*
  200GT (1962) 43
  200TS (1961) 42
  204cc Elite **44**
  250 Desmo (1974) *53*
  250 Racer (1966) 146
  350 Mk 3 (1974) 45
  500 Sport Desmo (1978) 45, 46
  500SL Pantah (1982) 46
  750GT (1973) 45
  750S (1974) 45
  900GTS (1978) 45
  Brisk (1962) 135
  Darmah SD900 (1978) 46
  Daytona (1963) 43; (1964) *53*
  Diana (1961) 43
  Elite (1963) 44
  Mike Hailwood Replica (1979) 46, *53*
  Mk 3D (1969) 44
  Scrambler 350 (1972) 44
  Sebring (1966) 44

Dürkopp Diana (1961) 153

E
EMC-Puch (1953) 143
Erskine-JAP 499cc (1952)
162
Excelsior 47
Autobyk (1948) 47
D9 (1936) 47
Manxman (1935) 141
Model 4 (1930) 47
Speedway Mk 1 (1933)
161
Speedway Mk II (1947)
161
Speedway Mk III (1950)
161
TT Replica (1929) 141

F
FB Mondial Ex-Works 250
Gran Premio (1956/57)
127
Francis-Barnett 47, *54*
58 Falcon (1951) 47
71 Cruiser (1954) *54*
81 Falcon (1959) 47
Model 85 Trials (c1960)
118

G
Garelli KL100 (1977) 47
Gilera 48
50 Trial (1972) 48
125 OSPI (1989) 48
Racing Special (1972)
147
Gitan 125 Scirocco (1951)
48
Giulietta Sports Moped
(1975) 135
Greeves
25 Sports Twin (1961) 48
Hawkstone (1959) 118
Scottish (1958) 118

H
Hagan 350 Grass Track
Bike (c1960) *125*
Harley-Davidson 57–8
Electraglide (1975) 58
Model 18F with sidecar
(1918) 129
Model J (1920) 57;
(1927) 57
Model VLE (1933) 57
Road King (1997) 137
Special (1974) 58
V-twin (1930) 57
Heinkel
Tourist (1958) 151;
(1959) 152
Heldun Hawk (1969) 146
Henderson 58
De Luxe (1922) 58
Hesketh 59
V1000 (1979/1980) 59;
(1982) 59
Hewetson Vertical Single
(1898) 60
Honda 54, 60–1
750F2 (1976) 61
C77 (1963) *54*
C100 (1962) 60
CB350F (1975) 60
CB400F (1975) 60;
(1976) 60
CB750F2 (1976) 61
CBX 1000 Moto Martin
Tokyo (1980's) 61
CBX 1000B (1981) *54*
CBX 1000C (1982) 61

CBX 1000Z (1978) 61
CM400 Custom (1981)
61
CZ100 (1964) 132
ST70 (1974) 132
Works 250 Four (1964)
145
Z50 (1972) 132
Z50 Gorilla (1981) 133
Z50A (1971) 132
Z50J Gorilla (1981) 133

I
Indian *54*, 62
741B (1941) 130
751B (1941) *54*
Brave (1952) 62
Four (1940) 62
Sport Scout 75 (1940) 62
Itom 63
Competizione (1957)
144
Mk 8 (1960) 63; (1964)
63
Mk 9 (1967) 146
Tabor (1962) 63

J
Jackson Speedway 499cc
(c1952) 162
James *54*, 63
7 with Sidecar (1922) 156
Comet J10 (1952) 63
Commodore (1959) 63
M25S Super Swift
Sports (1964) *54*
JAP 64
2½hp (1904) 64
Jawa
500 (1967) 162
500 Ice Speedway Bike
(1968) *125*
Jawa-Hagon Grass
Track Bike (c1969) 162

K
Kawasaki *54*, 64–5
500 H1E (1974) 65
650 W1 (1968) 64
KR250 (1984) *54*
Works KR750 Model
602L (1976) 147
Z1B (1974) 65
Z400 (1973) 65
Z650B1 (1977) 65
Z1100A (1983) 65
Kerry 3½hp (1904) 66
Kreidler
50 GP (1980) 148
Works Replica (1971)
146

L
Lambretta
Lambrettino (1960) 135
LC125 (1953) 150
LD150 (1957) 151
Li150 Series 2 (1962) 153
Li150 Series 3 (1966) 154
Model D (1954) 150
Model F (c1953) 150
SX200 (c1966) 154
TV Series 1 (1957) 152
TV175 Series 2 (1959)
152
TV200 (1967) 154
Laverda 66
750 SF2 (1974) 66
Jota 120 (1982) 66
Montjuic Series 2 (1980)
66
Levis 67

211cc (1921) 67;
(1925) 67
As (1935) 67
Lube B25 (c1950) 67

M
Maico
250 Motocross Bike
(1959) *125*
Maicoletta M250 (1958)
151
Puissant Motocross
Bike (1968) *125*
mascots 163
Maserati/Itom GSB
Special (1958) 144
Matchless 68–9
CSR (1961) 69
G3L (1944) 68
G3LC Trials (1954) 116
G3LS (1954) 68; (1958)
69
G9 (1952) 68; (1959) 69
G11 (1956) 69
G50 (1959) *127*
G85CS (1966) *125*
Model X (1937) 68
T/5 (1930) 68
V-twin (1918) 68
Mattingly-JAP 499cc
(1956) 162
memorabilia *128*, 163
Messerschmitt Vespa
VS150 (c1955) 150
military motorcycles
129–31
Minerelli Racer (1972) 147
Minerva 70
211cc (1903) 70
Single (1904) 70
Monet-Goyon GZA-3
Tricycle (1923) *128*
monkey bikes 132–3
Monotrace 70
Type MM (1925) 70
mopeds 134–5
Moto Guzzi 55, 71–3
98 Zigolo Series 1
(1957) *55*
750S3 (1975) 72
850GT with Squire
Sidecar (1972) 158
850T3 PA (1982) 137
1000SP NT (1981) 73
Cardellino 65 (1954) 72
Galletto (1953) 71
Le Mans 1 (1977) 73
Lodola 235 (1962) 72
Lodola GT (1960) 72
Nuovo Falcone (1970)
55; (1971) 131, 137;
(1972) 72
V35 Imola Mk II (1984) 73
V35 Series II (1980) 73
V35II Police (1985) 137
V50 Series II (1980) 73
Moto Morini 55, 74–7
3½ Sport (1976) 75
350 Dart (1988) *55*, 77
350 Excalibur (1992) 77
350 Sport ES FD (1981)
76
350 Sport Valentini
(1976) 75
350 Strada (1975) 75
500 (1981) *55*
500 Camer (1981) 76
500/5 (1978) 75
500/5 Sport (1980) 76
500/5 Tour (1979) 76
500/6 Turismo (1983) *55*
501 Conguaro (1990) 77

Camel Series 1 (1981) 77
K2 Series 1 (1982) 77
KJ Kanguro Juniore
(1984) 77
Regularita (1964) 75
Tressette Sprint (1962)
74
TS125 (1955) 74
Motobi 71
125 (1960s) 71
650S (1971) 71
Sport (c1959) 71
Motosacoche Single
(1910) 78
MV Agusta *56*, 78–9
150GT (1971) 78
175CSS (1957) 78
350B (1973) 79
600 Four (1967) 78
750GT (1972) 79
750S (1974) *56*
750S America (1977) 79
Monza 861 Arturo Magni
(1978) 79

N
Neracar 2¼hp (1921) 80
New Imperial *56*, 80
6.8hp (1926) 80
350 (1937) 80
Grand Prix (1934) *126*
Model 46 (1937) *56*
Model 100 (1935) 80
Norman
B4 Sports (1961) 80
Nippy (1962) 135
Norton *56*, 81–4
16H (1924) *56*
19 (1928) 81
500T Trials (1950) 116
850 Commander
Roadster (c1972) *56*
Classic (1988) 84
Commando 750 **83**
Commando 750 Interpol
(1969) 83
Commando 850 Mk III
(1975) 84
Commando Café Racer
(1970) 83
Commando Interpol
(1972) 137
Commando Interstate
(1975) 84
CSI (1928) 81
Dominator 88 (1955) 82
Dominator 99 (1960) 82
ES2 (1939) 81; (1946)
81; (1960) 82
ES2 and Sidecar (1958)
128
International (1932) 141
International Model 30
(1957) *56*
Manx (1951) 143
Manx 30M (1959) 145
Manx M40 (1952) *126*
Mk II Commando (1974)
84; (1976) 84
Mk III Interstate (1976) 84
Model 7 (1950) 82
Model 18 (1924) 139
Model 18 Scrambler
(c1938) 115
Model 25 TT Replica
(1927) 139
Model 30 International
(1935) 81; (1948) 81;
(1949) 82
Model 40 Manx (1959)
145
Model 50 (1958) 82

Norton-Cosworth
Challenge (c1982) 148
P11 (1968) 83
Works Racer (1935) 142
NSU 85
501T with Sidecar
(1930) 157
Fox A1 (1950) 85
HK101 Kettenkrad
(1944) 130
Quickly Moped (1959)
134
Renn Maschine
(1905–10) 138
Single (1909) 85

O
OEC Blackburne (1922) 85
Ossa Enduro (1972) 85

P
Panther 86
Model 120 (1963) 86
Model 120 with Double-
Adult Busmar Sidecar
(1959) 158
P & M (1918) 86
Red Panther (1935) 86
Stroud Trials (1934) 114
Stroud Trials Mk I (1950)
115
police bikes 136–7
Praga 499cc (1928) 86
Puch 163

Q
Quadrant 3½hp (1906) 87

R
racing bikes 126–7, 138–48
Rajoot GTS (1979) 133
Raleigh 163
MT30 (1928) 87
Runabout (1964) 135
René-Gillet Model J (1933)
87
Rex-Acme 350cc (1926)
139
Rickman
Metisse Mk 4 (1975) 120
Rickman/Triumph
Special (1968) 128
Rotrax
Rotrax-JAP 499cc
(1950) 161
Speedway Bike (1977)
125
Royal Enfield 88–9, 121,
163
500 (c1955) 121
770cc (1914) 88
Bullet (1954) 121;
(1957) 89; (1960) 89
Bullet 500 (1959) 121
Bullet Replica (1955) 117
Bullet Trials (1959) 118
Clipper (1956) 88;
(1957) 89
Clipper Airflow (1959) 89
Crusader (1962) 121
Crusader Sports (1960)
89
Ex-Works Racer (1914)
138
Interceptor Series II
(1970) 89
Model 180 with Sidecar
(1924) 156
Model C (1942) 130
Model G (1949) 121
Model G2 (1950) 88
Model KX (1937) 88

Model S (1934) 88;
(1935) 88
Ulster (1939) 121
Royal Ruby Spring Frame
(1918) 90
Rudge 90
DT Speedway Bike
(1930) 125
Multi (1922) 90
overhead-valve JAP
engine 161
Special (1936) 90
TT Replica (1932) 141
Ulster (1938) 90
Rudge-Whitworth 163
Rumi Junior Gentleman
(1959) 90

S
scooters 149–54
Scott 91
Flying Squirrel (1928) 91;
(1957) 91; (1959) 91
Flying Squirrel Sports
(1929) 91
Sprint Special (1928) 122
Squirrel (1929) 91
Squirrel with Sidecar
(1919) 155
TT Replica (1929) 140
Two-Speeder (1929) 91
SGN Polini Special (1980s)
148
sidecars 128, 155–8
signs 128, 163
Singer 300cc (1912) 92
Sparkbrook 2fihp (1921) 92
specials 128, 159
speedway bikes 125,
160–2
Standard Ideal Touring
(1930) 92
Sunbeam 93–4, 122
2¾hp (1914) 93; (1925)
122
491cc (1923) 93
Li95 (1934) 94
Model 1 (1926) 93;
(1927) 93
Model 8 (1928) 94;
(1935) 94
Model 9 (1927) 94
Model 80 Works TT
(1928) 140
S7 (1948) 94, 122
S8 (1951) 94; (1955)
122; (1958) 94
S8 with Sidecar (1951)
158
Suzuki 96–7
AS50 (1969) 96
ASS100 (1971) 96
Dresda Suzuki GT750
Special (1975) 97
GSX750E (1983) 97
GSX1100ES (1983) 97
GT250 X7 (1979) 97
GT750A (1976) 97
GT750J (1972) 96
Italia Vallelunga 750/3
(1973) 96
RE5A (1976) 97
RV90 (1976) 133
TR500 (c1973) 127

T
Tandon Trials Model
(1957) 117
Terrot 350 (1933) 98
Tribsa Special (c1959) 159
Triton
Special (1956) 159;

(1970) 159
Stan Cooper Replica
(1950s) 128, 159
Triumph 98–106, 123–4
3T (1946) 99
3½hp Model D TT
Replica (1914) 98
3½hp Model R (Ricardo)
(1921) 99
5T Speed Twin (1950)
100; (1952) 101;
(1954/57) 101; (1956)
102
5TA Speed Twin (1959)
103; (1961) 103, 123;
(1962) 104
6T Thunderbird (1949)
100; (1952) 101; (1955)
101; (1958) 102; (1960)
137
100 (1938) 99
Cub (1958) 144
Cub Trials Conversion
(1959) 118
Model H (1915) 129
Model QA (1927) 99
Model SD with
Watsonian Sidecar
(1923) 156
Speed Twin **100**;
(1940) 123
T15 Terrier (1956) 102
T20 Cub (1955) 123
T20 Cub Trials (1963) 119
T20 S/C Super Cub
(1967) 104
T20 Tiger Cub (1958)
103; (1963) 104
T20M Mountain Cub
(1967) 104
T20SH Sports Cub
(1962) 103
T100 (1956) 102
T100R Daytona (1976)
106
T100SS (1967) 124
T120 Bonneville (1969)
105
T120R Bonneville (1960)
103; (1972) 105
T140 Bonneville
Executive (1983) 106
T140 Bonneville Special
(1979) 106
T140V Bonneville (1976)
106, 124
T150 Trident (1975) 105
T160 Trident (c1978)
124
Tiger 70 (1937) 99
Tiger 90 (1963) 104;
(1964) 123
Tiger 100 (1951) 101;
(1955) 102; (1958)
102, 123
Tiger 110 (1956) 102
Tiger 750 (c1977) 124
Touring (1912) 123
TR5 Trophy (1949)
100; (1950) 115
TR6 (1967) 104
TR6 Trophy (1958) 103
TR6C (1966) 104
TR25W (1969) 105
TRW (1952) 136;
(1964) 131
WD Model 3HW (c1940)
130
TWN FIP3 (1956) 134

U
Ultima Lyon (1921) 106

V
Velocette 107–10, 124
KSS Mk II (1936) 107;
(1948) 108
KTT Mk VII Racing
Motorcycle (1938) 142
KTT/KSS Special (1934)
159
LE Mk I Display Engine
and Shaft Drive (1948)
108
LE Mk III (1960) 109
MAC (1936) 124;
(1956) 108; (1957) 109
Model G2 (1922) 107
MOV (1937) 108;
(1948) 108
MSS (1956) 108
MSS Scrambler (1962)
119
Thruxton (1968) 110
Valiant Veeline (1959) 109
Venom (1956) 109;
(1960) 110
Venom Clubman (1962)
124
Venom/KSS Special
(c1961) 159
Viper (1960) 109;
(1964) 110
Vogue (1964) 110
Vespa
42C2 (1957) 151
42L2 (1955) 150
GS150 (1959) 152
GS160 Series 2 (1964)
153
Sportique (1960) 153;
(1962) 153
Sprint (1968) 154
SS180 (1969) 154
Victoria
Peggy (1956) 151
Sport Type 13 (1967)
111
Vincent 124
Grey Flash (1950) 126
Series C Rapide (1952)
124
Vincent-HRD 111–12
Black Lightning (1949)
143
Egli Vincent **112**
Rapide (1948) 111
Series A (1938) 111
Series C Comet (1951)
112
Series D 'Open' Black
Shadow (1955) 112

Y
Yale 7–8hp (1914) 113
Yamaha 113
OW48R (1981) 127
RD125DX (1980) 113
TD1 (1962) 145
VMX 1200 with
Hedingham XL (1985)
158
YDS3C (1965) 113

Z
Zenith Gradua with
Sidecar (1914) 155
Zündapp
Combinette De Luxe
(1955) 134; (1956)
134
Combinette Type 408
(1955) 134
K800W with sidecar
(1934) 129